Linguistics
and Literary History
Essays in Stylistics

Linguistics
and Literary History
Essays in Stylistics

By Leo Spitzer

NEW YORK

RUSSELL & RUSSELL · INC

1962

FOREWORD

THE following studies owe their birth to the kind invitation of the Department of Modern Languages and Literatures at Princeton University, extended to me at the behest of Professor Américo Castro, to give a lecture on the subject indicated by the title of the first essay, and to the further invitation of the Princeton University Press to expand the lecture (which is reproduced herein with the addition of some notes) into a book which would show some practical applications of my linguistic method to literature.

I dedicate this first book of mine printed in America, which is to continue the series of studies in stylistics previously published in Germany—*Aufsätze zur romanischen Syntax und Stilistik*, Halle (Niemeyer) 1918; *Stilstudien*, I-II, München (Hueber) 1928; *Romanische Stil- und Literaturstudien*, I-II, Marburg an der Lahn (Elwert) 1931—to Assistant Professor ANNA GRANVILLE HATCHER who is an outstanding American scholar in the too little cultivated field of syntax—which, in her case, is expanded into stylistic and cultural history—and who could thus teach me, not only the intricacies of English syntax and stylistics, but some of the more recondite features of American culture and of its particular moral, logical, and aesthetic aspirations: a knowledge without which all endeavors of the philologist to explain poetry to an American public must fail completely. For poetry has always been addressed to a public with which the poet felt himself to be united—so that the explanation of poetry, too, must needs be addressed to a public whose reactions the commentator is able to foresee. It is one of the benefits falling to the lot of the emigrant scholar that, however much his outward activity may be curtailed in the new country in comparison with his former situation, his inner activity is bound to be immensely enhanced and intensified: instead of writing as he pleases, after the usual fashion of the German scholar in particular (who is so well satisfied to live in the paradise of his ideas, whether this be accessible to his fellow men or not), he must, while trying to preserve his own idea of scholarship, continually count with his new audience, bearing in mind not only the conventional requirements but also those innermost strivings of the nation (inasmuch as it is given him to feel them) which, opposed to his nature as they may have seemed to him in the beginning, tend imperceptibly to become a second nature in him—indeed, to make shine by contrast his first nature in the clearest light. And, by so doing, he comes to feel enriched and to find that he has attained peace and happiness.

L.S.

THE JOHNS HOPKINS UNIVERSITY
SEPTEMBER 1945.

CONTENTS

Because the chapters listed above are intended to be read as articles one after the other, and consultation as a reference book is not envisaged, the author has decided that an index should not be included in the book.

I

LINGUISTICS AND LITERARY HISTORY[1]

THE title of this book is meant to suggest the ultimate unity of linguistics and literary history. Since my activity, throughout my scholarly life, has been largely devoted to the rapprochement of these two disciplines, I may be forgiven if I preface my remarks with an autobiographic sketch of my first academic experiences: What I propose to do is to tell you only my own story, how I made my way through the maze of linguistics, with which I started, toward the enchanted garden of literary history—and how I discovered that there is as well a paradise in linguistics as a labyrinth in literary history; that the methods and the degree of certainty in both are basically the same; and, that if today the humanities are under attack (and, as I believe, under an unwarranted attack, since it is not the humanities themselves that are at fault but only some so-called humanists who persist in imitating an obsolete approach to the natural sciences, which have themselves evolved toward the humanities)—if, then, the humanities are under attack, it would be pointless to exempt any one of them from the verdict: if it is true that there is no value to be derived from the study of language, we cannot pretend to preserve literary history, cultural history—or history.

I have chosen the autobiographical way because my personal situation in Europe forty years ago was not, I believe, essentially different from the one with which I see the young scholar of today (and in this country) generally faced. I chose to relate to you my own experiences also because the basic approach of the individual scholar, conditioned as it is by his first experiences, by his *Erlebnis*, as the Germans say, determines his method: *Methode ist Erlebnis*, Gundolf has said. In fact, I would advise every older scholar to tell his public the basic experiences underlying his methods, his *Mein Kampf*, as it were—without dictatorial connotations, of course.

I had decided, after college had given me a solid foundation in the classical languages, to study the Romance languages and particularly French philology, because, in my native Vienna, the gay and orderly, skeptic and sentimental, Catholic and pagan Vienna of yore was filled with adoration of the French way of life. I had always been surrounded by a French atmosphere and, at that juvenile stage of experience, had acquired a picture, perhaps overgeneralized, of French literature, which seemed to me definable by an Austrianlike mixture of sensuousness and reflection, of vitality and discipline, of sentimentality and critical wit. The moment when the curtain rose on a French play given by a French troupe, and the valet, in a knowing accent of psychological alertness, with his rich, poised voice, pronounced the words "Madame est servie," was a delight to my heart.

But when I attended the classes of French linguistics of my great teacher Meyer-Lübke no picture was offered us of the French people, or of the Frenchness of their language: in these classes we saw Latin *a* moving, according to relentless phonetic laws, toward French *e* (*pater* > *père*); there we saw a new system of declension spring up from nothingness, a system in which the six Latin cases came to be reduced to two, and later to one—while we learned that similar violence had been done to the other Romance languages and, in fact, to many modern languages. In all this, there were many facts and much rigor in the establishment of facts, but all was vague in regard to the general ideas underlying these facts. What was the mystery behind the refusal of Latin sounds or cases to stay put and behave themselves? We saw incessant change working in language—but why? I was a long while realizing that Meyer-Lübke was offering only the *pre*-history of French (as he established it by a comparison with the other Romance languages), not its history. And we were never allowed to contemplate a phenomenon in its quiet being, to look into its face: we always looked at its neighbors or at its predecessors—we were always looking over our shoulder. There were presented to us the relationships of phenomenon *a* and phenomenon *b*; but phenomenon *a* and phenomenon *b* did not exist in themselves, nor did the historical line *a - b*.

In reference to a given French form, Meyer-Lübke would quote Old Portuguese, Modern Bergamesque and Macedo-rumanian, German, Celtic, and paleo-Latin forms; but where was reflected in this teaching my sensuous, witty, disciplined Frenchman, in his presumably 1000 years of existence? He was left out in the cold while we talked about his language; indeed, French was not the language of the Frenchman, but an agglomeration of unconnected, separate, anecdotic, sense-less evolutions: a French historical grammar, apart from the word-material, could as well have been a Germanic or a Slav grammar: the leveling of paradigms, the phonetic evolutions occur there just as in French.

When I changed over to the classes of the equally great literary historian Philipp August Becker, that ideal French-man seemed to show some faint signs of life—in the spirited analyses of the events in the *Pèlerinage de Charlemagne*, or of the plot of a Molière comedy; but it was as if the treat-ment of the contents were only subsidiary to the really scholarly work, which consisted in fixing the dates and his-torical data of these works of art, in assessing the amount of autobiographical elements and written sources which the poets had supposedly incorporated into their artistic produc-tions. Had the *Pèlerinage* to do with the Xth crusade? Which was its original dialect? Was there any epic poetry, Mero-vingian or other, which preceded Old French epic poetry? Had Molière put his own matrimonial disillusionment into the *Ecole des femmes*? (While Becker did not insist on an affirmative conclusion, he considered such a question to be a part of legitimate literary criticism.) Did the medieval farce survive in the Molière comedy? The existing works of art were stepping-stones from which to proceed to other phenom-ena, contemporary or previous, which were in reality quite heterogeneous. It seemed indiscrete to ask what made them works of art, what was expressed in them, and why these expressions appeared in France, at that particular time. Again, it was prehistory, not history, that we were offered, and a kind of materialistic prehistory, at that. In this attitude of positivism, exterior events were taken thus seriously only to evade the more completely the real question: Why did the phenomena *Pèlerinage* and *Ecole des femmes* happen at all? And, I must admit, in full loyalty to Meyer-Lübke, that he taught more of reality than did Becker: it was unquestionable that Latin *a* had evolved to French *e*; it was untrue that Molière's experience with the possibly faithless Madeleine Béjart had evolved to the work of art *Ecole des femmes*. But, in both fields, that of linguistics as well as that of literary history (which were separated by an enormous gulf: Meyer-Lübke spoke only of language and Becker only of literature), a meaningless industriousness prevailed: not only was this kind of humanities not centered on a particular people in a particular time, but the subject matter itself had got lost: Man.[2] At the end of my first year of graduate studies, I had come to the conclusion, not that the science offered *ex cathedra* was worthless but that I was not fit for such studies as that of the irrational vowel -*i*- in Eastern French dialects, or of the *Subjektivismusstreit* in Molière: never would I get a Ph.D.! It was the benignity of Providence, exploiting my native Teutonic docility toward scholars who knew more than I, which kept me faithful to the study of Romance philology. By not abandoning prematurely this sham science, by seeking, instead, to appropriate it, I came to recognize its true value as well as my own possibilities of work—and to establish my life's goal. By using the tools of science offered me, I came to see under their dustiness the fingerprints of a Friedrich Diez and of the Romantics, who had created these tools; and henceforth they were not dusty any more, but ever radiant and ever new. And I had learned to handle many and manifold facts: training in handling facts, brutal facts, is perhaps the best education for a wavering, youthful mind.

And now let me take you, as I promised to do, on the path that leads from the most routinelike techniques of the linguist toward the work of the literary historian. The different fields will appear here in the ascending order, as I see them today, while the concrete examples, drawn from my own activity, will not respect the chronological order of their publication.

Meyer-Lübke, the author of the comprehensive and still final etymological dictionary of Romance languages, had taught me, among many other things, how to find etymologies; I shall now take the liberty of inflicting upon you a concrete example of this procedure—sparing you none of the petty drudgery involved. Since my coming to America, I have been curious about the etymology of two English words, characterized by the same "flavor": *conundrum* "a riddle the answer to which involves a pun; a puzzling question," and *quandary* "a puzzling situation." The NED attests *conundrum* first in 1596; early variants are *conimbrum, quonundrum, quadrundum*. The meaning is "whim" or "pun." In the seventeenth century it was known as an Oxford term: preachers were wont to use in their sermons the baroque device of puns and conundrums, e.g. "Now all House is turned into an Alehouse, and a pair of dice is made a Paradice; was it thus in the days of Noah? Ah no." This baroque technique of interlarding sermons with puns is well known from the *Kapuziner-Predigt*, inspired by Abraham a Santa Clara, in Schiller's *Wallenstein's Lager*: "Der *Rheinstrom* ist worden zu einem *Peinstrom*," etc.

The extraordinary instability (reflecting the playfulness of the concept involved) of the phonetic structure: *conundrum - conimbrum - quadrundrum*, points to a foreign source, to a word which must have been (playfully) adapted in various ways. Since the English variants include among them a -*b*- and a -*d*- which are not easily reducible to any one basic sound, I propose to submit a French word-family which, in its different forms, contains both -*b*- and -*d*-: the French *calembour* is exactly synonymous with *conundrum* "pun." This *calembour* is evidently related to *calembredaine* "nonsensical or odd speech," and we can assume that *calembour*, too, had originally this same general reference. This word-family goes back probably to Fr. *bourde* "tall story" to which has been added the fanciful, semipejorative prefix *cali-*, that can be found in *à califourchon* "straddling" (from Latin *quadrifurcus*, French *carrefour* "crossroads": the *qu-* of the English variants points to this Latin etymon). The French ending -*aine* of *calembredaine* developed to -*um*: *n* becomes *m* as in *ransom* from French *rançon*; *ai* becomes *o* as in *mitten* (older *mitton*) from French *mitaine*. Thus *calembourdane*, as a result of various assimilations and shortenings which I will spare you, becomes *colundrum, *columbrum and then conundrum, conimbrum, etc. Unfortunately, the French word-family is attested rather late, occurring for the first time in a comic opera of Vadé in 1754. We do find, however, an équilbourdie "whim" as early as 1658 in the Muse normande, a dialectal text. The fact is that popular words of this sort have, as a rule, little chance of turning up in the (predominantly idealistic) literature of the Middle Ages; it is, therefore, a mere accident that English conundrum is attested in 1596 and French calembour only in 1757; at least, the chance appearance of équilbourdie in the dialectal text of 1658 gives us an earlier attestation of the French word-family. That the evidently popular medieval words emerge so late in literature is a fact explainable by the currents prevalent in literature; the linguist must take his chances with what literature offers him in the way of attestation. In view of the absolute evidence of the equation conundrum = calembredaine we need not be intimidated by chronological divergencies—which the older school of etymologists (as represented by the editors of the NED) seem to have overrated.

After conundrum had ceased to be a riddle to me, I was emboldened to ask myself whether I could not now solve the etymology of the word quandary—which also suggested to me a French origin. And, lo and behold: this word, of unknown origin, which is attested from about 1580 on, revealed itself etymologically identical with conundrum! There are English dialect forms such as quándorum quóndorum which serve to establish an uninterrupted chain: calembredaine becomes conimbrum conundrum quonundrum quandorum and these give us quandary.[3]

Now what can be the humanistic, the spiritual value of this (as it may have seemed to you) juggling with word forms? The particular etymology of conundrum is an inconsequential fact; that an etymology can be found by man is a miracle. An etymology introduces meaning into the meaningless: in our case, the evolution of two words in time—that is, a piece of linguistic history—has been cleared up. What seemed an agglomeration of mere sounds now appears motivated. We feel the same "inner click" accompanying our comprehension of this evolution in time as when we have grasped the meaning of a sentence or a poem—which then become more than the sum total of their single words or sounds (*poem* and *sentence* are, in fact, the classical examples given by Augustine and Bergson in order to demonstrate the nature of a stretch of *durée réelle*: the parts aggregating to a whole, time filled with contents). In the problem which we chose, two words which seemed erratic and fantastic, with no definite relationships in English, have been unified among themselves and related to a French word-family.

The existence of such a loan-word is another testimony to the well-known cultural situation obtaining when medieval England was in the sway of French influence: the English and French word-families, although attested centuries after the Middle Ages, must have belonged to one Anglo-French word-family during that period, and their previous existence is precisely proved by proving their family relationship. And it is not by chance that English borrows words for "pun" or "whim" from the witty French, who have also given *carri-witchet* "quibble" and (perhaps: see the NED) *pun* itself to English. But, since a loan-word rarely feels completely at home in its new environment, we have the manifold variations of the word, which fell apart into two word-groups (clearly separated, today, by the current linguistic feeling): *conundrum-quandary*. The instability and disunity of the word-family is symptomatic of its position in the new environment.

But the instability apparent in our English words had already been characteristic of *calembredaine - calembour*, even in the home environment: this French word-family, as we have said, was a blend of at least two word-stems. Thus we must conclude that the instability is also connected with the semantic content: a word meaning "whim, pun" easily behaves whimsically—just as, in all languages throughout the world, the words for "butterfly" present a kaleidoscopic instability. The linguist who explains such fluttery words has to juggle, because the speaking community itself (in our case, the English as well as the French) has juggled. This juggling in itself is psychologically and culturally motivated: language is not, as the behavioristic, antimentalistic, mechanistic or materialistic school of linguists, rampant in some universities, would have it: a meaningless agglomeration of corpses: dead word-material, automatic "speech habits" unleased by a trigger motion. A certain automatism may be predicated of the use of *conundrum* and *quandary* in contemporary English, and of *calembour, calembredaine* in contemporary French (though, even today, this automatism is not absolute, since all these words have still a connotation of whimsicality or fancifulness and are, accordingly, somewhat motivated). But this is certainly not true for the history of the words: the linguistic creation is always meaningful and, yes, clear-minded: it was a feeling for the appositeness of nomenclature which prompted the communities to use, in our case, two-track words. They gave a playful expression to a playful concept, symbolizing in the word their attitude toward the concept. It was when the creative, the Renaissance, phase had passed that English let the words congeal, petrify, and split into two. This petrification is, itself, due to a decision of the community which, in eighteenth-century England, passed from the Renaissance attitude to the classicistic attitude toward language, which would replace creativity by standardization and regulation. Another cultural climate, another linguistic style. Out of the infinity of word-histories which could be imagined we have chosen only one, one which shows quite individual circumstances, such as the borrowing of a foreign word by English, the original French blend, the subsequent alterations and restrictions; every word has its own history, not to be confused with that of any other. But what repeats itself in all word-histories is the possibility of recognizing the signs of a people at work, culturally and psychologically. To speak in the language of the homeland of philology: *Wortwandel ist Kulturwandel und Seelenwandel*; this little etymological study has been humanistic in purpose.

If we accept the equation: *conundrum* and *quandary* = *calembredaine*—how has this been found? I may say, by quite an orthodox technique which would have been approved by Meyer-Lübke—though he would not, perhaps, have stopped to draw the inferences on which I have insisted. First, by collecting the material evidence about the English words, I was led to seek a French origin. I had also observed that the great portion of the English vocabulary which is derived from French has not been given sufficient attention by etymologists; and, of course, my familiarity with the particular behavior of "butterfly words" in language was such as to encourage a relative boldness in the reconstruction of the etymon. I had first followed the inductive method—or rather a quick intuition—in order to identify *conundrum* with *calembredaine*; later, I had to proceed deductively, to verify whether my assumed etymon concorded with all the known data, whether it really explained all the semantic and phonetic variations; while following this path I was able to see that *quandary* must also be a reflection of *calembredaine*. (This to-and-fro movement is a basic requirement in all humanistic studies, as we shall see later.) For example, since the French word-family is attested later than is the English, it seemed necessary to dismiss the chronological discrepancies; fortunately—or, as I would say, providentially—the Normandian *équilbourdie* of 1658 turned up! In this kind of gentle blending together of the words, of harmonizing them and smoothing out difficulties, the linguist undoubtedly indulges in a propensity to see things as shifting and melting into each other—an attitude to which you may object: I cannot contend more than that this change was *possible* in the way I have indicated, since it contradicts no previous experience; I can say only that two unsolved problems (the one concerning the prehistory of *conundrum*, the other that of *calembredaine*) have, when brought together, shed light on each other, thereby enabling us to see the common solution. I am reminded here of the story of the Pullman porter to whom a passenger complained in the morning that he had got back one black shoe and one tan; the porter replied that, curiously enough, a similar discovery had been made by another passenger. In the field of language, the porter who has mixed up the shoes belonging together is language itself, and the linguist is the passenger who must bring together what was once a historical unit. To place two phenomena within a framework adds something to the knowledge about their common nature. There is no mathematical demonstrability in such an equation, only a feeling of inner evidence; but this feeling, with the trained linguist, is the fruit of observation combined with experience, of precision supplemented by imagination—the dosage of which cannot be fixed a priori, but only in the concrete case. There is underlying such a procedure the belief that this is the way things happened; but there is always a belief underlying the humanist's work (similarly, it cannot be demonstrated that the Romance languages form a unity going back to Vulgar Latin; this basic assumption of the student in Romance languages, first stated by Diez, cannot be proved to the disbeliever).[4] And who says belief, says suasion: I have, deliberately and tendentiously, grouped the variants of *conundrum* in the most plausible order possible for the purpose of winning your assent. Of course, there are more easily believable etymologies, reached at the cost of less stretching and bending: no one in his senses would doubt that French *père* comes from Latin *pater*, or that this, along with English *father*, goes back to an Indo-European prototype. But we must not forget that these smooth, standard equations are relatively rare—for the reason that a word such as "father" is relatively immune to cultural revolutions or, in other words, that, in regard to the "father," a continuity of feeling, stretching over more than 4000 years, exists in Indo-European civilization.

Thus our etymological study has illuminated a stretch of linguistic history, which is connected with psychology and history of civilization; it has suggested a web of interrelations between language and the soul of the speaker. This web could have been as well revealed by a study of a syntactical, a morphological evolution—even a phonetic evolution of the type "*a* becomes *e*," wherein Meyer-Lübke had failed to see the *durée réelle*, exclusively concerned as he was with *l'heure de la montre*: his historical "clock time."

Now, since the best document of the soul of a nation is its literature, and since the latter is nothing but its language as this is written down by elect speakers, can we perhaps not hope to grasp the spirit of a nation in the language of its outstanding works of literature? Because it would have been rash to compare the whole of a national literature to the whole of a national language (as Karl Vossler has prematurely tried to do) I started, more modestly, with the question: "Can one distinguish the soul of a particular French writer in his particular language?" It is obvious that literary historians have held this conviction, since, after the inevitable quotation (or misquotation) of Buffon's saying: *"Le style c'est l'homme,"* they generally include in their monographs a chapter on the style of their author. But I had in mind the more rigorously scientific definition of an individual style, the definition of a linguist which should replace the casual, impressionistic remarks of literary critics. Stylistics, I thought, might bridge the gap between linguistics and literary history. On the other hand, I was warned by the scholastic adage: *individuum est ineffabile*; could it be that any attempt to define the individual writer by his style is doomed to failure? The individual stylistic deviation from the general norm must represent a historical step taken by the writer, I argued: it must reveal a shift of the soul of the epoch, a shift of which the writer has become conscious and which he would translate into a necessarily new linguistic form; perhaps it would be possible to determine the historical step, psychological as well as linguistic? To determine the beginning of a linguistic innovation would be easier, of course, in the case of contemporary writers, because their linguistic basis is better known to us than is that of past writers.

In my reading of modern French novels, I had acquired the habit of underlining expressions which struck me as aberrant from general usage, and it often happened that the underlined passages, taken together, seemed to offer a certain consistency. I wondered if it would not be possible to establish a common denominator for all or most of these deviations; could not the common spiritual etymon, the psychological root, of several individual "traits of style" in a writer be found, just as we have found an etymon common to various fanciful word formations?[5] I had, for example, noticed in the novel *Bubu de Montparnasse* of Charles-Louis Philippe (1905), which moves in the underworld of Parisian pimps and prostitutes, a particular use of *à cause de*, reflecting the spoken, the unliterary language: "Les réveils de midi sont lourds et poisseux. . . . On éprouve un sentiment de déchéance *à cause* des réveils d'autrefois." More academic writers would have said "en se rappelant des réveils d'autrefois. . . ," "à la suite du souvenir. . . ." This, at first glance, prosaic and commonplace *à cause de* has nevertheless a poetic flavor, because of the unexpected suggestion of a causality, where the average person would see only coincidence: it is, after all, not unanimously accepted that one awakes with a feeling of frustration from a noon siesta *because* other similar awakenings have preceded; we have here an assumed, a poetic reality, but one expressed by a prosaic phrase. We find this *à cause de* again in a description of a popular celebration of the 14th of July: "[le peuple], *à cause de* l'anniversaire de sa délivrance, laisse ses filles danser en liberté." Thus, one will not be surprised when the author lets this phrase come from the mouth of one of his characters: "Il y a dans mon coeur deux ou trois cent petites émotions qui brûlent *à cause de toi*." Conventional poetry would have said "qui brûlent pour toi"; "qui brûlent *à cause de toi*" is both less and more: more, since the lover speaks his heart better in this sincere, though factual manner. The causal phrase, with all its semipoetic implications, suggests rather a commonplace speaker, whose speech and whose habits of thought the writer seems to endorse in his own narrative.

Our observation about *à cause de* gains strength if we compare the use, in the same novel, of other causal conjunctions, such as *parce que*: for example, it is said of the pimp's love for his sweetheart Berthe: "[il aimait] sa volupté particulière, quand elle appliquait son corps contre le sien. . . . Il aimait cela qui la distinguait de toutes les femmes qu'il avait connues *parce que* c'était plus doux, *parce que* c'était plus fin, et *parce que* c'était sa femme à lui, qu'il avait eue vierge. Il l'aimait *parce qu*'elle était honnête et qu'elle en avait l'air, et pour toutes les raisons qu'ont les bourgeois d'aimer leur femme." Here, the reasons why Maurice loved to embrace his sweetheart (*parce que c'était doux, fin, parce que c'était sa femme a lui*) are outspokenly classified or censored by the writer as being *bourgeois*; and yet, in Philippe's narrative, the *parce que* is used as if he considered these reasons to be objectively valid.

The same observation holds true for the causal conjunction *car*: in the following passage which describes Maurice as a being naturally loved by women: "Les femmes l'entouraient d'amour comme des oiseaux qui chantent le soleil et la force. Il était un de ceux que nul ne peut assujettir, *car* leur vie, plus forte et plus belle, comporte l'amour du danger."

Again, it can happen that a causal relationship is implied without the use of a conjunction, a relationship due to the gnomic character adherent, at least in that particular milieu, to a general statement—the truth of which is, perhaps, not so fully accepted elsewhere: "Elle l'embrassa à pleine bouche. *C'est une chose hygiénique* et bonne entre un homme et sa femme, qui vous amuse un petit quart d'heure avant de vous endormir." (Philippe could as well have written "car. . . ," "parce que c'est une chose hygiénique. . . .") Evidently this is the truth only in that particular world of sensuous realism which he is describing. At the same time, however, the writer, while half-endorsing these bourgeois platitudes of the underworld, is discreetly but surely suggesting his criticism of them.

Now I submit the hypothesis that all these expansions of causal usages in Philippe cannot be due to chance: there must be "something the matter" with his conception of causality. And now we must pass from Philippe's style to the psychological etymon, to the radix in his soul. I have called the phenomenon in question "pseudo-objective motivation": Philippe, when presenting causality as binding for his characters, seems to recognize a rather objective cogency in their sometimes awkward, sometimes platitudinous, sometimes semipoetic reasonings; his attitude shows a fatalistic, half-critical, half-understanding, humorous sympathy with the necessary errors and thwarted strivings of these underworld beings dwarfed by inexorable social forces. The pseudo-objective motivation, manifest in his style, is the clue to Philippe's *Weltanschauung*; he sees, as has also been observed by literary critics, without revolt but with deep grief and a Christian spirit of contemplativity, the world functioning wrongly with an appearance of rightness, of objective logic. The different word-usages, grouped together (just as was done with the different forms of *conundrum* and *quandary*) lead toward a psychological etymon, which is at the bottom of the linguistic as well as of the literary inspiration of Philippe.

Thus we have made the trip from language or style to the soul. And on this journey we may catch a glimpse into a historical evolution of the French soul in the twentieth century: first we are given insight into the soul of a writer who has become conscious of the fatalism weighing on the masses, then, into that of a section of the French nation itself, whose faint protest is voiced by our author. And in this procedure there is, I think, no longer the timeless, placeless philology of the older school, but an explanation of the concrete *hic et nunc* of a historical phenomenon. The to-and-fro movement we found to be basic with the humanist has been followed here, too: first we grouped together certain causal expressions, striking with Philippe, then hunted out their psychological explanation, and finally, sought to verify whether the element of "pseudo-objective motivation"[6] concorded with what we know, from other sources, about the elements of his inspiration. Again, a belief is involved— which is no less daring than is the belief that the Romance languages go back to one invisible, basic pattern manifest in them all: namely, the belief that the mind of an author is a kind of solar system into whose orbit all categories of things are attracted: language, motivation, plot, are only satellites of this mythological entity (as my antimentalistic adversaries would call it): *mens Philippina.* The linguist as well as his literary colleague must always ascend to the etymon which is behind all those particular so-called literary or stylistic devices which the literary historians are wont to list. And the individual *mens Philippina* is a reflection of the *mens Franco-gallica* of the twentieth century; its ineffability consists precisely in Philippe's anticipatory sensitivity for the spiritual needs of the nation.

Now, it is obvious that a modern writer such as Philippe, faced with the social disintegration of humanity in the twentieth century, must show more patent linguistic deviations, of which the philologist may take stock in order to build up his "psychogram" of the individual artist. But does Philippe, a stranded being broken loose from his moorings, transplanted, as it were, into a world from which he feels estranged—so that he must, perforce, indulge in arbitrary whimsicality—represent only a modern phenomenon? If we go back to writers of more remote times, must it not be that we will always find a balanced language, with no deviations from common usage?

It suffices to mention the names of such dynamic writers of older times as Dante or Quevedo or Rabelais to dispel such a notion. Whoever has thought strongly and felt strongly has innovated in his language; mental creativity immediately inscribes itself into the language, where it becomes linguistic creativity; the trite and petrified in language is never sufficient for the needs of expression felt by a strong personality. In my first publication, "Die Wortbildung als stilistisches Mittel" (a thesis written in 1910), I dealt with Rabelais' comic word-formations, a subject to which I was attracted because of certain affinities between Rabelaisian and Viennese (Nestroy!) comic writing, and which offered the opportunity of bridging the gap between linguistic and literary history. Be it said to the eternal credit of the scholarly integrity of Meyer-Lübke that he, in contrast to the antimentalists who would suppress all expressions of opposition to their theories, recommended for publication a book with an approach so aberrant from his own. In this work I sought to show, for example, that a neologism such as *pantagruélisme*, the name given by Rabelais to his stoic-epicurean philosophy ("certaine gayeté d'esprict, conficte en mépris des choses fortuites") is not only a playful outburst of a genuine gaiety, but a thrust from the realm of the real into that of the unreal and the unknown—as is true, in fact, of any nonce-word. On the one hand, a form with the suffix -*ism* evokes a school of serious philosophic thought (such as *Aristotelianism, scholasticism*, etc.) ; on the other, the stem, *Pantagruel*, is the name of a character created by Rabelais, the half-jocular, half-philosophical giant and patriarchal king. The coupling of the learned philosophical suffix with the fanciful name of a fanciful character amounts to positing a half-real, half-unreal entity: "the philosophy of an imaginary being." The contemporaries of Rabelais who first heard this coinage must have experienced the reactions provoked by any nonce-word: a moment of shock followed by a feeling of reassurance: to be swept toward the unknown frightens, but realization of the benignly fanciful result gives relief: laughter, our physiological reaction on such occasions, arises precisely out of a feeling of relief following upon a temporary breakdown of our assurance. Now, in a case such as that of the creation *pantagruélisme*, the designation of a hitherto unknown but, after all, innocuous philosophy, the menacing force of the neologism is relatively subdued. But what of such a list of names as that concocted by Rabelais for the benefit of his hated adversaries, the reactionaries of the Sorbonne: *sophistes, sorbillans, sorbonagres, sorbonigenes, sorbonicoles, sorboniformes, sorboniseques, niborcisans, sorbonisans, saniborsans*. Again, though differently, there is an element of realism present in these coinages: the Sorbonne is an existing reality, and the formations are explainable by well-known formative processes. The edition of Abel Lefranc, imbued with his positivistic approach, goes to the trouble of explaining each one of these formations: *sorboniforme* is after *uniforme*, *sorbonigene* after *homogène*, while *niborcisans, saniborsans* offer what, in the jargon of the linguists, is called a metathesis. But by explaining every coinage separately, by dissolving the forest into trees, the commentators lose sight of the whole phenomenon: they no longer see the forest—or rather the jungle which Rabelais must have had before his eyes, teeming with viperlike, hydralike, demonlike shapes. Nor is it enough to say that the scholarly Rabelais indulges in humanistic word lists with a view to enriching the vocabulary—in the spirit of an Erasmus who prescribed the principle of *copia verborum* to students of Latin—or that Rabelais' rich nature bade him make the French language rich; the aesthetics of richness is, in itself, a problem; and why should richness tend toward the frightening, the bottomless? Perhaps Rabelais' whole attitude toward language rests upon a vision of imaginary richness whose support is the bottomless. He creates word-families, representative of gruesome fantasy-beings, copulating and engendering before our eyes, which have reality only in the world of language, which are established in an intermediate world between reality and irreality, between the nowhere that frightens and the "here" that reassures. The *niborcisans* are as yet an entity vaguely connected with the *sorbonisans*, but at the same time so close to nothingness that we laugh—uneasily; it is *le comique grotesque* which skirts the abyss. And Rabelais will shape grotesque word-families (or families of word-demons) not only by altering what exists: he may leave intact the forms of his word material and create by juxtaposition: savagely piling epithet upon epithet to an ultimate effect of terror, so that, from the well known emerges the shape of the unknown—a phenomenon the more startling with the French, who are generally considered to inhabit an orderly, clearly regulated, well-policed language. Now, of a sudden, we no longer recognize this French language, which has become a chaotic word-world situated somewhere in the chill of cosmic space. Just listen to the inscription on the *abbaye de Thélème*, that Renaissance convent of his shaping, from which Rabelais excludes the hypocrites:

> Cy n'entrez pas, hypocrites, bigots,
> Vieux matagotz, marmiteux, borsoufles,
> Torcoulx, badaux, plus que n'estoient les Gotz,
> Ny Ostrogotz, precurseurs des magotz,
> Haires, cagotz, cafars empantouflez,
> Gueux mitoufles, frapars escorniflez,
> Befflez, enflez, fagoteurs de tabus;
> Tirez ailleurs pour vendre vos abus.

The prosaic commentators of the Lefranc edition would explain that this kind of rather mediocre poetry is derived from the popular genre of the *cry* (the harangue of a barker), and overloaded with devices of the *rhétoriqueur* school. But I can never read these lines without being frightened, and I am shaken in this very moment by the horror emanating from this accumulation of -*fl*- and -*got*- clusters—of sounds which, in themselves, and taken separately, are quite harmless, of words grouped together, bristling with Rabelais' hatred of hypocrisy—that greatest of all crimes against life. A *cry*, yes, but in a more extensive meaning of the word: it is the gigantic voice of Rabelais which cries to us directly across the gulf of the centuries, as shattering now as at the hour when Rabelais begot these word-monsters.

If, then, it is true that Rabelais' word-formation reflects an attitude somewhere between reality and irreality, with its shudders of horror and its comic relief, what of Lanson's famous statement on Rabelais in general, which is repeated in thousands of French schools and in most of the Lanson-imbued seminars of French throughout the world: "Jamais réalisme plus pur, plus puissant et plus triomphant ne s'est vu"? Well, it is simply wrong. I have not time to develop here the conclusions which would round out the utterly anti-realistic picture of Rabelais that stands out in his work; it could be shown that the whole plot of Rabelais' epic, the fantastic voyage of fantastic people to the oracle of the priestess Bacbuc (whose ambiguous response: *"Trinc!"* is just a nowhere word) as well as the invention of detail (e.g. Panurge's speech on debtors and lenders, in which the earthy Panurge drives forward, from his astute egoistic refusal to live without debts, to a cosmic, utopian vision of a paradoxical world resting on the universal law of indebtedness)—that everything in Rabelais' work tends toward the creation of a world of irreality.

Thus, what has been disclosed by the study of Rabelais' language, the literary study would corroborate; it could not be otherwise, since language is only one outward crystallization of the "inward form," or, to use another metaphor: the lifeblood of the poetic creation[7] is everywhere the same, whether we tap the organism at "language" or "ideas," at "plot" or at "composition." As regards the last, I could as well have begun with a study of the rather loose literary composition of Rabelais' writings and only later have gone over to his ideas, his plot, his language. Because I happened to be a linguist it was from the linguistic angle that I started, to fight my way to his unity. Obviously, no fellow scholar must be required to do the same. What he must be asked to do, however, is, I believe, to work from the surface to the "inward life-center" of the work of art: first observing details about the superficial appearance of the particular work (and the "ideas" expressed by a poet are, also, only one of the superficial traits in a work of art);[8] then, grouping these details and seeking to integrate them into a creative principle which may have been present in the soul of the artist; and, finally, making the return trip to all the other groups of observations in order to find whether the "inward form" one has tentatively constructed gives an account of the whole. The scholar will surely be able to state, after three or four of these "fro voyages," whether he has found the life-giving center, the sun of the solar system (by then he will know whether he is really permanently installed in the center, or whether he finds himself in an "excentric" or peripheric position). There is no shadow of truth in the objection raised not long ago by one of the representatives of the mechanist Yale school of linguists against the "circularity of arguments" of the mentalists: against the "explanation of a linguistic fact by an assumed psychological process for which the only evidence is the fact to be explained."[9] I could immediately reply that my school is not satisfied with psychologizing one trait but bases its assumptions on several traits carefully grouped and integrated; one should, in fact, embrace *all* the linguistic traits observable with a given author (I myself have tried to come as close as possible to this requirement of completeness in my studies on Racine, Saint-Simon, Quevedo [in *RSL*]). And the circle of which the adversary just quoted speaks is not a vicious one; on the contrary, it is the basic operation in the humanities, the *Zirkel im Verstehen* as Dilthey has termed the discovery, made by the Romantic scholar and theologian Schleiermacher, that cognizance in philology is reached not only by the gradual progression from one detail to another detail, but by the anticipation or divination of the whole—because "the detail can be understood only by the whole and any explanation of detail presupposes the understanding of the whole."[10] Our to-and-fro voyage from certain outward details to the inner center and back again to other series of details is only an application of the principle of the "philological circle." After all, the concept of the Romance languages as based on one Vulgar Latin substratum, and reflected in them although identical with none—this has been reached by the founder of Romance philology, Diez, the pupil of the Romantics, precisely by means of this "philological circle," which allowed him to sit installed in the center of the phenomenon "Romance Languages," whereas Raynouard, his predecessor, by identifying one of the Romance varieties, Provençal, with Proto-Romance, found himself in an excentric position, from which point it was impossible to explain satisfactorily all the outward traits of Romance. To proceed from some exterior traits of Philippe's or Rabelais' language to the soul or mental center of Philippe and Rabelais, and back again to the rest of the exterior traits of Philippe's and Rabelais' works of art, is the same *modus operandi* as that which proceeds from some details of the Romance languages to a Vulgar Latin prototype and then, in reverse order, explains other details by this assumed prototype—or even, from that which infers from some of the outward, phonetic and semantic appearances of the English word *conundrum* to its medieval French soul, and back to all its phonetic and semantic traits.

To posit a soul of Rabelais which creates from the real in the direction of the unreal is, of course, not yet all that is desirable in order to understand the whole phenomenon: the Rabelaisian entity must be integrated into a greater unit and located somewhere on a historical line, as Diez, in a grandiose way, did with Romance—as we have tried to do, on a minor scale, with *calembredaine - conundrum*. Rabelais may be a solar system which, in its turn, forms part of a transcending system which embraces others as well as himself, others around, before, and after him; we must place him, as the literary historians would say, within the framework of the history of ideas, or *Geistesgeschichte*. The power of wielding the word as though it were a world of its own between reality and irreality, which exists to a unique degree with Rabelais, cannot have sprung out of nothingness, cannot have entirely ebbed after him. Before him there is, for example, Pulci, who, in his *Morgante Maggiore*, shows a predilection for word-lists, especially when he has his facetious knights indulge in name-calling. And, with Pulci, the Rabelaisian tendency to let language encroach on reality, is also to be found: when he retells, in half-facetious vein, the story immortalized by Turoldus of the battle of Roncevaux, we learn that the Saracens fell under the blows of the Christian knights in a trice: they stayed not upon the order of their dying but died at once: not tomorrow, or the day after tomorrow, nor the day after the day after tomorrow, nor the day after the day after the day after tomorrow: not *crai e poscrai, o poscrilla, o posquacchera*. In this sequel of gurgling and guttural sounds, the words *crai* and *poscrai* are genuine Italian reflections of the Latin words *cras* and *posteras*; but *poscrilla, posquacchera* are popular fantasy words.[11] The onomatopoeias with which popular language likes to juggle have here been used by a reflective poet for purposes of grotesque art: we can see here the exact point of transition of popular language into literature. Pulci believes in the ideals of Christian orthodox knighthood less full-heartedly than did Turoldus, for whom the heroic and religious values were real, and who must needs subordinate his language to the expression of these values. The word-world, admitted to a work of art by Pulci, was not yet available to Turoldus, or even to Dante (the "etymological puns" of the *Vita nuova* are quite another matter: they are only "illustrations," just as had been true of the puns of the Church Fathers).[12] The appearance of this intermediate world is conditioned by a belief in the reality of words, a belief which would have been condemned by the "realists" of the Middle Ages. The belief in such vicarious realities as words is possible only in an epoch whose belief in the *universalia realia* has been shaken. It is this phantasmagoric climate, casually evoked by Pulci, in which Rabelais will move easily and naturally, with a kind of cosmic independence. It is the belief in the autonomy of the word which made possible the whole movement of Humanism, in which so much importance was given to the word of the ancients and of the Biblical writers; it is this belief which will in part explain the extraordinary development of mathematics in the sixteenth and seventeenth centuries—i.e. of the most auton-omous language that man has ever devised.

Now, who are the descendants of Rabelais? French clas-sical literature, with its ideal of the *mot juste*, of the *mot mis à sa place*, broke away from the Renaissance tradition of the autonomy of the word. But undercurrents persisted, and I would say that Balzac, Flaubert (in his Letters), Théophile Gautier (in his *grotesqueries*), Victor Hugo (in his *William Shakespeare*), and Huysmans are, to a certain extent, de-scendants of Rabelais in the nineteenth century. In our own time, with Ferdinand Céline, who can build a whole book out of invectives against the Jews ("Bagatelles pour un mas-sacre"), we may see language exceed its boundaries: this book, in the words of André Gide, is a "chevauchée de Don Quichotte en plein ciel . . ."; "ce n'est pas la réalité que peint Céline; c'est l'hallucination que la réalité provoque." The fol-lowing sample of Celinian inspiration makes a pseudo-Rabe-laisian effect, and can be compared with the apocalyptic in-scription over the portal of Thélème: "Penser 'sozial!' cela veut dire dans la pratique, en termes bien crus: 'penser juif! pour les juifs! par les juifs, sous les juifs!' Rien d'autre! Tout le surplus immense des mots, le vrombissant verbiage socialitico-humanitaro-scientifique, tout le cosmique cara-fouillage de l'impératif despotique juif n'est que l'enrobage mirageux, le charabia fatras poussif, la sauce orientale pour ces encoulés d'aryens, la fricassée terminologique pour rire, pour l'adulation des 'aveulis blancs,' ivrognes rampants, in-touchables, qui s'en foutrent, à bite que veux-tu, s'en mystifi-ent, s'en baffrent à crever."

Here, evidently, the verbal creation, itself a *vrombissant verbiage* (to use the alliterative coinage of Céline), has im-plications more eschatological than cosmic: the word-world is really only a world of noisy words, clanking sounds, like so many engines senselessly hammering away, covering with their noise the fear and rage of man lonely in the doomed modern world. Words and reality fall apart. This is really a *voyage au bout du monde*: not to the oracle of Bacbuc but to chaos, to the end of language as an expression of thought.

The historical line we have drawn (we may call it the

evolution of an idea: the idea of "language become autonomous"), which is marked by the stages Pulci - Rabelais - Victor Hugo - Céline, is paralleled or crossed by other historical lines with other names located on the historical ladder. Victor Hugo is not Rabelais, although there may be Hugoesque traits in Rabelais, Rabelaisian traits in Hugo. We must not confuse a historical line with a solar system resting in itself: what appeared to us central in Rabelais may be peripheric in Victor Hugo, and the reverse. Every solar system, unique in itself, undefinable (*"ineffabile"*) to a certain extent, is traversed by different historical lines of "ideas," whose intersection produces the particular climate in which the great literary work matures—just as the system of a language is made up of the intersections of different historical lines of the *calembredaine - conundrum* variety.

Thus we started with a particular historical line, the etymology of a particular word-family, and found therein evidences of a change of historical climate. Then we considered the change of a whole historical climate as expressed in the innovations, linguistic and literary, of writers of two different epochs (the twentieth and the sixteenth), finally to arrive at the point of positing theoretically self-sufficient systems: the great works of art, determined by different historical developments and reflecting in all their outward details, linguistic as well as literary, their respective central "sun." It is obvious that, in this paper, I have been able to give you only scattered samples, the conclusions from which I have loaded, and perhaps overloaded, with an experience resulting from hundreds of such to-and-fro voyages—all directed by the same principles, but each one bound for an unpredictable goal. My personal way has been from the observed detail to ever broadening units which rest, to an increasing degree, on speculation. It is, I think, the philological, the inductive way, which seeks to show significance in the apparently futile, in contrast to the deductive procedure which begins with units assumed as given—and which is rather the way followed by the theologians who start from on high, to take the downward path toward the earthly maze of detail, or by the mathematicians, who treat their axioms as if these were God-given.

In philology, which deals with the all-too-human, with the interrelated and the intertwined aspects of human affairs, the deductive method has its place only as a verification of the principle found by induction—which rests on observation.

But, of course, the attempt to discover significance in the detail,[13] the habit of taking a detail of language as seriously as the meaning of a work of art—or, in other words, the attitude which sees all manifestations of man as equally serious—this is an outgrowth of the preestablished firm conviction, the "axiom," of the philologian, that details are not an inchoate chance aggregation of dispersed material through which no light shines. The philologian must believe in the existence of some light from on high, of some *post nubila Phoebus*. If he did not know that at the end of his journey there would be awaiting him a life-giving draught from some *dive bouteille*, he would not have commenced it: "Tu ne me chercherais pas si tu ne m'avais pas déjà trouvé," says Pascal's God. Thus, humanistic thought, in spite of the methodological distinction just made, is not so completely divorced from that of the theologian as is generally believed; it is not by chance that the "philological circle" was discovered by a theologian, who was wont to harmonize the discordant, to retrace the beauty of God in this world. This attitude is reflected in the word coined by Schleiermacher: *Weltanschauung*:[14] "die Welt anschauen": "to see, to cognize the universe *in its sensuous detail*." The philologian will then continue the pursuit of the microscopic because he sees therein the microcosmic; he will practice that "*Andacht zum Kleinen*" which Jacob Grimm has prescribed; he will go on filling his little cards with dates and examples, in the hope that supernal light will shine over them and bring out the clear lines of truth. The Humanist believes in the power bestowed on the human mind of investigating the human mind. When, with scholars whose goal and whose tool are thus identical, the faith in the human mind, as a tool and as a goal, is broken, this can only mean a crisis in the humanities—or, should I say, in the *Divinities*? And this is the situation today. A man without belief in the human mind is a stunted human being—how can he be a Humanist? The humanities will be restored only when the Humanists shed their agnostic attitudes, when they become human again, and share the belief of Rabelais' humanistic and religious king: "sapience n'entre point en ame malivole; et science sans conscience n'est que ruine de l'ame"—or, to go back to the Augustinian wording: "Non intratur in veritatem nisi per charitatem."[15]

* *
*

In the essays to follow I have made an attempt to apply the principle of the "philological circle" to various authors of different nations and periods, applying it in varying degree and manner and in combination with other methods. But these articles are conceived not only as illustrations of my procedure, but as independent contributions to the understanding of the writers treated therein: contributions which should prove readable for any cultured person interested in the style of works of art.[16] For if my procedure should have any value, this must be revealed in the new results, the scholarly progress, attained by its means: the philological circle should not imply that one moves complacently in the circle of the already-known, in a *piétinement sur place*. Thus each single essay is intended to form a separate, independent unit: I hope that the repetitions of theoretical and historical statements which are the unavoidable consequence of this manner of presentation, will be felt by the reader rather as recurrent *leitmotifs* or *refrains* destined to emphasize a constancy and unity of approach.

Before putting to the test the method of the "philological circle" already delineated, I should like to warn the reader that he must not expect to find, in my demonstration of this method, the systematic step-by-step procedure which my own description of it may have seemed to promise.[17] For, when I spoke in terms of a series of back-and-forth movements (first the detail, then the whole, then another detail, etc.), I was using a linear and temporal figure in an attempt to describe states of apperception which, in the mind of the humanist, only too often co-exist. This gift, or vice (for it has its dangers), of seeing part and whole together, at any moment, and which, to some degree, is basic to the operation of the philological mind, is, perhaps, in my own case, developed to a particular degree, and has aroused objections from students and readers—in Germany, where the synthetic capacities of the public are, in general, superior to their analytic capacities, as well as in America where the opposite obtains. A very understanding but critical ex-student of mine, an American, once wrote me: "To establish a behavioristic technique which would reveal the application of your method is, it seems to me, beyond your possibilities. You know the principles that motivate you, rather than any 'technique' that you rigorously follow. Here, it may be a memory from boyhood, there an inspiration you got from another poem; here, there and everywhere it is an urge in you, an instinct backed up by your experience, that tells you immediately: 'this is not important; this is.' At every second you are making choices, but you hardly know that you make them: what seems right to you must be immediately right. And you can only show by doing; you see the meaning as a whole from the beginning; there are almost no steps in your mental processes; and, writing from the midst of your thoughts you take it for granted that the reader is with you and that what is self-evident to you as the next step (only, it's not the next step, even: it's already included, somehow) will also be so to him."

These words, obviously, offer a picture of the limitations of a particular individual temperament. But much of what my correspondent says is given with the operation of the circle—when this is applied, not to routine reading, on the one hand, or to the deductions of schematic linguistics on the other, but to a work of art: the solution attained by means of the circular operation cannot be subjected to a rigorous rationale because, at its most perfect, this is a negation of steps: once attained, it tends to obliterate the steps leading up to it (one may remember the lion of medieval bestiaries who, at every step forward, wiped out his footprints with his tail, in order to elude his pursuers!).

Why do I insist that it is impossible to offer the reader a step-by-step rationale to be applied to a work of art? For one reason, that the first step, on which all may hinge, can never be planned: it must already have taken place. This first step is the awareness of having been struck by a detail, followed by a conviction that this detail is connected basically with the work of art; it means that one has made an "observation,"—which is the starting point of a theory, that one has been prompted to raise a question—which must find an answer. To begin by omitting this first step must doom any attempt at interpretation—as was the case with the dissertation (mentioned in note I of my article on Diderot) devoted to the "imagery" of Diderot, in which the concept "imagery" was based on no preliminary observation but on a ready-made category applied from without to the work of art.

Unfortunately, I know of no way to guarantee either the "impression" or the conviction just described: they are the results of talent, experience, and faith. And, even then, the first step is not to be taken at our own volition: how often, with all the theoretical experience of method accumulated in me over the years, have I stared blankly, quite similar to one of my beginning students, at a page that would not yield its magic. The only way leading out of this state of unproductivity is to read and reread,[18] patiently and confidently, in an endeavor to become, as it were, soaked through and through with the atmosphere of the work. And suddenly, one word, one line, stands out, and we realize that, now, a relationship has been established between the poem and us. From this point on, I have usually found that, what with other observations adding themselves to the first, and with previous experiences of the circle intervening, and with associations given by previous education building up before me (all of this quickened, in my own case, by a quasi-metaphysical urge toward solution) it does not seem long until the characteristic "click" occurs, which is the indication that detail and whole have found a common denominator—which gives the etymology of the writing.[19] And looking back on this process (whose end, of course, marks only the conclusion of the *preliminary* stage of analysis), how can we say when exactly it began? (Even the "first step" was preconditioned.) We see, indeed, that to read is to have read, to understand is equivalent to having understood.[20]

I have just spoken of the importance of past experience in

the process of understanding the work of art—but as only one of the intervening factors. For experience with the "circle" is not, itself, enough to enable one to base thereupon a program applicable to all cases. For every poem the critic needs a separate inspiration, a separate light from above (it is this constant need which makes for humility, and it is the accumulation of past enlightenments that encourages a sort of pious confidence). Indeed, a Protean mutability is required of the critic, for the device which has proved successful for one work of art cannot be applied mechanically to another: I could not expect that the "trick of the five *grands*" (which I shall apply to an ode of Claudel's) would work for the "récit de Théramène," or that proper names, which will serve as a point of departure in my article on Cervantes, would play any part in the study on Diderot. It is, indeed, most trying for the experienced teacher to have to watch a beginner re-use and consequently mis-use, a particular clue that had served the teacher when he was treating a quite different writer—as though a young actor were to use the leer of Barrymore's Richard III for his performance of Othello. The mutability required of the critic can be gained only by repeated experiences with totally different writers; the "click" will come oftener and more quickly after several experiences of "clicks" have been realized by the critic. And, even then, it is not a foregone conclusion that it will inevitably come; nor can one ever foretell just when and where it will materialize ("The Spirit bloweth . . .").

The reason that the clues to understanding cannot be mechanically transferred from one work of art to another lies in the fact of artistic expressivity itself: the artist lends to an outward phenomenon of language an inner significance (thereby merely continuing and expanding the basic fact of human language: that a meaning is quite arbitrarily—arbitrarily, at least, from the point of view of the current usage of the language—associated with an acoustic phenomenon); just *which* phenomena the literary artist will choose for the embodiment of his meaning is arbitrary from the point of view of the "user" of the work of art. To overcome the impression of an arbitrary association in the work of art, the reader must seek to place himself in the creative center of the artist himself—and re-create the artistic organism. A metaphor, an anaphora, a staccato rhythm may be found anywhere in literature; they may or may not be significant. What tells us that they are important is only the feeling, which we must have already acquired, for the whole of the particular work of art.

And the capacity for this feeling is, again, deeply anchored in the previous life and education of the critic, and not only in his scholarly education: in order to keep his soul ready for his scholarly task he must have already made choices, in ordering his life, of what I would call a moral nature; he must have chosen to cleanse his mind from distraction by the inconsequential, from the obsession of everyday small details— to keep it open to the synthetic apprehension of the "wholes" of life, to the symbolism in nature and art and language. I have sometimes wondered if my "explication de texte" in the university classroom, where I strive to create an atmosphere suitable for the appreciation of the work of art, would not have succeeded much better if that atmosphere had been present at the breakfast table of my students.

NOTES

1. Text of an address, originally entitled "Thinking in the Humanities," delivered to the Department of Modern Languages and Literatures of Princeton University, to which some notes and an epilogue have been added.

It is paradoxical that professors of literature who are too superficial to immerse themselves in a text and who are satisfied with stale phrases out of a manual, are precisely those who contend that it is superfluous to teach the aesthetic value of a text of Racine or Victor Hugo: the student will, in some way or another, come to grasp its beauty without any direction—or, if he is incapable of doing so, it is useless to talk about it. But there are hidden beauties which do not reveal themselves at the first exploratory attempts (as the apologetic theologians know); in fact, all beauty has some mysterious quality which does not appear at first glance. But there is no more reason for dodging the description of the aesthetic phenomenon than of any natural phenomenon. Those who oppose the aesthetic analysis of poetic works seem to affect at times the susceptibility of a sensitive plant: if one is to believe them, it is because they cherish so deeply the works of art, it is because they respect their chastity, that they would not deflower, by means of intellectual formulas, the virginal and ethereal quality of works of art, they would not brush off the shimmering dust from the wings of these poetic butterflies! I would maintain, on the contrary, that to formulate observations by means of words is not to cause the artistic beauty to evaporate in vain intellectualities; rather, it makes for a widening and a deepening of the aesthetic taste. Love, whether it be love for God, love for one's fellow men, or the love of art, can only gain by the effort of the human intellect to search for the reasons of its most sublime emotions, and to formulate them. It is only a frivolous love that cannot survive intellectual definition; great love prospers with understanding.

2. The presentation of so great a scholar as Meyer-Lübke from the only angle which concerns us here is necessarily one-sided; for a more complete evaluation of his scholarship, as well as for a picture of his personality, I may refer the reader to my paper, "Mes souvenirs sur Meyer-Lübke" in *Le français moderne*, VI, 213. As for Philipp August Becker, my few remarks have given no real idea of his exuberant personality—which seldom penetrated into his scholarship; his was an orgiastic nature which somehow did not fit into the traditional pattern of a scholar. A story told me by Walther von Wartburg may illustrate this: Becker, who was rather given to the worship of Bacchus-Dionysos, used to invite his colleagues at Leipzig to a certain popular inn for copious libations. One night, after many hours of merrymaking, he realized that the bourgeois patrons sitting around him were shocked by his exuberance; immediately turning to his colleagues, he remarked: "And now I want to tell you something about early Christian hymns!" For almost an hour he talked, to the delight, not only of his colleagues but also of the crowd of *Spiessbürger* who had gradually drawn closer to him, enthralled by the eloquence of this greybeard bard who was reviving the spirit of Saint Ambrosius in a tavern.

3. These etymologies have appeared in the *Journal of English and Germanic Philology*, XLII, 405; there I suggested also the possibility of a *calembourd-on* as etymon, but today I prefer *calembredaine* to that unattested formation.

4. In fact, Ernst Lewy would destroy the unity of "Romance Languages" by placing French and Spanish, along with Basque and Irish, in an Atlantic group of languages, and Rumanian within the Balkan group (see my discussion in *Anales de l'Inst. de lingüística de Cuyo*, II). Again, there is the Russian school of "Japhetists" who believe not in "families" but in "systems" of languages, and who make bold to discover in any given language certain primeval basic "elements" of the prelogical period in human speech (see Malkiel's article in *Language*, XX, 157).

5. Perhaps the transition from a particular historical line in language, as traced by an etymology, to the self-contained system of a work of literature, may seem violent to the reader: in the first case the "etymon" is the "soul of the nation" at the moment of the creation of the word; in the second, it is the "soul of one particular author." The difference, as Professor Singleton has pointed out to me, is that between the unconscious will of the nation that creates its language, and the conscious will of one member of the nation who creates wilfully and more or less systematically. But, apart from the fact that there are rational elements in popular linguistic creations, and irrational ones in those of the creative artist— what I would point out here is the relationship, common to both, between the linguistic detail and the soul of the speaker(s), and the necessity, in both cases, of the to-and-fro philological movement.

Perhaps a better parallel to the system of a work of art would be the system of a language at a definite moment of its evolution. I attempted just such a characterization of a linguistic system in my article on Spanish in *Stilstudien*, I.

6. This study has been published in *Stilstudien*, II.

The method I have been describing in the text is, of course, one that is followed by all of us when we must interpret the correspondence of someone with whom we are not well acquainted. For several years I had been in correspondence with a German emigrant in France whom I did not know personally and whose letters had given me the impression of a rather self-centered person who craved a cozy and congenial environment. When she was finally rescued to another country, she published a book of memoirs, a copy of which was sent me. On the cover of the book I saw pictured the window of the room she had occupied in Paris; behind this window, in the foreground, was a great cat looking out upon the Cathedral of Notre Dame. A great part of the book itself was taken up with this cat, and I had not read far before I found—without great surprise—several sentences such as "blottie dans un fauteuil, j'éprouvai un tel bonheur, je me sentis si bien à mon aise sous ce soleil doux qui me faisait ronronner à la manière des chats." Evidently a catlike existence was the deep-felt aspiration of this emigrant who, in the midst of world catastrophe, had lost the feeling of protectedness and had had to seek protection in herself.

7. We could here also be reminded of Goethe's simile (in *Die Wahlverwandtschaften*, II, 2): "We have learned about a special arrangement of the English Navy: all ropes of the Royal Fleet, from the strongest to the thinnest, have a red thread woven into them in such a way that it cannot be taken out without completely raveling the rope, so that even the smallest particle is stamped as the property of the Crown. Similarly, Ottilia's diary is pervaded by a thread of affection and attachment which connects every part and characterizes the whole of it." In this passage Goethe has formulated the principle of inner cohesion as it exists in a

sensitive writer. It is the recognition of this principle which enabled Freud to apply his psychoanalytical finds to works of literature. While I do not wish to disavow the Freudian influence in my earlier attempts at explaining literary texts, my aim today is to think, not so much in terms of the all-too-human "complexes" which, in Freud's opinion, are supposed to color the writing of the great figures of literature, but of "ideological patterns," as these are present in the history of the human mind.

Mr. Kenneth Burke, in his book *Philosophy of Literary Form* (Louisiana, 1940), has worked out a methodology of what he calls the "symbolic" or "strategic" approach to poetry—an approach which comes very close to the Freudian one (and to my own, as far as it was influenced by Freud), and which consists of establishing emotional clusters. When Mr. Burke finds such clusters in Coleridge, for example, and observes their constancy in the writings of this poet, he will claim to have found a factual, observable, irrefutable basis for the analysis of the structure of the work of art in general.

What I would object to in this method is that it can, obviously, be applied only to those poets who do, in fact, reveal such associational clusters —which is to say, only to those poets who do allow their phobias and idiosyncrasies to appear in their writing. But this must exclude all writers before the eighteenth century, the period in which the theory of the "original genius" was discovered and applied. Before this period, it is very difficult to discover, in any writer, "individual" associations, that is to say, associations not prompted by a literary tradition. Dante, Shakespeare, Racine are great literary "individuals," but they did not (or could not) allow their style to be permeated by their personal phobias and idiosyncrasies (even Montaigne, when portraying himself, thought of himself as "l'homme"). When a student of mine, working on the style of Agrippa d'Aubigné, was influenced by Professor Burke's book to apply the method of "emotional clusters" to that sixteenth-century epic poet, and was able, indeed, to find a series of antithetical associations, such as "milk - poison," "mother - serpent," "nature - unnatural" used in reference to pairs represented by the Catholic Catherine de Medicis and her Protestant opponents, I had to point out to him that these particular associational patterns (which had reminded him of Joyce) were all given by classical and Scriptural tradition: D'Aubigné merely gave powerful expression to age-old ideological motifs that transcended his personal, nervous temperament: the starting point for his "mère non-mère" was, obviously, the Greek μήτηρ ἀμήτωρ. Recently, I have had occasion also to point out the same truth in regard to the sixteenth-century poet Guevara, whose style has been explained by Freudian frustration.

8. Under the noble pretext of introducing "history of ideas" into literary criticism, there have appeared in recent times, with the approval of the departments of literary history, academic theses with such titles as "Money in Seventeenth-Century French (English, Spanish etc.) Comedy," "Political Tendencies in Nineteenth-Century French (English, Spanish etc.) Literature." Thus we have come to disregard the philological character of the discipline of literary history, which is concerned with ideas couched in linguistic and literary form, not with ideas in themselves (this is the field of history of philosophy) or with ideas as informing action (this is the field of history and the social sciences). Only in the linguistico-

literary field are we philologians competent qua scholars. The type of dissertations cited above reveals an unwarranted extension of the (in itself commendable) tendency toward breaking down departmental barriers, to such a degree that literary history becomes the gay sporting ground of incompetence. Students of the department of literature come to treat the complex subjects of a philosophical, political, or economic nature with the same self-assurance that once characterized those Positivists who wrote on "The Horse in Medieval Literature." But while it is possible for the average person to know "what a horse is" (if less so what "a horse in literature" is), it is much more difficult for a student of literature to know "what money is" (and still more so what "money in literature" is). In fact, this new type of thesis is only an avatar of the old positivistic thesis; but, while the original positivism was motivated by a sincere respect for competence, the neo-positivists now would administer the death-blow to scholarly competence.

9. Cf. my article in *Modern Philological Quarterly*: "Why Does Language Change?" and the polemics resulting therefrom in *Language*, xx, 45 and 245.

10. Cf. Schleiermacher, *Sämtl. Werke*, III, 3, p. 343. "Über den Begriff der Hermeneutik mit Bezug auf F. A. Wolfs Andeutungen und Arts Lehrbuch"—a speech delivered in 1829. Schleiermacher distinguishes between the "comparative" and the "divinatory" methods, the combination of which is necessary in "hermeneutics," and since hermeneutics falls into two parts, a "grammatical" and a "psychological" part, both methods must be used in both parts of hermeneutics. Of the two methods, it is the divinatory which requires the "Zirkelschluss." We have been dealing here with the *Zirkelschluss* in the "divination" of the psychology of authors; as for "grammatical divination," any college student who attempts to parse a Ciceronian period is constantly using it: he cannot grasp the construction except by passing continuously from the parts to the whole of the sentence and back again to its parts.

Dr. Ludwig Edelstein has called my attention to the Platonic origin of Schleiermacher's discovery: it is in *Phaedo* that Socrates states the importance of the whole for the cognition of the parts. Accordingly, it would appear that I err in adopting Schleiermacher's "theological" approach and that I am undiplomatic in asking for an approach so at variance with that which is traditional in the humanities (when Dewey reproved the Humanists for the residues of theology in their thinking, they made haste to disavow any theological preoccupation—while I take the stand of saying: "Yes, we Humanists are theologians!"); would it not, I am asked, be better to show the irrationalism inherent in any rational operation in the humanities, than to demand the overt irrationalism of religion which our secular universities must thoroughly abhor? My answer is that Socrates himself was a religious genius and that, through Plato, he is present in much of Christian thought. As concerns the necessity, for the scholar, of having recourse to religion, cf. the conclusive reasoning of Erich Frank in his book *Philosophical Understanding and Religious Truth* (1945).

The traditional view of the "viciousness" of the philological circle is unfortunately held in an otherwise brilliant attack against "the biographical fashion in literary criticism" (University of California Publications, in *Classical Philology*, XII, 288) by Professor Harold Cherniss: in his argument against the philologians of the Stefan George school who, though not dealing with the outward biography of artists, believe that the inner form of the artist's personality can be grasped in his works by a kind of intuition, Cherniss writes: "The intuition which discovers in the writings of an author the 'natural law' and 'inward form' of his personality, is proof against all objections, logical and philological; but, while one must admit that a certain native insight, call it direct intelligence or intuition as you please, is required for understanding any text, it is, all the same, a vicious circle to intuit the nature of the author's personality from his writings and then to interpret those writings in accordance with the 'inner necessity' of that intuited personality. Moreover, once the intuition of the individual critic is accepted as the ultimate basis of all interpretation, the comprehension of a literary work becomes a completely private affair, for the intuition of any one interpreter has no more objective validity than that of any other."

I believe that the word "intuition" with its deliberate implication of extraordinary mystic qualities on the part of the critic, vitiates not only the reasoning of the Stefan George school but also that of their opponents. The "circle" is vicious only when an uncontrolled intuition is allowed to exercise itself upon the literary works; the procedure from details to the inner core and back again is not in itself at all vicious; in fact, the "intelligent reading" which Professor Cherniss advocates without defining it (though he is forced to grant rather uncomfortably that it is "a certain native insight, call it direct intelligence or intuition as you please") is based precisely on that very philological circle. To understand a sentence, a work of art, or the inward form of an artistic mind involves, to an increasing degree, irrational moves—which must, also to an increasing degree, be controlled by reason.

Heidegger, in *Sein und Zeit*, I, 32 ("Verstehen und Auslegung"), shows that all "exegesis" is circular, i.e. is a catching up with the "understanding," which is nothing else than an anticipation of the whole that is "existentially" given to man: "Zuhandenes wird immer schon aus der Bewandtnisganzheit der verstanden. . . . Die Auslegung gründet jeweils in einer *Vorsicht*, die das in Vorhabe Genommene auf eine bestimmte Auslegbarkeit hin 'anschneidet.' . . . Auslegung ist nie ein voraussetzungsloses Erfassen eines Vorgegebenen. . . . Alle Auslegung, die Verständnis beistellen soll, muss schon das Auszulegende verstanden haben. . . . *Aber in diesem Zirkel ein vitiosum sehen und nach Wegen Ausschau halten, ihn zu vermeiden, ja ihn auch nur als unvermeidliche Unvollkommenheit 'empfinden,' heisst das Verstehen von Grund aus missverstehen* [the italics are the author's]. . . . Das Entscheidende ist nicht aus dem Zirkel heraus-, sondern in ihn nach der rechten Weise hineinzukommen. . . . In ihm verbirgt sich eine positive Möglichkeit ursprünglichsten Erkennens, die freilich in echter Weise nur dann ergriffen ist, wenn die Auslegung verstanden hat, dass ihre erste, ständige und letzte Aufgabe bleibt, sich jeweils Vorhabe, Vorsicht und Vorgriff nicht durch Einfälle und Volksbegriffe vorgeben zu lassen, sondern in deren Ausarbeitung aus den Sachen selbst her das wissenschaftliche Thema zu sichern. Der 'Zirkel' im Verstehen gehört zur Struktur des Sinnes, welches Phänomen in der existenzialen Verfassung des Daseins, im auslegenden Verstehen verwurzelt ist."

This "Vorsicht," this anticipation of the whole, is especially necessary for the understanding of philosophical writing. Franz Rosenzweig, "Das neue Denken" (in *Kleinere Schriften*, 1937) writes: "The first pages of philosophical books are held by the reader in special respect. . . . He thinks they [such books] ought to be 'especially logical,' and by this he means that each sentence depends on the one that precedes it, so that if the famous one stone is pulled, 'the whole tumbles.' Actually, this is nowhere less the case than in philosophical books. Here a sentence does not follow from its predecessor, but much more probably from its successor. . . . Philosophical books refuse such methodical ancien-régime strategy; they must be conquered à la Napoleon, in a bold thrust against the main body of the enemy; and after the victory at this point, the small fortresses will fall of themselves." (I owe this quotation to Kurt H. Wolf's article, "The Sociology of Knowledge" in *Philosophy of Science*, x; Wolf calls the anticipatory understanding of wholes a "central attitude": "In our everyday social interaction we constantly practice the central-attitude approach without which we could not 'know' how to behave toward other persons, or how to read a book, to see a picture, or to play or listen to a piece of music. . . .") What Heidegger, Rosenzweig, and Wolf describe is the method of the humanities which Pascal has called the "esprit de finesse" (as contrasted to the "esprit géométrique").

For the students in Romance Gröber formulated the idea of the philological circle (without mentioning the "circle" itself) in *Gröber's Grundriss* 1/3 (1888) : "Absichtslose Wahrnehmung, unscheinbare Anfänge gehen dem zielbewussten Suchen, dem allseitigen Erfassen des Gegenstandes voraus. Im sprungweisen Durchmessen des Raumes hascht dann der Suchende nach dem Ziel, Mit einem Schema unfertiger Ansichten über ähnliche Gegenstände scheint er das Ganze erfassen zu können, ehe Natur und Teile gekannt sind. Der vorschnellen Meinung folgt die Einsicht des Irrtums, nur langsam der Entschluss, dem Gegenstand in kleinen und kleinsten vorsichtigen Schritten nahe zu kommen, Teil und Teilchen zu beschauen und nicht zu ruhen, bis die Überzeugung gewonnen ist, dass sie nur so und nicht anders aufgefasst werden müssen."

It is also true of the comparative linguist who establishes his "phonetic laws" on the basis of "evident etymologies," which themselves are based on those "phonetic laws," that he moves in a circle, in the words of Zupitza, *Zeitschr, f. vergl. Sprachwissenschaft*, xxxvii (1904) p. 387: "Unsere wissenschaft kommt aus einem kreislauf nicht heraus: sie geht von evidenten gleichungen aus, entnimmt diesen ihre gesetze und prüft an diesen gesetzen jene gleichungen, die ihre grundlage bilden." And even elementary language teaching must move in a circle: R. A. Hall in *Bull. of the American University Professors*, xxxi, 6, advocating the modern "direct method" as preferable to the old "reading method," writes: "When he [the student] has learnt a sufficient number of examples, the linguistic analysis becomes simply a series of obvious deductions from what he has learned; it helps him to perceive the patterns inherent in what he already knows, and tells him how far he can go in extending these patterns to new material." The inference from "patterns" is nothing but an anticipation of a whole deduced from the known examples.

11. This point has been entirely overlooked in the treatment of the passage by an antimentalist; see my article in *Italica*, xxi, 154.

12. This is not to say that the puns and repetitions used by Rabelais do not historically develop from the same devices used by the Fathers and the medieval writers. Rabelais' facetious etymology *Beauce* = "[je trouve]

beau ce," and his repetition of words, such as *moine moinant de moinerie*, are scholastic devices—only that they are used by him in an antimedieval manner, informed by a worldly spirit and, most important of all, by the consciousness of the autonomy of a "word world."

13. I have often wondered how historians of literature could make such sweeping statements, as they are wont to do, on the whole of the literary work of a poet, or of a period, without descending into the detail of texts (and into the linguistic detail). Goethe speaks pertinently ("Einleitung in die Propyläen") of the "Anschauung" necessary for the concrete apperception of works of art: "Um von Kunstwerken eigentlich und mit wahrem Nutzen für sich und andere zu sprechen, sollte es freilich nur in Gegenwart derselben geschehen. Alles kommt aufs Anschauen an; es kommt darauf an, dass bei dem Worte, wodurch man ein Kunstwerk zu erläutern hofft, das Bestimmteste gedacht werde, weil sonst gar nichts gedacht wird. Daher geschieht es so oft, dass derjenige, der über Kunstwerke schreibt, bloss im Allgemeinen verweilt. . . ."

The same seems to have been felt by Santayana in regard to the field of philosophy; in *The Middle Span*, p. 155, he has the following to say about the habits of his Harvard students during the last decades of the nineteenth century: "I doubt that the texts were much studied directly in those days at Harvard. The undergraduates were thinking only of examinations and relied on summaries in the histories of philosophy and on lecture notes. . . . Philosophy can be communicated only by being evoked: the pupil's mind must be engaged dialectically in the discussion. Otherwise, all that can be taught is the literary history of philosophy, that is, the *phrases* that various philosophers have rendered famous. To conceive what those phrases meant or could mean would require a philosophical imagination in the public which cannot be demanded. All that usually exists is familiarity with current phrases, and a shock, perhaps of pleased curiosity but more often of alarm and repulsion, due to the heterodoxy of any different phrases." It is needless to add that a "literary history" which is satisfied with enumerating the "phrases" (whether famous or not) used by a writer (philosophical or otherwise), without establishing any connection between them and the mainspring of the writer's inspiration, is sham literary history.

14. According to Gundolf, in his essay on Schleiermacher. According to A. Götze, *Euphorion* 1924, however, the word was not previously coined by him, but is a creation of his period.

15. Even with philologians (who are not by nature apt to be insensitive to literary values, as are so many of the so-called "linguists") one can discern "unhumanistic" prejudices. For example, Professor Entwistle ("Idealistic Extensions of Linguistics" in *Miscel·lania Fabra*, Buenos Aires, 1943) maintains that the linguistic interpretation of poetry implies the crossing of an intellectual frontier: the philologian has to deal not with "science" which treats of things that can be measured and weighed, not with "unambiguous facts" which can be tested by anyone, but with "knowledge" irreducible to "scientific" treatment—to which belongs hermeneutics, the study of the poet's meaning: this meaning cannot be treated in the "old assertive language" of the positivistic linguist, and still less can be the elusive significance of a poetic text, which transcends the poet's conscious intention. By such distinctions Professor Entwistle is perpetuating the nineteenth-century rift between positivistic science

and wisdom. As concerns what Entwistle considers to be the purely scientific part of philology—such as the phonetic laws, which he ranks with the facts testable by everyone—I wonder if the formulation of a phonetic law is not as much of a speculation as is the attempt to discover the significance of a poetic passage; and is it really true that a phonetic law can be tested by anyone who has not had a preparation for this type of study? It can be done only to the same extent, I should think, which would hold true for the establishment of the meaning of a poetic passage. And as for the unconscious intentions of the poet, I simply would not advise the interpreter to concern himself with them. As a matter of fact, the example of "unconscious poetic intention" offered by Mr. Entwistle seems to me to show how little he has grasped the purpose of philological studies: of the passage from the *Aeneid* in which Aeneas sees depicted on the walls of Carthage the Trojan war and his father's deeds:

> En Priamus! Sunt hic etiam sua praemia laudi;
> sunt lacrimae rerum, et mentem mortalia tangunt.
> Solve metus; feret haec aliquam tibi fama salutem.

Entwistle writes: "The sense of the second last line, in its context, seems to be encouraging [he has translated it: "tears are shed for his misfortunes and his death moves men's minds to pity"]: it is better to be remembered sorrowfully than to be forgotten altogether. Yet *sunt lacrimae rerum* means something other and more moving than that. There is music and intensity in the line beyond anything Vergil may have consciously meant. . . . 'Nature's tears and the mortal sadness of mankind' has been discovered in that music by posterity, and, I think, justly so." But it can be *proved* by the philologist that Vergil *meant* (and it is only with conscious meaning that the philologian is concerned) the first, the "lesser" of the two meanings mentioned (as is indicated by the two anaphoric *sunt's* which suggest a parallelism of arguments leading to the encouraging final line). The second meaning which has been attached to the line by posterity is an error due to its isolated consideration out of context (which led to the misinterpretation of *rerum* as "Nature" instead of "misfortunes," an error comparable to the famous misinterpretation of Buffon's "le style c'est l'homme même"—or even to many witty or punning misinterpretations of certain poetic lines (e.g. when the line of Schiller's Maid of Orleans: "Johanna geht und nimmer kehrt sie wieder" is facetiously interpreted to mean that never again will she sweep the floor). To the philologian this secondary graft or palimpsest imposed upon the original text may be historically quite interesting, but it has to be discarded from his interpretation of the given work of art. There is no music in Vergil's poetry but that which he put in it—but, by the same token, it is also necessary that this music be retained and not destroyed, as it is by such a translation as "tears are shed for *his* misfortunes and *his* death": the indefinite quality of "misfortune" and "death" should be preserved. Vergil's poetic music consists in the procedure of expanding the particular example of Priam's fate to that of man (and, similarly, *mortalia* should not be concretized to "death" but left as "the mortal fate"); it is the general gnome, so indissolubly linked by Vergil with the particular case, that posterity has arbitrarily detached (and, in addition to this antipoetic first move, has misinterpreted—this time poetically, in the manner mentioned above).

In this, as in the following studies, the reader will find me polemizing against the views of fellow scholars. I have sometimes been accused of raising up straw men just to knock them down, instead of being satisfied with offering my own picture of the phenomenon in question. My answer is that, in matters stylistic as well as in factual questions of literary history or linguistics, the *consensus omnium* is a desideratum, the only path to which is the discussion of the pros and cons of theories different from one's own, which enable us to vindicate the relative superiority of our own theory. The greater the objective certainty that a stylistic explanation can claim, the more we will have overcome that impressionism which, until recently, has seemed the only alternative to the positivistic treatment of literature.

16. The frequent occurrence, in my text, of quotations in the original foreign language (or languages) may prove a difficulty for the English reader. But since it is my purpose to take the word (and the wording) of the poets seriously, and since the convincingness and rigor of my stylistic conclusions depends entirely upon the minute linguistic detail of the original texts, it was impossible to offer translations.

17. Perhaps I should make it clear that I am using the word "method" in a manner somewhat aberrant from common American use: it is for me much more a "habitual procedure of the mind" (Lalande, *Vocabulaire de la philosophie*, s.v. *méthode* 1) than a "program regulating beforehand a series of operations . . . in view of reaching a well-defined result" (*ibid.* 2). As used by me it is nearly synonymous with *Erlebnis*, and consequently would correspond relatively to what is called in America "approach," were it not for the volitional and even "strategic" nuance, in this word, of military siege or of tracking down a quarry, by which it may be historically explained.

In this connection I may quote a passage from a letter of Descartes to Mersenne (*Oeuvres*, ed. Adam-Tannery, I, 347): "Mais ie n'ay sceu bien entendre ce que vous objectez touchant le titre [Discours de la Méthode]; car ie ne mets pas *Traité de la Methode*, mais *Discours de la Methode*, ce qui est le mesme que *Preface ou Advis touchant la Methode*, pour monstrer que ie n'ay pas dessein de l'enseigner, mais seulement d'en parler. Car comme on peut voir de ce que i'en dis, elle consiste plus en Pratique qu'en Theorie, & ie nomme les Traitez suivans des *Essais de cette Methode*, pource que ie pretens que les choses qu'ils contiennent n'ont pû estre trouvées sans elle, & qu'on peut connoistre par eux ce qu'elle vaut."

18. If I were to give one piece of advice to our students of literary history, it would be substantially the same as that which Lanson, touring the United States forty years ago, gave to the students of his time who were then, as they are now, only too eager to rush to their big libraries to find in the many books of "secondary literature" an alibi for getting away from the "primary" texts they should study: "*Read your texts!*" My "circular method" is, in fact, nothing but an expansion of the common practice of "reading books": reading at its best requires a strange cohabitation in the human mind of two opposite capacities: contemplativity on the one hand and, on the other, a Protean mimeticism. That is to say: an undeflected patience that "stays with" a book until the forces latent in it unleash in us the recreative process.

19. Sometimes it may happen that this "etymology" leads simply to a characterization of the author that has been long accepted by literary historians (who have not needed, apparently, to follow the winding path

I chose), and which can be summed up in a phrase which smacks of a college handbook. But, to make our own way to an old truth is not only to enrich our own understanding: it produces inevitably new evidence, of objective value, for this truth—which is thereby renewed. A *comédie-proverbe* of Musset is based, after all, on a commonplace saying: was it a waste of time to illustrate so wittily "il faut qu'une porte soit ouverte ou fermée"?

20. The requirement at St. John's for the Hundred Great Books is good, I believe, in so far as it may encourage the "click" to repeat itself in an accelerated manner—if, of course, it has come about in the first experiences: to have read these hundred books "without click" would be equivalent to not having read a single book.

2

LINGUISTIC PERSPECTIVISM IN THE
DON QUIJOTE

Argumentum: Here, the procedure will be to start from a particular feature of Cervantes' novel which must strike any reader: the instability and variety of the names given to certain characters (and the variety of etymological explanations offered for these names), in order to find out what may be Cervantes' psychological motive behind this polyonomasia (and polyetymologia). I see this as a deliberate refusal on the part of the author to make a final choice of one name (and one etymology): in other words, a desire to show the different aspects under which the character in question may appear to others. If this be true, then such a relativistic attitude must tinge other linguistic details in the novel; and, indeed, it is surely such an attitude that is behind the frequent debates (particularly between Quijote and Sancho), which never end conclusively, over the relative superiority of this or that word or phrase. It is as if language in general was seen by Cervantes from the angle of perspectivism. With this much settled, it will not be difficult to see (what, in fact, has been recognized by Castro) that perspectivism informs the structure of the novel as a whole: we find it in Cervantes' treatment of the plot, of ideological themes as well as in his attitude of distantiation toward the reader.

And yet, beyond this perspectivism, we may sense the presence of something which is not subject to fluctuation: the immovable, immutable principle of the divine—which, perhaps, to some extent, is reflected in the earthly *artifex* himself: the novelist who assumes a near-divine power in his mastery of the material, in his own unshaken attitude toward the phenomena of his world (and even in his aloofness from the reader). And it is in this glorification of the artist that the main historical significance of the Spanish masterpiece is to be seen.

UCH, though not too much, has been written about Cervantes' master novel. Yet, we are still far from understanding it in its general plan and in its details as well as we do, for instance, Dante's *Commedia* or Goethe's *Faust*—and we are relatively further from an understanding of the whole than of the details. The main critical works of recent years, which represent gigantic strides forward toward the understanding of the whole, are, in my opinion, Américo Castro's *El pensamiento de Cervantes* (Madrid, 1925), in which the themes of Cervantes' poetry of ideas are stated, and Joaquín Casalduero's article in *Revista de filología hispánica*, II, 323 "La composición de 'El Ingenioso Hidalgo Don Quijote de la Mancha,' " in which the artistic architecture of the novel, as based on the themes recognized by Castro, is pointed out. As for the style of the novel, Helmut Hatzfeld, in his book *Don Quijote als Wortkunstwerk* (Leipzig, 1927), has attempted to distinguish different "styles" determined by previous literary traditions (the pastoral or chivalric styles, the style of Boccaccio, etc.)—without, however, achieving what I should call an integration of the historical styles into one Cervantine style in which the personality of the writer would manifest itself. Perhaps it is better not to break up the unity of a work of art into historical units which, in any case, are extraneous to Cervantes and, instead, to proceed according to a method by which one would seek to move from the periphery toward the center of the artistic globe—thus remaining within the work of art. Any one outward feature, when sufficiently followed up to the center, must yield us insight into the artistic whole, whose unity will thus have been respected. The choice of the particular phenomenon, then, would appear to be of secondary importance: any single one must, according to my ideology, give final results.

Accordingly, I shall choose certain linguistic phenomena (of, at first glance, slight importance for Cervantes' artistic cosmos) which I shall attempt to reduce to a common denominator, later to bring this into relationship with the "pensamiento," the *Weltanschauung* of Cervantes.

Any reader of the *Quijote* is struck by the instability of the names of the main characters of the novel: in the first chapter we are told by Cervantes that the protagonist has been called, by the sources of "this so truthful story," alternatively Quixada, Quesada, or Quixana (this last, according to Cervantes, being the best "conjecture"); from this assortment the "ingenioso hidalgo" chose, before starting his knightly career, the name that he was to bear in the whole book: Quijote. When, at the end, he is cured of the fever of quixotism and repudiates *Amadis de Gaula* and the rest of the novels of chivalry, he recovers his unpretentious prosaic original name (II, 74): "ya no soy don Quixote de la Mancha, sino Alonso Quixano a quien mis buenas costumbres me dieron renombre de Bueno"; and the final scene of his Christian death and regeneration seems rounded out by a kind of rebaptism, as this "loco" becomes a "cuerdo" (the change of name is thrice mentioned in this final chapter, as if the author wanted to din it into our heads that the old Adam is dead); in his will, "Quixano" calls his niece Antonia by the name Quixana, as if to emphasize that he is now a "bourgeois rangé" to the extent of having a family bearing his own (everyday) name. The first-mentioned name Quixada is also used in recognition of the reasonable side of the protagonist's nature: earlier (I, 5) he was referred to, by an acquaintance who knew him in the days before his madness, as "Señor Quixada." Again, just as Quesada, Quixada, or Quixana became a Quijote when he fancied himself a knight, so, when his chivalric dreams seemed about to give way to those of pastoral life, he imagines himself to be called "el pastor Quijotiz" (and his companion, Sancho Panza, "el pastor Pancino").[1] In another episode, Dorotea, who plays the role of Princess Micomicona (I, 30), feigns that her presumptive rescuer is called "[si mal no me acuerdo,] don Azote o don Jigote." And the Countess Trifaldi jocundly endows him with the superlative for which she seems to have a predilection: "Quijotísimo." As for his epithet "de la Mancha," this is coined (I, I) after Amadis de Gaula. Later, he will be called by the name, first given him by Sancho, "el caballero de la Triste Figura," still later by "el caballero de los Leones" (in II, 27-29, this change is strongly emphasized, and a certain character is rebuked by Sancho for having disregarded the distinction).[2]

It is obviously required by chivalric decorum that whoever enters the sphere of the knight Don Quijote must also change his or her name: Aldonza Lorenza > Dulcinea ("nombre a su parecer músico y peregrino y significativo"), Tolosa > doña Tolosa, la Molinera > doña Molinera (I, 3), and the anonymous nag receives the name of Rocinante ("nombre a su parecer alto, sonoro y significativo": note the parallel wording appearing in the justifications for the names given to Dulcinea and to the nag); incidentally, the ass from which Sancho is inseparable is not deemed worthy of a change of name that would be indicative of a change of rank. Although Sancho Panza, the peasant squire, undergoes no change of name similar to that of his master,[3] and is resolved always to remain (governor or no governor) plain Sancho without the addition of "don" (II, 4), there is some uncertainty in regard to his name, too, since, in the text of Cide Hamete Benengali, the Arabian chronicler whose manuscript Cervantes purports to have found at the moment when other sources gave out (I, 5), there is a picture of thick-set Sancho with "la barriga grande, el tallo corto, y las zancas largas," bearing the inscription: "Sancho Zancas."

It is, however, in regard to the name of Sancho's wife, that the greatest confusion obtains: Sancho calls her first "Juana Gutiérrez mi oislo" (I, 7); a few lines later, he ponders whether a crown would fit "la cabeza de Mari Gutiérrez"—which change the more intelligent commentators, seeking to avoid bringing the charge of inconsistency against Cervantes, rightly explain by the fact that *Mari* had come to represent simply a generic and interchangeable name for women. But in II, 5, Sancho's wife calls herself Teresa Cascajo; from then on she is either Teresa Panza or Teresa Sancho, "mujer de Sancho Panza"; of the name Teresa itself she says (II, 5): "Teresa me pusieron en el bautismo, nombre mondo y escueto. . . ." Evidently we have to do with a woman named Juana Teresa Gutiérrez, who becomes a Juana Panza or Teresa Panza when called after her husband, or . . . Cascajo when called after her father. Occasionally, however, according to the mood of the situation, she may be called "Teresaina" (II, 73) or "Teresona" (II, 67: because of her "gordura").[4]

There are other cases, slightly different from those enumerated so far, in which the ignorance and weak memory of Sancho seem to create a "polyonomasia": here we can hardly think in terms of different traditions offered by chroniclers (as in the case of the names of Quijote), or of popular variation (as in that of the names of Sancho's wife): Sancho must multiply names simply because all the forms of names that he retains are only approximations to the real ones; they are variable because he cannot take a firm hold on them; he indulges in what linguists call "popular etymologies," i.e. he alters names according to the associations most convenient to his intellectual horizon. Sometimes he offers several variations, but even when only one alteration is involved, the effect of polyonomasia still remains because of the fact that the real name is also present in the reader's mind. Mambrino (I, 19-21), of whose helmet he speaks, becomes "Malandrino" (a "moro"), "Malino" (=the Evil One), or "Martino" (a common first name); Fortinbras > feo Blas (I, 15), Cide Hamete Benengeli > ". . . Berengena" (II, 2; this Sancho justifies with the remark: ". . . los moros son amigos de berenjenas"[5]), Señora Rodriguez de Grijalva > Señora González (II, 31), Magalona > "la señora Magellanes o Magalona" (II, 41). A similar alteration of names is practiced by the *ama* who (I, 7) contends that the books which we know to have fallen prey to the *auto-da-fé* (I, 6) had been ravished by the sorcerer Muñaton: Don Quijote corrects this to "Frestón." "Never mind Frestón or Tritón," answers the *ama*, "provided it is a name ending in -*ton*": word forms that are unalterable for the learned Don Quijote are quite exchangeable in the mind of the uncultured *ama*.

The names of the Countess Trifaldi are in a class by themselves since, in addition to the instability of names conditioned by a masquerade, there are involved the alterations to which Sancho is prone: here there coexist polyonomasias of the first and second degrees. The Countess is first (II, 36) introduced to us (by her messenger Trifaldi de la Barba) as "la condesa Trifaldi, por otro nombre llamada la Dueña Dolorida"; one of the two names is her authentic one, the other her "name within the world of romance" (just as Don Quijote is also the "Caballero de la Triste Figura"). When she appears in the pageant (II, 38) of the *carro triunfal* her name "Trifaldi" is given the following explanation: "la cola, o falda, o como llamarla quisieren, era de tres colas"; the "mathematical" (geometrical) figure of her skirt with three flounces (or trains?) is so striking that every spectator must interpret her name as "la Condesa de las Tres Faldas." But the scrupulous chronicler Benengeli who, like Cervantes, seems to care about even the minor details of the fiction-within-the-fiction, is said by Cervantes to have stated that the character was really called "la Condesa *Lobuna*"—allegedly because of the presence of wolves in her domain (he adds that, according to onomastic traditions in princely houses she would have been called "la Condesa Zorruna" if foxes had been prevalent in her domain)—but that she had dropped this name in favor of the more novel one derived from the form of her skirt. Now, this etymology of the name "Trifaldi," as stated by the chronicler (and as made evident to the eye of the spectators who see the masquerade skirt), had been somewhat anticipated by Sancho's popular etymology in II, 37: "esta condesa Tres Faldas o Tres Colas (que en mi tierra faldas y colas, colas y faldas todo es uno)." Ultimately we are presented with an array of (possible) names for the same character: "la Condesa Trifaldi, de Tres Faldas, de Tres Colas (the latter name would be due to what the modern linguist in his jargon calls "synonymic derivation"), Lobuna ("Zorruna" again being a "synonymic derivate"[6]), Dueña Dolorida—a list as impressive as that of the names of Don Quijote.

Now those commentators who, in general, take the line of emphasizing the satiric intent of Cervantes, will point out that the variety of names attributed to the protagonist by Cervantes is simply an imitation of the pseudohistorical tendencies of the authors of chivalric novels who, in order to show their accurateness as historians, pretend to have resorted to different sources.[7] In the case of the names of Sancho's wife,

some commentators point out, as we have seen, that the polyonomasia is due to the onomastic habits of the period; in the
alterations of the name "Mambrino" they usually see a satire
on Sancho's ignorance; in the case of the Condesa Trifaldi
I have seen no explanation (Rodríguez Marín's edition points
out possible "historical" sources for the costume itself of "tres
colas o faldas"). But, evidently, there must be a common pattern of thought behind all these cases, which would explain
(1) the importance given to a name or change of name, (2)
the etymological concern with names, (3) the polyonomasia
in itself.

Now it happens that just these three features are well
known to the medievalist (less, perhaps, to students of Renaissance literature): they ultimately derive from Biblical
studies and from ancient philology: one need only think of
Saint Jerome's explanation of Hebrew names or of Isidore's
"Etymologies"—and of the etymologizing habits of all great
medieval poets. The names in the Bible were treated with
seriousness; in the Old Testament the name, or rather the
names of God were all-important (*Exodus* VI, 2-3: "I am
Iahve, and I have appeared to Abraham, Isaak and Jacob as *El
Schaddai*, under the name of Jahve I was not known to
them," cf. *ibid.*, III, 14); the many *nomina sacra* revealed the
many aspects through which the divine might make itself felt
(cf. *PMLA*, LVI, 13 seq.). Nor does the importance of the
name decrease with the New Testamentary divinity (Christ is
Immanuel). And, in the New Testament, a tendency appears
which will have great influence on medieval chivalry: the
change of name subsequent to baptism will be imitated by the
change of name undergone by the newly dubbed knight. In all
these sacred (or sacramental) names or changes of names,
etymology plays a large part, because the true meaning (the
etymon) may reveal eternal verities latent in the words—indeed, it was possible for many etymologies to be proposed for
the same word, since God may have deposited different meanings in a single term: polyonomasia and polyetymology. Both
these techniques are generally applied to a greater degree to
proper names than to common nouns—because the former,
"untranslatable" as they are by their nature, participate more

in the mysterious aspect of human language: they are less motivated. In proper names the medieval mind could see reflected more of the multivalence of the world full of arcana. The Middle Ages were characterized by an admiration as well for the correspondence between word and thing as for the mystery which makes this correspondence unstable.

By all this I do not mean to deny that Cervantes followed the models pointed out to us by the commentators: what I do say is that, in doing so, he was also following certain accepted medieval patterns (which, however, he submitted to a new interpretation: that of his critical intelligence). It is possible, for example, in the case of the name "Trifaldi," to see on the surface a medieval imagination at work: the name is given an interpretation (*Trifaldi = tres faldas*) which, from our modern linguistic or historical point of view, is evidently wrong but which would have delighted a medieval mind, ever ready to accept any interpretation offering a clarification of the mystery of words.[8] The ancient and medieval etymologies are indeed rarely those a modern linguist would offer, trained as he is to respect the formational procedures current in human language; the aim of those etymologies was to establish the connection between a given word and other existing words as an homage to God whose wisdom may have ordained these very relationships. The etymological connections that the medieval etymologist sees are direct relationships established between words vaguely associated because of their homonymic ring—not the relationships established by "historical grammar" or those obtained by decomposition of the word into its morphological elements.[9] In other words, we are offered edifying ideal possibilities, not deterministic historical realities; Isidore will connect *sol* and *solus* because of the ideological beauty of this relationship, not *sol* and ἥλιος as the comparative grammarian of today must do.

But, if the equation *Trifaldi = tres faldas* represents a "medieval" etymology, Cervantes himself did not take too seriously his own etymologizing: he must have been perfectly well aware of the historically real explanation—that which prompted him to coin the word. *Trifaldi* is evidently a regressive form from *Trifaldín*, which name, in turn, is the farcical

Italian *Truffaldino* "nome di personaggio ridicolo e basso di commedia" (Tomm.-Bellini); the reference to *truffare* "to cheat" is apposite, in our story, given the farcical episode intended to delude Don Quijote and Sancho. Thus the name of the messenger *Trifaldín* is (historically) not a diminutive of *Trifaldi*, as it might seem but, on the contrary, was preexistent, in Cervantes' mind, to the name of the mistress. The etymology of "tres faldas" is, historically speaking, entirely out of place. We have to face here the same para-etymological vein in which Rabelais (facetiously imitating medieval practice, while exemplifying the joyous freedom with which the Renaissance writer could play with words) explained the name *Gargantua* by *que grand tu as* [sc. *le gosier*]! and *Beauce* by [*je trouve*] *beau ce* [sc. *pays*]. In this story, the para-etymological play with names serves to underline the deceitfulness of outward evidence; what for Quijote and Sancho are wondrous events are, in reality, only *burlas* in a baroque world of histrionics and disingenuity.[10]

The disingenuous procedure of offering such "medieval" etymologies as would occur to his characters (for the simpleton Sancho as well as the learned Arab Benengeli are medieval primitives) is also exemplified in the case of the nag Rocinante, whose name is interpreted by Don Quijote[11] in the style of Isidore: the horse was a "rocín antes"—which may mean either "a nag before" ("previously a nag," "an erstwhile nag") or "a nag before all others": "antes de todos los rocines del mundo." Two explanations are given of one word, as was the general medieval practice[12]—not the *one* historically true significance according to which the name was actually coined: viz. *rocín* + the noble and "literary" participial ending *-ante*. Cervantes was perfectly aware of the correct etymology but he allowed his medieval Don Quijote to offer a more "significant" one. He knew also the explanation of the name *Quijote* (= *quij-* "jaw" + the comic suffix *-ote*, derived from *jigote* etc.), while his protagonist, who adopted this name, thought of it as patterned on *Lanzarote*.[18]

Thus we may conclude that, while, for the medieval world, the procedures of polyonomasia and polyetymologia amounted to a recognition of the working of the divine in the world,

Cervantes used the same devices in order to reveal the multivalence which words possess for different human minds: he who has coined the names put into them other meanings than those conceived of by the characters themselves: a *Trifaldín* who is for Cervantes a *truffatore*, a cheater or practical joker, is understood by Don Quijote and Sancho to be the servant of a Countess *Trifaldi* who wears a three-flounce skirt.

Perhaps this procedure is symptomatic of something basic to the texture of our novel; perhaps a linguistic analysis of the names can carry us further toward the center, allowing us to catch a glimpse of the general attitude of the creator of the novel toward his characters. This creator must see that the world, as it is offered to man, is susceptible of many explanations, just as names are susceptible of many etymologies; individuals may be deluded by the perspectives according to which they see the world as well as by the etymological connections which they establish. Consequently, we may assume that the linguistic perspectivism of Cervantes is reflected in his invention of plot and characters; and, just as, by means of polyonomasia and polyetymologia, Cervantes makes the world of words appear different to his different characters, while he himself may have his own, the coiner's, view of these names, similarly he watches the story he narrates from his own private vantage point: the way in which the characters conceive of the situations in which they are involved may be not at all the way in which Cervantes sees them—though this latter way is not always made clear to the reader. In other words, Cervantes' perspectivism, linguistic and otherwise,[14] would allow him qua artist to stand above, and sometimes aloof from, the misconceptions of his characters. Later we will have more to say about what lies behind this attitude of Cervantes; suffice it for us here, where we are given the first opportunity to look into the working of the (linguistic) imagination of the novelist, to have summarily indicated the relationship between his linguistic ambivalences and his general perspectivism.[14a]

If, now, we turn back for a moment to Sancho's mispronunciations of names—which, as we have seen, was one of the contributing factors to the polyonomasia of the novel—

we will recognize a particular application of Cervantes' linguistic perspectivism at work: to Sancho's uncultured mind, "Mambrino" must appear now as "Malino," now as "Martino," etc. In this, there is no suggestion of smugness on the part of Cervantes, as there might be with modern intellectual writers who would mock the linguistic "abuses" of ignorant characters; Cervantes presents "Malino," "Martino," etc., simply as the "linguistic appearances" of what, for Don Quijote, for example, can evidently be only Mambrino.[15] This lack of auctorial criticism in the face of so much linguistic relativity tends to shake the reader's confidence in established word usage. Of course, we are apt to rely on the correctness of Don Quijote's use of words and names; but who knows whether the knight, who is so often mistaken in his attempts to define reality (as he is precisely in his identification of the helmet of Mambrino), has hit this time upon the right name, whether this name is not as much of a dream as are the fantastic adventures he envisions (we are reminded of the baroque theme *par excellence* ". . . que los sueños sueños son")? Why should, then, "Mambrino" and not "Malino" or "Martino" be the name representing *reality*? The same insistence on "correctness" of word-usage, as applied to the nonexistent, occurs in the scene where Quijote listens to the *ama*'s cock-and-bull story of the theft of the books by "the sorcerer Muñaton," and finds nothing to correct therein but the name: not "Muñaton" but "Freston": Freston and Mambrino are names correct in irreality (in books), representing naught in reality. Evidently we are offered in Don Quijote a caricature of the humanist[16] who is versed in books and bookish names, but is unconcerned as to their valid relationship to reality (he has a pendant in the *licenciado*, to whom Don Quijote tells the fantastic story of his descent to the "cueva de Montesinos," and who is outspokenly qualified by Cervantes as a "humanista").[17]

In these two incidents we have a suggestion of a theme which informs our whole novel: the problem of the reality of literature. I belong with those critics who take seriously Cervantes' statement of purpose: "derribar la máquina mal fundada de los libros de caballería"; this statement, which indicts a particular literary genre, is, in fact, a recognition of the potential danger of "the book." And, in its larger sense, the *Quijote* is an indictment of the bookish side of Humanism,[18] a creed in which, seventy years earlier, Rabelais had so firmly believed, and an indictment of the "word-world" in which the Renaissance had delighted without qualms. Whereas the writers of the Renaissance were able to build up their word-worlds out of sheer exuberance, free to "play" linguistically because of their basic confidence in life—with the baroque artist Desengaño, disillusionment is allowed to color all things of the world, including books and their words, which possess only the reality of a *sueño*. Words are no longer, as they had been in the Middle Ages, depositories of truths nor, as they had been in the Renaissance, an expansion of life: they are, like the books in which they are contained, sources of hesitation, error, deception—"dreams."

The same linguistic perspectivism is present in Cervantes' treatment of common nouns. For the most part we have to do with the confusion, or the criticism, engendered by the clash of two linguistic standards determined mainly by social status.[19] Here, too, in this continuous give-and-take between cultured and uncultured speakers, there is given a suggestion of linguistic relativism that is willed by Cervantes. The opposition between two different ways of speech takes different forms: it may be Sancho who is interrupted and corrected by Don Quijote: in I, 32 [*hereje o*] *flemático* is corrected to *cismático*; in II, 7 *relucido* > *reducido*; II, 8 *sorbiese* > *asolviese*; II, 9 *cananeas* > *hacaneas*; II, 187 *friscal* > *fiscal*.[20] Particularly interesting are the cases in which the term used by Sancho and the correction offered by Quijote are in the relationship of etymological doublets (popular and learned developments of the same root): (I, 12): *cris - eclipse, estil - estéril* (how admirably has Cervantes anticipated the discoveries of nineteenth-century linguistics!). Again, it may be a question of Sancho's reaction to the language of the knight which the squire either misunderstands (in I, 8 Quijote's *homicidios* "murders" is transposed by Sancho into the more familiar, semipopular doublet *omecillos* "feuds") or fails to understand (in II, 29 Quijote must explain the meaning of *longincuos* ["por longincuos caminos"], which he "translates" by *apartados*). In general, Don Quijote shows more tolerance for linguistic ignorance (in regard to the *longincuos* just mentioned, he excuses Sancho with the words: "y no es maravilla que no lo entiendes, que no estás tu obligado a saber latín") than his uncultured associates (who seem more concerned with things than with words) do for linguistic pedantry: they often blame the knight for his *jerigonza* (I, 11), for his *griego* (I, 16). And, when Don Quijote reproves Sancho for his use of *abernuncio* instead of *abrenuncio*, the squire retorts: "Déjeme vuestra grandeza, que no estoy agora para mirar en sotilezas ni en letras mas o menos" (similarly, in II, 3, when the *bachiller* Sansón Carrasco corrects *presonajes* to *personajes*, Sancho remarks: "Otro reprochador de voquibles tenemos! Pues andense a eso y no acabaremos en toda la vida"). Sancho adopts the attitude of a Mathurin Régnier, opposing the "éplucheurs de mots"! It may happen that the same Sancho, the advocate of naturalness in language, turns purist for the moment[21] for the edification of his wife, and corrects her *revuelto* to *resuelto* (III, 5); but then he must hear from her lips—oh, relativity of human things!—the same reproach he was wont to administer to his master: "No os pongáis a disputar, marido, conmigo. Yo hablo como Dios es servido, y no me meto en más dibujos!" (here, she is referring to the language of God, Who, as Sancho himself had already claimed, is the great "Entendedor" of all kinds of speech).[22] Another example of the linguistic intolerance of the common people is the retort of the shepherd who has been corrected for having said *mas años que sarna* instead of ... *que Sarra*: "Harto vive la sarna," he answers, "y si es, señor, que me habéis de andar zaheriendo [='éplucher'] a cada paso los vocablos no acabaremos en un año." In this case Don Quijote apologizes, and admits that there is as much sense to the one as to the other expression (in other words, he is brought to recognize the wisdom of "popular etymology"). Indeed, Don Quijote the humanist is made to learn new words, popular graphic expressions unknown to him—such as terms descriptive of *naturalia turpia* which the high-minded knight was wont to eschew in his conversation (I, 48: *hacer aguas* "to urinate"; Sancho is triumphant: "Es posible que no entienda vuestra merced hacer aguas mayores o menores?"), or low argot expressions (I, 22: *gurapas, canario*, from the language of galley-slaves). And—the acme of shame for a humanist!—it may even happen that he has to be instructed in Latinisms by Sancho (with whom they appear, of course, in garbled form), as when he fails to understand his squire's remark: "quien infierno tiene *nula es retencia*" (I, 25): it is significant that Sancho the Catholic Positivist is more familiar with ecclesiastical Latin terms than is his master, the idealistic humanist. Thus, Don Quijote is shown not only as a teacher but also as a student of language; his word-usage is by no means accepted as an ideal. And the reader is allowed to suppose that, to Cervantes himself, the language of the knight was not above reproach: when, in his solemn challenges or declarations of love, Quijote indulges in archaic phonetics (*f* - instead of *h* -) and morphology (uncontracted verb forms), this is not so different from the *a Dios prazca* of Sancho, or the *voacé* of one of the captives.

It seems to me that Cervantes means to present the problem of the Good Language in all its possibilities, without finally establishing an absolute: on the one hand, Sancho is allowed to state his ideal of linguistic tolerance (II, 19): "Pues sabe que no me he criado en la corte ni he estudiado en Salamanca para saber si añado o quito alguna letra a mis vocablos, no hay para qué obligar al sayagués a que hable como el toledano, y toledanos puede haber que no las cortan en el aire en esto del hablar polido." On the other, Don Quijote may assert his ideal of an "illustrated language" (in the sense of Du Bellay): when Sancho fails to understand the Latinism *erutar* (II, 43), Don Quijote remarks: "*Erutar*, Sancho, quiere decir 'regoldar,' y este es uno de los mas torpes vocablos que tiene la lengua castellana, aunque es mas significativo. La gente curiosa se ha acogido al latín, y al *regoldar* dice *erutar*, y a los *regüeldos, erutaciones*; y cuando algunos no entienden sus términos, importa poco, que el uso los irá introduciendo con el tiempo, que con facilidad se entiendan; y esto es enriquecer la lengua, sobre quien tiene poder el vulgo y el uso." Thus, Don Quijote would create a more refined word-usage—though, at the same time, he realizes that the ultimate decision as to the enrichment of the language rests with the people; and he does not deny the expressivity of the popular expressions. Sancho's principle of linguistic expressivity, which is in line with his advocacy of the natural, of that which is inborn in man, must be seen *together* with Quijote's principle of linguistic refinement—which is a reflection of his consistent advocacy of the ideal: by positing the two points of view, the one problem in question is dialectically developed. It is obvious that in the passage on *erutar* we have a plea for a cultured language—though the ratification by the common people is urged. But this is not the same as saying that Cervantes himself is here pleading for linguistic refinement: rather, I believe, he takes no final stand but is mainly interested in a dialectical play, in bringing out the manifold facets of the problem involved. Sancho has a way of deciding problems trenchantly; Don Quijote is more aware of complexities; Cervantes stands above them both: to him, the two expressions *regoldar* and *erutar* serve to reveal so many perspectives of language.[23]

Within the framework of linguistic perspectivism fits also Cervantes' attitude toward dialects and jargons. Whereas, to Dante, all dialects appeared as inferior (though inferior in different degrees) realizations of a Platonic-Christian ideal pattern of language, as embodied in the *vulgare illustre*, Cervantes saw them as ways of speech which exist as individual realities and which have their justification in themselves. The basic Cervantine conception of perspectivism did not allow for the Platonic or Christian ideal of language: according to the creator of Don Quijote, dialects are simply the different reflections of reality (they are "styles," as the equally tolerant linguist of today would say), among which no one can take precedence over the other. Borgese, in "Il senso della letteratura italiana" (*Quaderni di domani*, Buenos Aires, 1933), speaks definitively of Dante's conception of the *vulgare illustre*: "Si veda nel *De vulgari eloquentia* com' egli si costruisca una lingua italiana che abbia carattere di perfezione divina, che sia, diremmo, una lingua celestiale e di angeli, di religione e di ragione; tanto che questa lingua, illustre, antica, cardinale, cortegiana, non si trova per natura in nessun luogo, e il parlare nativo di questo o di quel luogo, il dialetto di questa o quella città, è tanto più o meno nobile quanto più o meno s'avvicina a quell' ideale, così come un colore è più o meno cospicuo, più o meno luminoso, secondo che somigli al bianco o gli contrasti. Il bianco, il puro, il tutto-luce, l'astratto . . . da Dante è considerato . . . come tipo supremo del bello." Cervantes, on the contrary, delights in the different shades, in the particular gradations and nuances, in the gamut of colors between white and black, in the transitions between the abstract and the concrete. Hence we may explain the frequent excursions of Cervantes into what today we would call "dialectal geography" (I, 2): "un pescado que en Castilla llaman *abadejo* y en Andalucía *bacallao* y en otras partes *curadillo*, y en otras *truchuela*" (in fact, a modern Catalonian linguist, Montoliu, has been able to base his study of the synonyms for "mackerel" on this passage); I, 41 : "*Tagarinos* llaman en Berbería a los moros de Aragón, y a los de Granada *mudéjares*, y en el reino de Fez llaman a los mudéjares *elches.*"[24] In these lexicological variants, Cervantes must have seen not a striving toward the approximation of an ideal, but only the variegated phantasmagoria of human approaches to reality: each variant has its own justification, but all of them alike reflect no more than human "dreams." Don Quijote is allowed to expose the inadequacy of such chance designations, as appear in any one dialect, by punning on the word *truchuela* "mackerel": "Como hay muchas truchuelas, podrán servir de una trucha," where he interprets (or pretends to interpret) *truchuela* as "little trout." What, ultimately, is offered here is a criticism of the arbitrariness of any fixed expression in human language (*Sprachkritik*): the criticism which underlies the unspoken question, "Why should a mackerel be called a small trout?" Again, when Don Quijote hears the expression *cantor* used in reference to the galley-slaves, he asks the candid question (I, 22): "Por músicos y cantores van también a galeras?" Thus the literal interpretation of the expression serves to put into relief the macabre and ironic flavor of its metaphorical use [*cantar = cantar en el ansia* "to 'sing' under torture"]. Here we witness the bewilderment of Don Quijote, who tries to hold words to a strict account; we may, perhaps, sense a criticism of Quijote's too-literal approach toward language—but this, in itself, would amount to a criticism of the ambiguity of human speech. Cervantes is satisfied, however, merely to suggest the linguistic problem, without any didactic expansion.

A masterpiece of linguistic perspectivism is offered in the transposition, by Sancho, of the high-flown jargon of love contained in Don Quijote's letter to Dulcinea, of which the squire has remembered the spirit, if not the exact words. Sancho, like most primitive persons, has an excellent acoustic memory, "toma de memoria" and "tiene en su memoria" (in line with medieval practice, he does not "memorize," cf. my article on *decorar* in *RHF*, VI, 176, 283) but, in attempting to cope with Don Quijote's florid language, he must necessarily "transpose," remembering what he *thinks* Quijote has said. In this way, "soberana y alta señora" becomes "alta y sobajada señora"—which the barber corrects to ". . . sobrehumana o soberana": for this single term of address we are presented with three versions, resulting in a polyonomasia, as in the case of the proper names. Again, "de punto de ausencia y el llagado de las telas del corazon" > "el llego y falto de sueño y el ferido" (it is as though Sancho, while indulging in Isidorian etymologies, is shrewdly diagnosing his master). In such linguistic exchanges we have a parallel to the numerous dialogues between the knight and the squire which, as is well known, are inserted into the novel in order to show the different perspectives under which the same events must appear to two persons of such different backgrounds. This means that, in our novel, things are represented, not for what they are in themselves but only as things spoken about or thought about; and this involves breaking the narrative presentation into two points of view. There can be no certainty about the "unbroken" reality of the events; the only unquestionable truth on which the reader may depend is the will of the artist who chose to break up a multivalent reality into different perspectives. In other words: perspectivism suggests an

Archimedean principle outside of the plot—and the Archimedes must be Cervantes himself.

In the second chapter, the nickname "los del rebuzno" is loaded with a double-entendre: the Spanish variants of Gothamites draw on the doubtful art of braying for their proud war slogan: their banner bears the verse "no rebuznaron en balde | el uno y otro alcalde" (the "regidores" have been promoted to "alcaldes" in the course of history and—evidently—thanks to the compulsion of rhyme). Here, Don Quijote is entrusted by Cervantes with exploding the vanity of such sectional patriotism: the humanistic knight, in a masterful speech which includes a series of Spanish ethnical nicknames (which take the modern philologian, Rodríguez Marín, over four full pages to explain) : "los de la Reloja, los cazoleros, berenjeneros, ballenatos, jaboneros," shows the excessive vanity, originating in the flesh, not in the spirit, in the devil, not in true Catholicism, that is underlying the townspeople's attitude of resenting nicknames—i.e. of investing such trifling expressions of the language with disproportionate symbolic value. The Don Quijote who, on other occasions, is only too apt to introduce symbolism and general principles into everyday life, is here inspired by Cervantes to expose the vanity of misplaced symbolizing and generalization. The epithet "los del rebuzno" is thus made to shine with the double light of a stupidity—that wants to be taken seriously; of a local peculiarity—that aspires to "national" importance. The reader is free to go ahead and extend this criticism to other national slogans. That here Cervantes is endorsing Don Quijote seems beyond doubt since, when the novelist introduces this incident, he, speaking in his own right, attributes the adoption of the communal slogan to the activity of "the devil who never sleeps" and who is forever building "quimeras de no nada"—we might say: to a baroque devil who delights in deluding man. The chimeric and self-deluding quality of human vanity could hardly be illustrated more effectively than in this story, where the art of braying is first inflated and then deflated before our eyes, appearing as a "special language of human vanity."[25] And we may see in Cervantes' twofold treatment of the problem of nicknames another example of his baroque attitude (what is true, what is dream?)—this time, toward language. Is not human language, also, *vanitas vanitatum*, is it not sometimes a "braying" of a sort? Cervantes does not outspokenly say so.

The double point of view into which Cervantes is wont to break up the reality he describes may also appear in connection with one key-word, recurring throughout a given episode, upon which Cervantes casts two different lighting effects. We have a most successful example of this in the two chapters II, 25 and 27, where our interest is focused on the motif "braying like an ass." The connecting link between the two chapters is evidently "vanity": it is vanity that prompts the two *regidores* of the Mancha de Aragón to try to out-bray each other, as they search for the lost animal which they want to decoy and whose answering bray each seems to hear —only to learn, at the end, that the braying he heard was that of the other *regidor* (the ass, meanwhile, having died). It is vanity, again, that induces the townspeople—who, after this adventure, were called "los del rebuzno" by the inhabitants of neighboring villages—to sally forth to do battle with their deriders. And it is also due to vanity, on Sancho's part, that he, while deprecating, along with Don Quijote, the gift of imitating an ass, cannot refrain from showing off his own prowess in this regard before the townspeople—who straightway turn upon him in anger and beat him.

The vanity of "braying" shares with all other vanities the one characteristic that an inconsequential feature is invested with a symbolic value which it cannot, in the light of reason, deserve. Thus a duality (sham value vs. real value) offers itself to the artist for exploitation. In the first chapter, Cervantes has the two *regidores* address each other with doubtful compliments: "de vos a un asno, compadre, no hay alguna diferencia en cuanto toca al rebuznar" or "[you are the] más perito rebuznador del mundo." In the word *rebuznador*, there is a striving after the noble ring of *campeador, emperador*—which is drowned out by the blatant voice of the unregenerate animal: an ambivalence which exposes the hollow pretense.

There is one case in which Cervantes' perspectivism has

crystallized into a bifocal word-formation; in Don Quijote's remark: "eso que a ti te parece bacía de barbero me parece a mí el yelmo de Mambrino, y a otro le parecerá otra cosa" (I, 25),[26] there is contained a Weltanschauung which Américo Castro has, in a masterly fashion, recognized as a philosophical criticism (typical of the Renaissance) of the senses ("el engaño a los ojos"); and this vision finds its linguistic expression, highly daring for Cervantes' time, in the coinage *baciyelmo*, with which the tolerant Sancho concludes the debate about the identity of the shining object—as if he were reasoning: "if a thing appears to me as a, to you as b, it may be, in reality, neither a nor b, but $a + b$" (a similar tolerance is shown by Don Quijote a little later in the same episode, when he remarks, in the argument about the hypothetical nature of the hypothetical Mambrino: "Asi que, Sancho, deja ese caballo, o asno, o lo que quisieras que sea"; Quijote, however, does not go so far as to coin a *caballiasno*). Now, it is evident to any linguist that, when shaping *baciyelmo*, Cervantes must have had in mind an existing formation of the same type; and his pattern must have been that which furnished designations of hybrid animals—i.e. of a fantastic deviation from Nature—so that this quality of the fantastic and the grotesque is automatically transferred to the coinage *baciyelmo*; such a form does not guarantee the "actual" existence of any such entity $a + b$. In most cases, Cervantes must obey language, though he questions it: a basin he can only call "bacía," a helmet, only "yelmo"; with the creation of *baciyelmo*, however, he frees himself from linguistic limitations.[27] Here, as elsewhere, I would emphasize, more than Castro (whose task it was to show us the conformity to Renaissance thinking of what Cervantes himself has called his "espíritu lego"), the artistic freedom conquered by Cervantes. In the predicament indicated by (the paradigmatic) ". . . o lo que quisieras que sea," the artist has asserted his own free will.

Now, from what has been said it would appear that the artist Cervantes uses linguistic perspectivism only in order to assert his own creative freedom; and this linguistic perspectivism, as I have already suggested, is only one facet of the general spirit of relativism which has been recognized by most critics as characteristic of our novel.[28] Such perspectivism, however, had, in the age of Cervantes, to acknowledge ultimately a realm of the absolute—which was, in his case, that of Spanish Catholicism. Cervantes, while glorying in his role of the artist who can stay aloof from the "engaños a los ojos," the "sueños" of this world, and create his own, always sees himself as overshadowed by supernal forces: the artist Cervantes never denies God, or His institutions, the King and the State. God, then, cannot be attracted into the artist's linguistic perspectivism; rather is Cervantes' God placed above the perspectives of language, he is said to be, as we have seen, the supreme "Entendedor" of the language He has created—just as Cervantes, from his lower vantage-point, seeks to be. Perhaps we may assume with Cervantes the old Neo-platonic belief in an artistic Maker who is enthroned above the manifold facets and perspectives of the world.

The story of the *Cautivo* (i, 37 *seq.*), one of the many tales interpolated into the main plot, exemplifies linguistic perspectivism made subservient to the divine. The maiden betrothed to the ex-captive, who enters the stage dressed and veiled in Moorish fashion and who, without speaking a word, bows to the company in Moorish fashion, gives from the beginning the impression "que . . . devia de ser mora y que no sabía hablar cristiano" (note the expression *hablar cristiano* [instead of *hablar castellano*] which, with its identification of "Spanish" and "Christian," anticipates the religious motif basic to the story). Dorotea is the one to ask the all-important question: "esta señora es mora o cristiana?"—to which the Cautivo answers that she is a Moor in her costume and in her body, but in her soul, a great Christian, although not yet baptized—but "Dios será servido que presto se bautice" (again, we may see in this mention of God not only a conventional form but a suggestion of the main problem, which is the working of Divine Grace). The Cautivo, speaking in Arabic, asks his betrothed to lift her veil in order to show forth her enchanting beauty; when asked about her name, he gives it in the Arabic form: *lela Zoraida.* And now the Moorish girl herself speaks for the first time: "No, no Zoraida: María, María"—repeating this statement twice more (the last time half in Arabic, half in Spanish: "Sí, sí, María: Zoraida *macange* ['not at all']." The change of name which she claims—evidently in anticipation of the change of name which will accompany her baptism—is of deep significance; it is a profession of faith, of conversion. We will learn later that she must become a María because, since her early childhood, she had been taken under the mantle of the Virgin.

After this first appearance of "Zoraida-María," whose two names are nothing but the linguistic reflection of her double nature, the episode is interrupted by Don Quijote's speech on *armas y letras*; thus, after the briefest of introductions, we must lose sight for a while of Zoraida-María, the puzzle of whose twofold name and Januslike personality remains suspended in midair. The interruption is significant: Cervantes, in the episodic short stories, follows for the most part a technique opposed to that of the main plot: in the latter we are always shown first the objective reality of events, so that when they later become distorted after having passed through the alembic of Don Quijote's mind (Sancho, in general, remains more true to the reality he has experienced) we, from the knowledge we have previously gained, are proof against the knight's folly. But, in the short stories, on the contrary, Cervantes' technique is to tantalize us with glimpses into what seems an incredible situation, worthy of Quijote's own imagination (in our own story there suddenly appears before the group of Don Quijote's friends assembled in an inn, an exotic-looking woman, dressed in outlandish gear, with her companion who has to talk for her) and with all the connotations of the unreal; and the author is careful to protract our suspense to the utmost before giving us the solution of the initial puzzle. Thus the interpolations of these episodic short stories, whose reality is at least as fantastic as the most daring dreams of the mad knight, offer another revelation of the perspectivism of Cervantes; we have to do not only with the opposition between prosaic reality and fantastic dreams: reality itself can be both prosaic and fantastic. If, in the main plot, Cervantes has carried out his program of "derribar la máquina mal fundada" of the fantastic, he has taken care to rebuild this machinery in the by-stories. And our tale of the *Captive* is an excellent illustration of this rule.

When, after Don Quijote's speech, the Captive tells his story *ab ovo*, explaining how the startling fact of a "Zoraida-María" came to pass, we are allowed a glimpse into the historic reality of that hybrid world of Mohammedans and Christians, which was the equivalent in Cervantes' time of the *fronterizo* milieu of the romances—only, a more complicated variant because of the two different groups representative of the Mohammedan faith then facing the Spaniards: the Turks and the Arabs, the former the more ruthless type, the latter (to which Lela Marién and her father belong) the type more amenable to the Christian way of life. Indeed, the Arabs themselves seem to feel more akin to the Christian civilization than to the Turkish (the girl's father calls the Turks *canes*; it is ironic that later, after he has been deeply wronged by the Christians, he must call them *perros*).

As the Captive tells the story of the tragic events that took place against the background of the warring Turkish Empire, he embellishes his (Spanish-language) narrative with words from Turkish and Arabic, offering a linguistic mosaic that adds to the local color of his story. If we compare the Turkish words with the Arabic, we will note the sharpest of contrasts: the former are of a factual reference, narrowly descriptive, with no transcendental connotations (for the Turks are excluded from the possibility of Enlightenment by Grace): *leventes, bagarinos,.baño* (wrongly offered as a Turkish word for "prison"), *pasamaques, zoltanís, gilecuelco*; we find also the pejorative epithet *Uchalí Fartax* "que quiere decir en lengua turquesca el renegado tiñoso, porque lo era" (again, the *convenientia* between names and objects!). The Arabic words, on the contrary, are nearly always connected with things religious and, more specifically, with things Christian —so that a kind of transposition (or perspectivism) is achieved: "Lela Marién" instead of "Nuestra Señora la Vírgen María"; "Alá" for the Christian God, and also the' interjection "quelá" in the same reference; *nizarani* for "Christians"; *la zalá cristianesca* for "the Christian prayer," in which the adjective *cristianesco* (instead of *cristiano*), formed after *morisco, turquesco*, has something of the same transposed character, as if the Christian rites were seen from the outside. And, in addition to the linguistic medley offered the reader directly, there is a reference to the polyglot habits among the protagonists of the story. Zoraida, for example, chooses Arabic as the private language in which to talk and write to the Captive, but converses with the Christians (as also does her father) in the *lingua franca*—which language is characterized by the Captive as "lengua que en toda la Berberia, y aun en Constantinopla se habla entre cautivos y moros, que ni es morisca ni castellana ni de otra nacion alguna, sino una mezcla de todas las lenguas, con la cual todos nos entendemos," or "la bastarda lengua que . . . allí se usa": a characterization, it may be noted, which is not basically different from that offered in our times by Schuchardt ("Mischsprache," "Verkehrssprache"), the student of *lingua franca*, of the Creole languages etc., and the advocate of an international artificial language. Castilian, Turkish, Arabic, with reminiscences of *lingua franca*: why this Babelic confusion of tongues in our story? It does not suffice to appeal to the historical fact that these languages were actually spoken at the time in the Ottoman Empire, where Cervantes himself had lived as a captive: for, in addition to the foreign phrases that might serve simply for local color, we have to do evidently with an express concern for each individual language as such —to the extent that we are always informed in which language a certain speech, letter or dialogue was couched. It seems to me that Cervantes would point out that differences of language do not, by principle, hinder the working of Christian Grace—though he evidently grades the languages according to their penetrability by things Christian: Turkish is presented as on a lower level than Arabic—which lends itself so easily to the transposition of Christian concepts.[29] And this linguistic transposition of things Christian into things Moorish reflects only the transposed situation of a Moor who becomes a Christian; the story of the Captive and of Zoraida María shows Grace working toward the salvation of a disbeliever and toward the sacramental union, by a Christian mar-

riage, of two beings of different races: above the divergence
of race and language[30] God understands the Christian longing of Zoraida for the *Alá cristiano*. It was the Virgin Mary,
of whom she had learned from a Christian nurse, who inspired her to rescue the Christian soldier and to flee with him
to a Christian country in order there to be baptized and mar-
ried. When Zoraida speaks of Alá, every one knows that the
Christian God is meant—whose true nature shines through
the linguistic disguise. The same symbol is carried out on
another plane: when, from her window, Zoraida's white hand
is seen, adorned with Moorish jewels (*ajorcas*), waving a
Christian cross, the *ajorcas* are naturally overshadowed by
the cross.[31] Again, in the case of Zoraida's letters to the prisoners, written in Arabic but adorned with the sign of the
Cross, it is clear that these indications of different cultural
climates clearly express only one thing: her will to be a Christian. It is not the language, the gesture, the costume, or the
body that matter to Him, but the meaning behind all the exterior manifestations: the soul. God, Cervantes is telling us,
can recognize behind the "perspective" of a disbeliever, His
true faithful follower.

I cannot quite agree with Castro, who seems to see mainly
the human side of the episode, when he says (*El pensamiento
de Cervantes*, p. 147): "Amor y religión (ésta como envoltura
de aquél) llevan a Zoraida tras su cautivo," and considers
the story to be one of "armonía entre seres concordados."
Rather, I should say that religion is the kernel, love the en-
velopment; we have here a drama of Divine Grace working
against all possible handicaps and using the love between Moor
and Christian as a means to an end: the conversion of Zoraida
(and, incidentally, the return of a renegade[32] to the bosom
of the Church); therefore Cervantes has devised his story
against the background of the Spanish-Turkish wars, which
ended with the victory of the Spaniards at Lepanto and in
which, as Titian has represented it, Spain succors Christian
faith. I concur absolutely with Castro, however, when he goes
on to say that this story of abduction is the most violent and
the most tragic of all the episodes in the novel: Zoraida, in
her zeal to receive holy baptism and the sacrament of Chris-

tian marriage, must cheat her father, must see him subjected by her doings to the violence of the Christians who truss him up and finally leave him marooned on a desert island, where he cries out to his daughter, alternately cursing and beseeching her. Here is a good Arab, meek and truthful to Christians, who is thrown back to the Mohammedan god by the ruthless deed of his Christian daughter. That such sins may be committed for the rescue of a soul can only be explained, Cervantes seems to tell us, by the incalculable will of Providence. Why should these sins be made corollary to the salvation of the particular soul of Zoraida—while the soul of her father becomes thereby utterly lost to salvation? What whimsicality of God! I should say that this scene exhibits not so much the "abismos de lo humano," as Castro has it, but rather "abismos de lo divino." No harmonious earthly marriage could be concluded on the basis of such a terrifying violation of the Fourth Commandment; but God is able to put the laws of morality out of function in order to reach His own goal.

In our story, which is the story of a great deceit, the words referring to "deceit" take on a particularly subtle double-entendre. When, for example, Zoraida, in one of her letters to the Captive, says: "no te fíes de ningún moro, porque son todos *marfuzes*" of her Moslem coreligionists, she is using an originally Arabic word for "treacherous" which had come to be borrowed by the Spaniards probably to refer, primarily, to the treachery of the Mohammedans (meaning something like "false as a Moor"); the choice of this word, which sounds rather strange when used by an Arab, must mean that Zoraida is judging the Arabs according to Christian prejudices (it is ironical that, in this story, it is the Arabs who are faithful and kind, and the Christians who are "marfuzes"—although working toward a goal presumably willed by Providence). Again, the accusation of cheating is reversed when Zoraida, speaking as a Moor to the Christian captive, in the presence of her father, remarks: ". . . vosotros cristianos siempre mentís en cuanto decís, y os hacéis pobres por engañar a los moros"; here, where her judgment is, indeed, factually justified, she is actually speaking disingenuously—in order to further the stratagem planned by the Christians. The discrepancy between words and meaning, between judgment and behavior, has reached such proportions that we can view only with perplexity the "abismo del divino" which makes it possible that such evil means are accepted to further a noble purpose; the story offers us no way out but to try to share Zoraida's belief in the beneficent intervention of Lela Marién, who has prompted the good-wicked enterprise ("plega a Alá, padre mio, que Lela Marién, que ha sido la causa de que yo sea cristiana, ella te consuele en tu tristeza"). When Zoraida, speaking to her father, states of her deed "que parece tan buena como tú, padre amado, la juzgas por mala," we are offered basically the same perspectivistic pattern that we have noted in the case of the *baciyelmo*: it is implied, evidently, that Lela Marién knows of no perspectivism. There can be no doubt that what Cervantes is dealing with here is the tortuous and Jesuitic divinity that he was able to see in his time —whose decisions he accepts, while bringing out all the complications involved. Along with the submission to the divine there is instituted a tragic trial against it, a trial on moral grounds, and, on these grounds, the condemnation is unmitigated; the sacramental force of a father's curse is not entirely counterbalanced by the sacramental force of the Christian rites, the desire for which on Zoraida's part brought about the father's plight. Perhaps no writer, remaining within the boundaries of orthodox religion, has revealed more of the perplexities inherent in the theocratic order (a Nietzsche might have called this story an example of the immorality of God and have advocated the overthrow of such a God— whereas Cervantes quietly stays within the boundaries of the Christian fold). And this acme of submissive daring has been achieved by placing the divine beyond the perspectives which appear to the human eye.

Zoraida herself, for all her religious fervor, innocence, and supernatural beauty is, at the same time, capable of great wickedness. And again linguistic perspectivism is invoked in order to bring this side of her nature into relief. There is a moment when the band of fugitives pass the promontory called, after the mistress of Roderick, the last of the Gothic

Kings, *cabo de la Cava Rumia* ". . . de la mala mujer cristiana"; they insist, however, that to them it is not the "abrigo de mala mujer, sino puerto seguro de nuestro remedio." Now, when the name of this infamous woman, who sinned for love, is brought before the reader, he cannot fail to think of Zoraida—though, in the comparison with the Arabic prostitute "por quien se perdió España," the betrothed of the Captive must appear as a pure woman, who refused to live in a state of sin before her marriage. At the same time, however, Cervantes may wish us to realize how close was Zoraida to the abyss, and to see the ward of the Virgin, for a moment, under the perspective of la Cava.

* *
*

If we look back now over the development of this essay, we will see that we have been led from a plethora of names, words, languages, from polynomasia, polyetymologia and polyglottism, to the linguistic perspectivism of the artist Cervantes who knows that the transparence of language is a fact for God alone. And, at this point, I may be allowed to repeat, as a kind of epitomizing epilogue, the final passages of a lecture on the *Quijote* which I have given at several universities —which, I trust, will serve to round out the linguistic details I have pointed out earlier and to put them into relationship with the whole of the novel: a relationship which, in the course of our linguistic discussion, has already been tentatively indicated. After explaining that the *Quijote* appeals as well to children as to adults because of its combination of imagination and criticism, and that the modern genre of the critical novel, which started with a criticism of books and of a bookish culture (a criticism of the romances of chivalry) and came to be expanded to a new integration of the critical and the imaginative, was the discovery of Cervantes, I continued thus:

It is one of the great miracles of history (which is generally regarded deterministically by professional historians, who present individual phenomena as enclosed within tight compartments), that the greatest deeds sometimes occur at a place and a time when the historian would least expect them.

It is a historical miracle that, in the Spain of the Counter-Reformation, when the trend was toward the reestablishment of authoritarian discipline, an artist should have arisen who, thirty-two years before Descartes' *Discours de la méthode* (that autobiography of an independent philosophical thought, as Lanson has called it), was to give us a narrative which is simply one exaltation of the independent mind of man—and of a particularly powerful type of man: of the artist. It is not Italy, with its Ariosto and Tasso, not France with its Rabelais and Ronsard, but Spain that gave us a narrative which is a monument to the narrator qua narrator, qua artist. For, let us not be mistaken: the real protagonist of this novel is not Quijote, with his continual misrepresentation of reality, or Sancho with his skeptical half-endorsement of quixotism—and surely not any of the central figures of the illusionistic by-stories: the hero is Cervantes, the artist himself, who combines a critical and illusionistic art according to his free will. From the moment we open the book[33] to the moment we put it down, we are given to understand that an almighty overlord is directing us, who leads us where he pleases. The prologue of the whole work shows us Cervantes in the perplexity of an author putting the final touches to his work, and we understand that the "friend" who seemingly came to his aid with a solution was only one voice within the freely fabricating poet. And, on the last page of the book when, after Quijote's Christian death, Cervantes has that Arabian historian Cide Hamete Benegeli lay away his pen, to rest forever, on the top of the cupboard in order to forestall any further spurious continuation (after the manner of Avellaneda) of the novel, we know that the reference to the Arabian pseudo-historian is only a pretext for Cervantes to reclaim for himself the relationship of real father (no longer the "step-father," as in the prologue) to his book. Then the pen delivers itself of a long speech, culminating in the words: "For me alone Don Quijote was born and I for him; his task was to act, mine to write. For we alone are made for each other" ("Para mí solo nació Don Quijote, y yo para él; él supo obrar, y yo escribir; solos los dos somos para en uno"). An imperious *alone* (*solo[s]*) which only Cervantes could have said and in which all the Renaissance pride of the poet asserts itself: the poet who was the traditional immortalizer of the great deeds of historical heroes and princes. An Ariosto could have said the same words about the Duke of Ferrara.

The function of eulogizing princes was, as is well known, the basis of the economical situation of the Renaissance artist: he was given sustenance by the prince in return for the immortal glory which he bestowed upon his benefactor (cf. Zilsel, *Die Entstehung des Geniebegriffs*). But Don Quijote is no prince from whom Cervantes could expect to receive a pension, no doer of great deeds in the outer world (his greatness lay only in his warm heart), and not even a being who could be attested in any historical source—however much Cervantes might pretend to such sources. Don Quijote acquired his immortality exclusively at the hands of Cervantes —as the latter well knows and admits. Obviously, Quijote wrought only what Cervantes wrote, and he was born for Cervantes as much as Cervantes was born for him! In the speech of the pen of the pseudo-chronicler we have the most discreet and the most powerful self-glorification of the artist which has ever been written. The artist Cervantes grows by the glory which his characters have attained; and in the novel we see the process by which the figures of Don Quijote and Sancho become living persons, stepping out of the novel, so to speak, to take their places in real life—finally to become immortal historical figures. Thomas Mann, in a recent essay on the *Quijote* (in "Leiden und Grösse der Meister"), has said: "This is quite unique. I know of no other hero of a novel in world literature who would equally, so to speak, live off the glory of his own glorification ("ein Held, der von seinem Ruhm, von seiner Besungenheit lebte"). In the second part of the novel, when the Duke and Duchess ask to see the by now historical figures of Quijote and Panza, the latter says to the Duchess: "I am Don Quijote's squire who is to be found also *in the story* and who is called Sancho Panza—unless they have changed me in the cradle—I mean to say, at the printer's." In such passages, Cervantes willingly destroys the artistic illusion: he, the puppeteer, lets us see the strings of his puppet-show: "see, reader, this is not life, but a stage, a book: art; recognize the life-giving power of the artist as a thing distinct from life!"[34] By multiplying his masks (the friend of the prologue, the Arabian historian, sometimes the characters who serve as his mouthpiece), Cervantes seems to strengthen his grip on that whole artistic cosmos. And the strength of the grip is enhanced by the very nature of the protagonists: Quijote is what we would call today a split personality, sometimes rational, sometimes foolish; Sancho, too, at times no less quixotic than his master, is at other times incalculably rational. In this way, the author makes it possible for himself to decide when his characters will act reasonably, when foolishly (no one is more unpredictable than a fool who pretends to wisdom). At the start of his journey with Sancho, Don Quijote promises his squire an island kingdom to be ruled over by him, just as was done in the case of numerous squires in literature. But, acting on his critical judgment (of which he is not devoid), Don Quijote promises to give it to him immediately after their conquest—instead of waiting until the squire has reached old age, as is the custom in the books of chivalry. The quixotic side of Sancho accepts this prospective kingship without questioning its possibility, but his more earthly nature visualizes—and criticizes—the actual scene of the coronation: how would his rustic spouse Juana Gutiérrez look with a crown on her head? Two examples of foolishness, two critical attitudes: none of them is the attitude of the writer, who remains above the two split personalities and the four attitudes.

With the Machiavellian principle "divide and conquer" applied to his characters, the author succeeds in making himself indispensable to the reader: while, in his Prologue, Cervantes calls for a critical attitude on our part, he makes us depend all the more on his guidance through the psychological intricacies of the narrative: here, at least, he leaves us no free will. We may even infer that Cervantes rules imperiously over his own self: it was he who felt this self to be split into a critical and an illusionistic part (*desengaño* and *engaño*); but in this baroque Ego he made order, a precarious order, it is true, which was reached only once by Cervantes in all his works—and which was reached in Spain only by Cervantes (for Calderón, Lope, Quevedo, Gracián decided that the world is only illusion and dreams, "que los sueños sueño son"). And indeed only once in world literature has this precarious order come into being: later thinkers and artists did not stop at proclaiming the inanity of the world: they went so far as to doubt the existence of any universal order and to deny a Creator, or at least, when imitating Cervantes' perspectivism (Gide, Proust, Conrad, Joyce, Virginia Woolf, Pirandello),[35] they have failed to sense the unity behind perspectivism—so that, in their hands, the personality of the author is allowed to disintegrate. Cervantes stands at the other pole from that modern dissolution of the personality of the narrator: what grandeur there is in his attempt—made in the last moment before the unified Christian vision of the world was to fall asunder—to restore this vision on the artistic plane, to hold before our eyes a cosmos split into two separate halves: disenchantment and illusion, which, nevertheless, by a miracle, do not fall apart! Modern anarchy checked by a classical will to equipoise (the baroque attitude)! We recognize now that it is not so much that Cervantes' nature is split in two (critic and narrator) because this is required by the nature of Don Quijote, but rather that Don Quijote is a split character because his creator was a critic-poet who felt with almost equal strength the urge of illusionary beauty and of pellucid clarity.

To modern readers the "schizophrenic" Don Quijote might seem to be a typical case of social frustration: a person whose madness is conditioned by the social insignificance into which the caste of the knights had fallen, with the beginnings of modern warfare—just as, in Flaubert's *Un coeur simple*, we are meant to see as socially conditioned the frustrations of Félicité, the domestic servant, which lead to the aberration of her imagination. I would, however, warn the reader against interpreting Cervantes in terms of Flaubert, since Cervantes himself has done nothing to encourage such a sociological approach. Don Quijote is able to recover his sanity, if only on his death-bed; and his erstwhile madness is but one reflection of that generally human lack of reason—above which the author has chosen to take his stand.[36]

High above this world-wide cosmos of his making, in which

hundreds of characters, situations, vistas, themes, plots and subplots are merged, Cervantes' artistic self is enthroned, an all-embracing creative self, Naturelike, Godlike, almighty, all-wise, all-good—and benign: this visibly omnipresent Maker reveals to us the secrets of his creation, he shows us the work of art in the making, and the laws to which it is necessarily subjected. For this artist is Godlike but not deified; far be it from us to conceive of Cervantes as attempting to dethrone God, replacing Him by the artist as a superman. On the contrary, Cervantes always bows before the supernal wisdom of God, as embodied in the teachings of the Catholic Church and the established order of the state and of society. *Qua* moralist, Cervantes is not at all "perspectivistic."[37] Nor can we expect to find in Cervantes any of that romantic revolt of the artist against society. But, on the other hand, the artist Cervantes has extended, by the mere art of his narrative, the Demiurge-like, almost cosmic independence of the artist. His humor, which admits of many strata, perspectives, masks— of relativization and dialectics—bears testimony to his high position above the world. His humor is the freedom of the heights, no fate-bound dionysiac dissolution of the individual into nothingness and night, as with Schopenhauer and Wagner, but a freedom beneath the dome of that religion which affirms the freedom of the will. There is, in the world of his creation, the bracing air with which we may fill our lungs and by which our individual senses and judgment are sharpened; and the crystalline lucidity of an artistic Maker in its manifold reflections and refractions.

NOTES

1. And in that same pastoral game (II, 67) Sansón Carrasco would become "el pastor Sansonino" or "el pastor Carrascón (two names!), the barber > "Nicolás Miculoso" (after *Nemoroso*, as Quijote explains), *el Cura* > "el pastor Curiambro" (reminiscence of the giant Caraculiambro?); as for the name of Sancho's wife, however, the squire, who always pays heed to the *convenientia* of words and objects, agrees only to "Teresona" as the pastoral name for his fat Teresa. We see why he cannot agree to "Teresaina": this name, proposed by Sansón Carrasco (II, 73) is so evocative of the ethereal music of the flute (*dulzaina*) that Don Quijote must laugh at "la aplicacion del nombre."

2. A pendant to Quijote, the believer in an unreal order of virtue, is Cardenio, the lover who cannot face that injustice which so often obtains in the reality of love. Thus we will not be astonished to find that the onomastic pattern, dear to the romances of chivalry, represented by *Caballero de la Triste Figura* is also applied to Cardenio: he is alternatively called (by the shepherds who tell his story) *Roto de la Mala Figura, Caballero de la Sierra, Caballero del Bosque*—before he himself is allowed to state his simple, real name: "Mi nombre es Cardenio."

The importance of the *name* for the Middle Ages appears here most clearly; any knight of romance, Amadis or Perceval or Yvain, is presented as undergoing an inner evolution, whose outward manifestations are the different "adventures" which mark his career; and it is by virtue of these adventures that he acquires different names, each of which is revelatory of the particular stage attained; in this way, the evolution is clearly labeled for the reader. Yvain acquires a new dignity, so to speak, when he becomes the "Chevalier au Lion"; "Orlando innamorato" is a different person from "Orlando furioso." Consequently, a mistake in names is no slight mistake: it is a sin against the law of inner evolution which presides over the events of a heroic life. It is significant that Don Quijote speaks (I, 28) of "la ventura aquella de Amadís [de Grecia], *cuando se llamaba el Caballero de la Ardiente Espada*, que fué una de las mejores espadas que tuvo caballero en el mundo." It is precisely because this extraordinary sword distinguishes objectively one of the exemplary phases of the evolution of the knight that the name under which he appears has a somewhat objective, temporally definable validity.

3. In II, 2, Sancho reports with pride that, though Don Quijote and his beloved are being celebrated by the historiographer Cide Hamete Berengena [sic], under their fanciful names ("El ingenioso hidalgo," "Dulcinea del Toboso"), his name has suffered no such treatment: "que me mientan . . . *con mi mesmo nombre de Sancho Panza*."

4. Again, we have evidence of the importance of nomenclature: a change of suffix, in itself, may be equivalent to a change of linguistic perspective.

In another incident (I, 22), from one of the secondary episodes, we are told that, when the guard speaks of his prisoner, Ginés de Pasamonte, as "el famoso Ginés de Pasamonte, que por otro nombre llaman Ginesillo de Parapilla," the other retorts: "Señor Comisario, . . . no andemos ahora a deslindar nombres y sobrenombres. Ginés me llamo, y no Ginesillo, y Pasamonte es mi alcurnia, y no Parapilla, como voacé dice . . . algún día sabrá alguno si me llamo Ginesillo de Parapilla o no. . . . Yo haré que no me lo llamen." Again, just as in the case of Sancho's rebuke to the one who had altered Quijote's title, Cervantes takes occasion to show the natural indignation aroused by a violation of the "perspective" which the bearer of the name has chosen and under which he has a right to appear.

5. The same type of justification of a mispronunciation by the invention *ad hoc* of a (secondary) relationship is found in II, 3, when Sancho, in order to explain his version of the Arabic name *Benengeli* (i.e. Berengena), refers to the Moors' predilection for *berengenas*.

6. Sancho offers us another example of popular "synonymic derivation": *rata* "rate, installment of payment" has been understood by him as "rat," which, with him, must lead to *gata* "cat." As a matter of fact, the procedure by which developments take place in argot is not basically different from this: *dauphin* "dolphin" > "pimp" in French argot was interpreted as *dos fin* so that a *dos vert* could follow. The modern linguist would say that Sancho has the makings of an excellent subject for an inquirer such as Gilliéron, who wanted to seize, on the spot, the working of the popular imagination. When faced with the problem of language, Sancho is not lazy and passive, as he is in general (and in this incessant linguistic criticism and linguistic activity, side by side with inactivity in other realms of life, he is typically Spanish): he asks himself why the Spanish battlecry is *Santiago y cierra España!*: "Está por ventura España abierta, y de modo que es menester cerrarla, o qué ceremonia es esta?" Erroneously he seeks to interpret, by contemporary patterns, a way of speech obscured by historic development. While he does not know as much historical grammar as does Rodríguez Marín, the modern commentator of the *Don Quijote*, he shows himself to be aware of the basic problem of linguistics: the opaqueness of certain ways of speech.

7. Accordingly, this variety of names would be on one level with such pseudo-historical interruptions of the narrative as we have seen in I, 2, when Cervantes pretends to hesitate about which particular adventure of his protagonist to narrate first: it seems that there are some *autores* ("authors" or "authorities") who say that the adventure of Puerto Lápice was the first; others contend the same about that of the windmills, while Cervantes, himself, has ascertained, from the annals of La Mancha . . . etc.

We shall see later, however, that the pseudo-historical device has implications much more important than the parodying of chronicles.

8. It is in the medieval vein that Cervantes, in the Trifaldi episode (II, 39), has the name of the horse *Clavileño el Alígero* explained as follows: "cuyo nombre conviene con el ser de leño y con la clavija que trae en la frente y con la ligereza con que camina": *convenir, conveniencia* are the medieval (originally Ciceronian) expressions for "harmony"—as well as "grammatical accord," harmony between word and meaning, etc.

9. A characteristic trait of the ancient and medieval etymological procedures was to explain by compounds where the modern linguist would assume derivation: Thus Eng. *dismal* was explained by *dies mali* instead of as a derivative from OF *disme* "dime" (cf. *MLN*, LVII, 602). In the same vein is the decomposition of the derivative *Truff-ald-[ino]* into the two parts *tri + fald-*. Compare also Sancho's decomposition (II, 3) of *gramática* into *grama* (the herb) + *tica* (the meaning of the latter word has not yet been elucidated by commentators).

10. The trick intended for the protagonists is revealed in the midst of the pageant, when the majordomo, who plays the countess, corrects himself: "a este su criado, *digo, a esta su criada.*"

It may be stated that such baroque effects are on the increase in the second part of the *Quijote*, where pageants, *burlas* and *truffe* flourish (cf. "Las bodas de Camacho y Guiteria"). In Part I we are shown the aggressive Don Quijote and his grumbling but faithful follower Sancho challenging the outward world—meeting, in their adventures, with a flux of humanity in a series of chance encounters against the fluid background of roadsides and inns. In Part II, however, the couple appear rather as being challenged than as challenging the world—and this world, the world of the big city, the world of the aristocracy, is now more formidable, more firmly constituted. The resistance of the first environment was not sufficient to bring about the necessary cure of the knight: Quijote must be brought to face the criticism of the higher spheres of society, where he is victimized with sophisticated *burlas*. The aristocrats play theater for Don Quijote and Sancho (in a way that may remind us of Shakespeare's Sly—and the "governorship" of Sancho resembles Sly's temporary courtship). And theater, like *sueño*, is bound to end with an awakening from illusion. This is a baroque theme.

If Mr. Stephen Gilman (*RFH*, v, 148) is right in claiming for Avellaneda's continuation of the *Quijote* a baroque style, it might be apposite to add that Cervantes himself, whether prompted by his competitor or not (and I personally think, rather not), went the same path of "baroquization" in his own continuation of the story.

11. Don Quijote himself explains words according to an Isidorian scheme: e.g. when he takes it upon himself to explain *albogues* (II, 67), he begins by describing the "res" designated by the word ("albogues son unas chapas . . ."), and follows this with the etymon: it is originally Arabic, he says, as the prefix *al-* suggests. Don Quijote cannot stop here, however; giving full rein to his associative imagination, he goes on to mention other Arabic words in Spanish likewise characterized by *al-*, and ends by including certain loan-words with a termination in *-i*.

12. The same "twofold pattern" is followed for the etymology of the (legendary, medieval) island of which Sancho is to become the ruler (II, 45): "la ínsula Baratería, o ya porque el lugar se llamaba Baratario o ya por el barato con que se le había dado el gobierno"; here, the first etymology is the formal or tautological one which Cervantes slyly proposes (in order to remain faithful to the dichotomy) as an alternative to the second—which is the historically "real" etymology.

13. My reason for believing that the hidalgo had *Lanzarote* in mind when he changed his name, is found in the episode of I, 2, where Don Quijote adapts the text of the old *romance* to his own situation, substituting his own name for that of the protagonist: "Nunca fuera caballero/ De damas tan bien servido/ Como fuera don Quijote/ Cuando de su aldea vino." The suffix *-ote* (as in *monigote, machacote*) has a comic ring for the reader but not, evidently, for the coiner of the name.

We have a somewhat similar bivalence in the case of the name *Rocinante* —though here, of course, it is not the suffix but the radical which provides the comic effect. The noble connotation of *-ante*, that participial ending which had dropped out of current use in Old Romance languages, is to be found, with a nuance of high distinction, in such epic names as OF *Bali-*

gant, Tervagant, and in common nouns such as OF *aumirant* (Sp. *almirante*) and Sp. *emperante* (found along with *emperador* in the *Libro de buen amor*). Thus, our learned knight, with his "epic imagination," came naturally by his predilection for such a pattern of nomenclature.

As for the factual etymology of the word *quijote* (< OF *cuissot* "cuissart") this has been established by Malkiel, *Language,* XXI, 156. Mr. Malkiel, however, confuses historical linguistics with the study of a work of art when he writes: "The etymology of this word naturally aroused the curiosity of Cervantes." In reality, Cervantes has not shown himself interested in the etymology of the common noun *quijote,* but in that of the proper name *Quijote;* and the latter was not, for him, derived from OF *cuissot,* but from *Lanzarote,* and from the group *Quijada, Quijano* (whatever the origin of these may be).

14. As a non-linguistic example of such perspectivism, we may point to the passage made famous by Hume: two kinsmen of Sancho, called upon to give their opinion of a hogshead of wine, find it excellent, in the main, except for a peculiar flavor—on which they disagree. The one insists it has a leathery taste, the other, a metallic taste. When they have finally drunk their way to the bottom of the cask, they find a rusty iron key with a leather strap attached.

14a. It is not astonishing that Dostoievski, that great absolutist who delighted in showing up the relativity in human affairs, should have imitated the polyonomasia of Cervantes: In *Crime and Punishment,* the monomaniac Raskolnikov (whose name, related to *raskolnik* "heretic," suggests his monomania) has a friend named *Razumichin* (related to *razum* "reason"), who is the flexible, optimistic, helpful, and loquacious defender of reason: his flexibility of mind is mirrored in the alterations to which his name is subjected by other characters in the novel: *Vrazumichin* (to *vrazumlyaty* "to explain") and *Rassudkin* (to *rassudok* "judgment").

15. Sancho, who appears so often as the representative of that Catholic positivism which takes the world, as it is, as God-given, without envisaging the possibility of a more ideal order, expresses his linguistic doubts about the mysterious, significant, and musical names of Quijote's making, just as he usually (though not always) suspects the *arcana* of the world of enchantment that his master visualizes: (I, 28): ". . . no eran fantasmas ni hombres encantados, como vuestra merced dice, sino hombres de carne y de hueso *como nosotros,* y todos, según los oí nombrar . . . tenían sus nombres: que el uno se llamaba Pedro Martínez y el otro Tenorio Hernández, y el Ventero oí que se llamaba Juan Palomeque el Zurdo." When he hears from Quijote's lips the fantastic names of beings from a world he does not believe to exist, he tries to bring these names down to earth, to adapt them to his homely environment. And in I, 29, when it is explained to him that the princess Micomicona is called so after her estate Micomicón in Guiney, Sancho is happy only when he can find a parallel in the names of the common people he knows, such as Pedro de Alcalá, Juan de Úbeda, Diego de Valladolid, who are named after their birthplaces.

Evidently, the names in the world of Don Quijote must be, in opposition to the homespun names of Sancho's world, the more grandiloquent the less they cover of reality: they are of the grotesque, that is the comically frightening kind, that distinguishes the names of Pulci's and Rabelais'. giants: we find (I, 18) Caraculiambro de Malindranía; el grande emperador Alifarfarón, señor de la grande isla Trapobana; Pentapolín del Arremangado Brazo; Espartafilando del Bosque, duque de Nestria; (1, 30) Pandafilando de la Fosca Vista—which last is transposed by Sancho (in accord with the feeling he has acquired for linguistic correspondences between his master's speech and his own: $f > h$, *-ando* $>$ *-ado*) into *Pandahilado*; similarly, the poetic name *Fili* becomes, with Sancho, *hilo* (1, 23): Sancho's capacity of transposition is the linguistic equivalent of his capacity for adopting the fanciful schemes of Don Quijote. Another aspect of Sancho's positivistic approach is his lack of that symbolic feeling so characteristic of his master. He gauges symbolic actions according to their "positive" or pragmatic value in actual life: when Don Quijote invites him, in order to symbolize the Christian democracy of men, to sit at his table with him and the shepherds, Sancho refuses because of the inconvenience of having to be on his best behavior at the master's table. On the other hand (for Cervantes knows always an "on-the-other-hand"), Sancho's unmystical attitude is capable of producing good results: he is, during his governorship, able to uncover the swindle involving the money concealed in the staff, precisely because he disregards the symbolic value of the staff.

16. For us to apply this label to the knight striving to revive a medieval chivalric world, in the midst of his contemporary world of mass armies employing firearms, may seem surprising to the reader. But the humanistic world was a continuation of the medieval world: and what Don Quijote seeks to revive and reenact are humanistic dreams of antiquarians. The humanist tends to revive, by the strength of his imagination, a more beautiful past, regardless of how it may fit into his time; this is the ideal strength and the weakness of any humanist, and Cervantes has described both aspects.

17. It has not been sufficiently emphasized that Cervantes, as so often happens (e.g. in the case of the diptychs Marcela - Don Quijote, Cardenio - Don Quijote, el Cautivo - el Oidor; or in Don Quijote's speech on "armas y letras"), is proceeding by offering pendant pictures when he opposes to Don Quijote's vision in *la cueva de Montesinos* the speech of the *licenciado* on the humanistic books which he intends to write. Both turn to the past: the one seeks to relive it in the present, the other, to exhume it and transmit it through his books; both attempts, illustrating the same pattern of thought, are equally futile. Don Quijote's account of his visions is welcomed by the *licenciado* as a new "source" for his complication of fanciful lore—while these same visions have been inspired by that same sort of lore.

18. Cervantes himself must have been vulnerable to the humanistic "book-virus": he tells us that he used to pick up every printed scrap of paper—surely not, like Saint Francis, because some sacred words might be on it, but in order to live through the printed words a vicarious existence, in the fashion of his Don Quijote, i.e. as a "novel-reader."

Cervantes must also, like any humanist, have delighted in the deciphering of old documents: he tells us of the adventure of having Benengeli's Arabic deciphered for his benefit; in the story of the *Cautivo*, the Arabic letter of Lela Zoraida is puzzled out; and, in 11, 39, a Syriac text is referred to: "escritas en lengua siríaca unas letras, que habiéndose declarado en la candayesca, y ahora en la castellana, encierran esta sentencia." To be polyglot is to delight in many perspectives.

[78]

19. It could be said, of nearly every character in the *Quijote*, that he appears located at his own particular linguistic level, somewhere along a hierarchic ladder. The duchess, for example, who is quite conscious of her social and linguistic superiority over Sancho, and who takes care to distinguish her speech from his (II, 32: "la flor de las ceremonias, o cirimonias, *como vos decís*") must be shown her inferiority, at least in matters linguistic, to Don Quijote: when the latter has occasion to speak of "la retórica ciceroniana y *demostina*," the duchess asks about the significance of the last word, remarking "que es vocablo que no he oído en todos los días de mi vida," and is taunted by her husband: "habéis andado deslumbrada en tal pregunta." Thus the same character has a chance to snub and be snubbed linguistically—as well as otherwise.

On the other hand we may ask ourselves: does Cervantes the super-humanist smile here at the reader over the head of the humanistic character Don Quijote? For the adjective *demostino* (an evidently popular haplology for *demostenino* "of Demosthenes") is incorrectly formed. Is Cervantes here revindicating again for himself a position above his protagonist by having Quijote the scholar make elementary mistakes?

Even when the characters lapse into a foreign language, there is a difference according to social classes—the standard "second language" in Cervantes' time being Italian. Don Quijote, being a Spanish humanist, must, of course, know Italian: he expressly states (II, 52) that he knows "somewhat" of Tuscan and can sing some stanzas of Ariosto; he examines a printer as to his knowledge of Italian vocabulary ("does he know that *pignatta* corresponds to Sp. *olla*?"); and he occasionally inserts Italian forms into his facetious speeches: II, 24: "Notable *espilorchería*, como dice el italiano"; II, 25: "Dígame vuestra merced, señor adivino: *que peje pillamo*?" Here we have rather far-fetched idioms by which the humanist Quijote shows how conversant he is with the nuances that are better expressed in Italian than in Spanish.

We also find, in our novel, Italianisms used in the speech of the lower strata of society, where they seem to suggest the language of conviviality: the Ventero says of Maese Pedro (II, 25): ". . . es hombre galante (como dicen en Italia) y bon compaño"; in the drinking scene between Sancho, his ex-companion Ricote, and the other pseudo-pilgrims, a *lingua franca* version of Italian is used at the height of their merriment (II, 44): "Español y Tudesqui tuto uno: bon compaño"—(Sancho:) "Bon compaño, juradí." Clemencín and Rodríguez Marín are therefore wrong when they object to a *caro patron mio* in the mouth of Sancho (II, 23); this is not humanistic Italian but the language of plain people indulging in exuberant gaiety.

Thus we have two types of Italianate Spanish, according to social strata.

20. Compare, for other mispronunciations of Sancho (II, 68): *trogloditas > tortolitas, bárbaros > barberos, antropófagos > astropajos, scitas > perritas a quien dicen cita cita.*

21. It was to be expected that when Sancho became governor he would establish a linguistic level of his own, above that of his subjects. And, in fact, he once satirizes the way of speaking of a peasant by ironically carrying further a grammatical mistake of the latter; the scene in question could not be better analyzed than in the words of Morel-Fatio (*Rom.*, XVI,

476) : "Lorsque le paysan vient conter son cas au gouverneur de Barataria, il cherche dans sa mémoire le mot juridique qui exprime décemment l'acte qu'il a commis [that is, *yacer* 'to lie, sleep with'], et au lieu de 'hizo que *yoguiesemos*,' imparfait du subjonctif dont il n'avait conservé qu'un vague souvenir, il dit *yogasemos* . . . comme si l'infinitif était *yogar*. Sancho, qui, depuis qu'il est gouverneur, s'étudie à parler correctement, saisit avec joie l'occasion de souligner une grosse faute grammaticale chez un de ses semblables : 'Faites en sorte, mon brave homme, de ne plus *yogar* avec personne,' dit-il avec un sourire protecteur et appuyant sur le mot. Il y a là une finesse qu'ont dû sentir la plupart des lecteurs du *Don Quichotte*." Sancho, the perpetrator of so many linguistic sins, is not insensitive to those committed by his subjects; his linguistic personality varies according to his interlocutor.

22. This idea, which is a medieval one, is clearly expressed by Sancho when his wife contends that, since the time he became a member of the knight-errantry, she is no longer able to understand him (II, 5) : "Basta que me entienda Dios, mujer, que el es el entendedor de todas cosas." The same reliance on God appears in II, 7, when Sancho, whose remark, "yo soy tan fócil" (*fócil* evidently representing a combination of *dócil* + *facil*) has not been understood by Quijote, explains : "soy tan así"; when this does not help, he exclaims : "Pues si no me puede entender, no sé como lo diga; no sé mas, y Dios sea conmigo." The coinage *fócil*, however nonexistent it may be in common language, covers the reality of Sancho's inner being, which is defined simply as "being as he is," and which he trusts God may recognize.

(Don Quijote, himself, must admit [II, 20] that Sancho, in spite of his "rústicos términos," would make a good preacher; and Sancho concurs boastfully, immediately introducing a solecism : "Bien predica quien bien vive, y no sé otras *tologías*.")

23. The attitude of Cervantes toward the popular adages is no different from that toward popular words : Sancho is given to piling up such stereotyped word material indiscriminately; Don Quijote, who is himself prone to quote adages, admires Sancho's spontaneity and fluency in this regard, as well as the original and natural wisdom which they reveal— though he advocates more restraint in their use; Cervantes does not commit himself one way or the other.

24. In the *entremés* "Los habladores" a character is made to accumulate synonyms in different languages : "Una criada se llama en Valencia *fadrina*, en Italia *masara*, en Francia *gaspirria*, en Alemania *filomiquia*, en la corte *sirvienta*, en Vizcaya *moscorra*, y entre pícaros *daifa*." Here we have the raw material (*copia verborum*) on which Cervantes will draw in the *Quijote*.

25. The raw material from which Cervantes drew the first episode is, according to Rodríguez Marín, a folk-tale (I would say, of the *Schildbürger*-tale variety). But, obviously, the introduction therein of the baroque element is a Cervantine touch. It is also in line with this element that the chimeric expedition of the townspeople, who are bent on conquering the whole countryside, should end in the beating administered to Sancho—a victory which, if they had been familiar with the ancient Greek custom, says Cervantes, they would have celebrated by raising a monument, a "trofeo."

26. The same pattern is evident in other passages : what is the *cueva*

de Montesinos for Quijote is a "pit of hell" for Sancho: " 'Infierno le llamáis?' dijo Don Quijote," ii, 22.

27. Linguistically speaking, *baciyelmo* fits into the group of *dvandva* formations designating hybrids in Spanish: *marimacho, serpihombre* (Góngora) : an object, like an animate being, may present a hybrid aspect, and be represented by the same pattern: *arquibanco, catricofre* (and *baciyelmo*). As Miss Hatcher will show, in a forthcoming article, this Renaissance type in Spanish word-formation goes ultimately back to Greek: ἀνδρογύνης—τραγέλαφος, in Latinized form: *masculo-femina, hircocervus*—and *tunico-pallium*. Thus Cervantes has expressed his perspectivistic vision in a word-formational pattern of the Renaissance reserved for hybrids.

28. Interesting, in connection with Cervantes' linguistic perspectivism, are the many puns that appear in the *Quijote*: (i, 2) Don Quijote calls the innkeeper a *castellano* because the inn appears to him as a *castillo* in which he will be dubbed knight; but the innkeeper thinks that he has been called a "Castilian" "por haberle parecido de los sanos [the toughs] de Castilla." i, 3: "No se curó ['did not care'] el harriero destas razones (y fuera mejor que se curase porque fuera curarse ['be cured'] en salud)." ii, 36 [Someone takes money] "no para tomar el mono ['because of having taken the donkey'] sino la mona ['in order to get tipsy']." ii, 66: when the lackey says to Sancho, "tu amo debe de ser un loco," the squire answers: "Como debe? No debe nada a nadie; que todo lo paga, y más cuando la moneda es locura."

The pun is a bifocal manner of expression which relaxes and relativizes the firmness with which language usually appears to speaking man.

Sometimes the "word-world," in Renaissance fashion, encroaches on outward reality. The word *donas* in the phrase *ni dones ni donas* is an entirely fantastic formation, without any reality behind it (since the feminine of *don* is *doña* or *dueña*) : it is to be explained as an extraction from *don(es)* and susceptible of usage in connection with this word alone —just as *ínsulos* is possible only in the phrase *ni ínsulas ni ínsulos*. Such formations are intended to exclude from consideration all possible varieties of the species denoted by the radical—a tendency to be found in many languages: cf. Turk. *šapka yok mapka yok* "[I have] no cap no nothing" (*mapka* being a nonce-word patterned on *šapka*). But by the very creation of a name for that which exists only at the moment it is denied, the non-existent entity is endowed with a certain (fantastic) reality.

29. In the story of Ana Félix, the Christian daughter of the Morisco Ricote, we see again how closely connected are language and faith: she explains (ii, 53) : "Tuve una madre cristiana . . . mamé la Fé catolica con la leche; criéme con buenas costumbres; ni en la lengua ni en ellas jamás, a mi parecer, di señales de ser morisca." The reader should note the expression *mamar la fé con la leche* : the same expression is used in Cervantes (ii, 16) of the mother tongue: "todos los poetas antiguos escribieron en la lengua que mamaron con la leche"; and Castro has pointed out the origin of this metaphor (Bembo, *Della volgar lingua* 1525: ". . . nella latina [sc. *lingua*] essi [the Romans] tutti nascevano et quella insieme col latte dalle nutriei loro beeano. . ."). Here, we are at the bottom of the concept of *Muttersprache, langue maternelle, mother tongue*, which ultimately go back to an Augustinian concept: the Christian learns the name of God from his mother ("hoc nomen salvatoris mei . . . in ipso adhuc lacte matris

tenerum cor meum biberat") : the "name of God" is the most important and the most intimate linguistic knowledge the mother can impart to her child; thus (and this is in harmony with Christianity, which, in general, tends to present spiritual truths behind a human veil), the concept of "mother tongue" is vitally connected with that of maternal religion (cf. *Monatshefte für deutschen Unterricht*, XXXVI, 120).

30. In the other Moorish story in our novel, that of the expelled Ricote who, having fled to Germany, comes back in the disguise of a German pilgrim to Spain (II, 44) ; the exile mixes German (*Guelte! Guelte!*) into his Spanish—a language which he knows as well as does Sancho, whose "neighborhood shopkeeper" he had been. Cervantes describes Sancho's inability to understand the Germanate jargon of Ricote, whose identity he fails at first to recognize. Later, the pilgrim throws aside his incognito and hails Sancho "en voz alta y muy castellana"; "Ricote, sin tropezar nada en su lengua morisca, en la pura castellana le [to Sancho] dijo las siguientes palabras." In the ensuing drinking scene, Sancho, in his mellow tipsiness, finally ends up by speaking the esperanto of *lingua franca*. In this episode we must infer that the difficulties of linguistic understanding are all artificially contrived : here are *Ricote el morisco* and *Sancho el bueno*, who have lived side by side for many years and who are quite able to understand each other perfectly, who have the same habits of living, eating, and drinking—and are separated from each other only by the (arbitrary) fact of the Morisco's exile.

Ricote is as good a Spaniard as is Sancho (perhaps also a more gifted one : this comes out in his ironic question, so natural with emigrants who, returning to their mother country, see themselves in a position inferior to their merits: "Faltaban hombres más hábiles para gobernadores que tú eres?"), and his daughter is a perfect Christian; nevertheless, as exiles, they have been the victims of an arbitrary death-blow. But, by his exile, Ricote has not only learned to say *guelte* instead of *limosna*: he has come to know religious tolerance as he saw it practiced in Augsburg, in the heart of Protestantism. No bolder words could have been written, in Counter-Reformation Spain, about religious freedom, than are expressed here by Ricote. Nevertheless, the same Ricote bows submissively before the expulsion of the Moors by the Spanish King and his minister, which has plunged him and his family into despair and misery. Cervantes seems here more interested in the dialectic play of arguments, in the facets and perspectives of the problem, than in giving a decision on the moral issue. To the Spanish subject-matter of the novel, the stories of Moorish emigrants, renegades, and converts add a new perspective, that of Spain seen from the outside—a perspective of "spiritual geography."

31. The same double light is cast on the *caña*, that angling rod dropped by Zoraida to the captives, which is first only a utensil, an astute device, and then becomes a symbol of the miracle ("milagro") of a twofold salvation.

32. In this tale, the "renegade" develops before our eyes and gradually comes to take on stature; he shows his eagerness to help in the escape of the prisoners: after his repentance, when he swears by the cross to change from a "foul" member of the Church to a true member, the Christian fugitives put themselves "en las manos de Dios y en las del renegado" (as though God's hands used those of the renegade for His purposes). Later, it is true, his plan is abandoned for another one ("Dios, que lo ordenaba

de otra manera, no dió lugar al buen deseo que nuestro renegado tenía")
but, nevertheless, he is saved along with the whole party and succeeds in
his desire "a reducirse por medio de la santa Inquisición al gremio san-
tísimo de la Iglesia."

33. In this connection, we should consider the famous opening sentence
of the novel: "En un lugar de la Mancha de cuyo nombre no quiero acor-
darme." All the explanations hitherto offered (the silly autobiographical one: Cervantes had personal reasons for not wanting to remember the
name); that based on literary history, proposed by Casalduero (Cervantes
opposes his novel to the romances of chivalry, which claimed to know
exactly wherefrom their heroes hailed); the folkloristic one of María
Rosa Lida (the sentence is in line with the beginning of folk-tales) fail
to take into sufficient consideration the functional value, for the novel,
of the attitude of the author expressed therein—which, in my opinion, is
the glorification of the freedom of the artist. Even if, for example, Mme.
Lida should be right, the transfer of a sentence traditional in folk-tales
into this particular novel of Cervantes could give the transferred sentence
a new meaning, just as certain folklorisms adopted by Goethe or Heine
become more than folklorisms in the lyrical poetry of these poets. By the
deliberate assertion of his free will to choose the motifs of his plot, to
emphasize or disregard what detail he pleases (and "no quiero" expresses
deliberate disregard), Cervantes has founded that genre of "subjective
story-telling" which, before him, is found at its incipient stage with Boccaccio and which, later, was to inspire Goethe (in the beginning of the
Wahlverwandtschaften: "Eduard—so nennen wir einen reichen Baron im
besten Mannesalter—Eduard hatte . . ."), Laurence Sterne, Fielding, Mel-
ville ("Call me Ishmael!").

In an address to the Baltimore Goethe Society, entitled "Laurence
Sterne's *Tristram Shandy* and Thomas Mann's *Joseph the Provider*"
(later published in *M.L.Qu.*, VIII, 101 *seq.*), Professor Oskar Seidlin
pointed out the presence, in both these modern works, of some of the
same comic devices (change of names, assumption of fictional sources,
introduction of "relativizing dialogues," etc.) which I have been dis-
cussing as characteristic of Cervantine perspectivism. Since Thomas
Mann himself had stated in 1942 that, during the composition of his
Joseph he had had two books as his steady companions, *Tristram Shandy*
and *Faust*, the stylistic congruences between the German and the English
novel are easily explained. On the other hand, the devices of Sterne which
reappear with Mann were, in turn, borrowed from Cervantes; and, in this
connection, it is relevant to note that, in 1935, Thomas Mann had published his essay on the *Don Quijote*: thus the Cervantine climate may have
acted doubly upon him: directly as well as indirectly. And, though the
idea expressed in *Joseph the Provider* that the world is "Jehovah's Jest"
would not have occurred to Cervantes, who glorified the "artist beneath
the dome of God," the great *Entendedor*, the Spanish poet could have
subscribed to Mann's idea of "artistic lightness" as man's consolation (*loc.
cit.*, New York edition, p. 357): "For lightness, my friend, the artful jest,
that is God's very best gift to man, the profoundest knowledge we have
of this complex, questionable thing called life. God gave it to humanity
so that life's terribly serious face might be forced to wear a smile. . . .
Only in lightness can the spirit of men rise above them [the questions
put to us by life]: with a laugh at being faced with the unanswerable,

perhaps he can make even God Himself, the great Unanswering, to smile."

It is interesting that Thomas Mann who, in his *Buddenbrooks*, was still the pure representative of what Walzel has called "objective narration" (in the Spielhagen style), has from the time of his *Magic Mountain* developed consistently in the direction of Cervantine "story-telling" technique; this evolution must be due, not only to the general change in literary trends that has been taking place, but also to Mann's growing consciousness of the triumphant part the artist is called upon to play in modern society.

In this connection I may cite also the opening line of E. M. Forster's novel *Howard's End* (1910) : "One may as well begin with Helen's letters to her sister," on which Lionel Trilling, *E. M. Forster* (1943) remarks: "Guiding his stories according to his serious whim . . . Forster takes full and conscious responsibility for his novels, refusing to share in the increasingly dull assumption of the contemporary novelist, that the writer has nothing to do with the story he tells, and that, *mirabile dictu*, through no intention of his own, the story has chosen to tell itself through him. Like Fielding, he shapes his prose for comment and explanation. He summarizes what he is going to show, introduces new themes when and as it suits him."

34. I realize that this is an opinion contrary to that of the writers of the Enlightenment who, in their treatment of the *Don Quijote*, made much of Cervantes' own classicistic pronouncement that art imitates nature. Locke, for example, has written: "Of all the books of fiction, I know none that equals Cervantes's 'History of Don Quijote,' in usefulness [!], pleasantry, and a constant decorum. And indeed no writings can be pleasant, which have not nature at the bottom, and are not drawn after copy." And Sydenham, the English Hippocrates and founder of modern clinical treatment, is reported to have advised young medical students to read the *Don Quijote* instead of books on medicine—because (as Professor Edelstein shows, in *Bulletin of the History of Medicine*, suppl. 3, 1944, p. 54) he evidently thought the Spanish novel offered a deterrent example of a person who views the world in the light of his preconceived ideas instead of that of facts—with which alone Dr. Sydenham was concerned.

Needless to say, my historical interpretation is also at the other pole from the poetic vision of an Unamuno who believes that this story was dictated to Cervantes' pen by the suprapersonal and perennial Spanish character, by the innate Spanish will to immortality by suffering and the "sentimiento trágico de la vida" as embodied in the figures of the quasi-saint Nuestro Señor Don Quijote de la Mancha and of his evangelical squire. In my opinion, it is Cervantes the "artistic dictator," who dictated the story to his pen, and Cervantes, no half-christian like Unamuno, knew how to distinguish the earthly plane from the transcendental. On the former plane he obeyed his own *sovereign reason*. He does, then, not belong to the family of Pascal and Kierkegaard, but to that of Descartes and Goethe.

35. Pirandello's perspectivism is in this respect different from that of Cervantes: with the latter, it is the *author* who looks for his characters, not the reverse.

I beg also to disagree with those critics who compare Cervantes with El Greco because of the novelist's "modern impressionism." We must be clear about the meaning of the term "impressionism." Cervantes never offers *his own* impressions of outward reality, as does the modern artist of the impressionistic school; he presents simply the impressions which his characters may have had—and, by juxtaposing these different impressions, he implicitly criticizes them all. The program of the modern impressionist, on the other hand, makes impossible the intervention of the critical sense into what he sees. As for the impressionism of El Greco, while this involves no criticism of reality as does that of Cervantes (since the ultimate reality he portrays is the divine), it does offer the evanescent reflections of the divine—which may, of course, have prepared the public for the perception of the evanescent in this world, i.e. for modern "impressionistic" perception.

36. Professor Auerbach, in his book *Mimesis* (Bern, 1946), p. 319, states the lack, in the *Don Quijote* (as in the whole literature of the *siglo de oro*) of any "problematische Erforschung der zeitgenössischen Wirklichkeit," of any "Bewegung in den Tiefen des Lebens," of any search into the social motivations of Don Quijote's madness, and of the life of his age—the underlying idea being that the "real" motivations of life are those of sociology, not of morality, on which Cervantes has based his novel (though, as we have said, he offers us the conflict between different moral standards). The attitude of this critic, which seems to abound in the sense of Carl Becker ("the historian has become the successor of the theologian") is, in my opinion, contingent on the presupposition that moral values are obsolete in a modern world given to the sociological explanation of history.

37. It should perhaps be pointed out here that "perspectivism" is inherent in Christian thought itself. The pair Don Quijote - Sancho Panza is, after all, a Cervantine replica of the medieval characters Solomon and Marcolf, in whom the wisdom of the sage and that of the common man are contrasted (we may also see in Sancho Panza's *refranes* a later version of the *proverbes au vilain*). Such an exemplary contrast is derived from the evangelic truth that the common man has access to wisdom, as well as the learned man; that the spirit, if not the letter, of the law can be understood by anyone. Here, we have an example of "medieval gradualism," according to which the social or mental level of Christ's followers is ultimately irrelevant. It is for this reason that, in medieval mystery plays, lofty scenes treating the life of Christ may alternate with scurrilous scenes in which shepherds or clowns are allowed to express their "point of view," on the august events in question, in their own unregenerate rustic speech. In this "gradualism," perspectivism is implied; and, to the perspectivism which Cervantes found in the medieval tradition, he added only the artistic aloofness of a Renaissance thinker.

THE "RÉCIT DE THÉRAMÈNE"*

Argumentum: This time I shall not, according to my usual procedure, start from a detail (of style) but shall first seek to establish the meaning of the whole (the tragedy) before coming to the *récit* itself, and to the linguistic details therein. Since, in this case, we are dealing with a division of a work of art, rather than with the work of art as a whole (as with Cervantes), it is obvious that this division must be first placed rightly within the whole before any treatment of linguistic detail can be considered. In some cases (compare the chapter on Claudel), it is possible to state this relationship in a single sentence, and then

* For the convenience of the reader, the text in question is here inserted:

THÉSÉE

Théramène, est-ce toi? Qu'as-tu fait de mon fils?
Je te l'ai confié dès l'âge le plus tendre.
Mais d'où naissent les pleurs que je te vois répandre?
Que fait mon fils?

THÉRAMÈNE

O soins tardifs et superflus!
Inutile tendresse! Hippolyte n'est plus.

THÉSÉE

Dieux!

THÉRAMÈNE

J'ai vu des mortels périr le plus aimable,
Et j'ose dire encor, seigneur, le moins coupable.

THÉSÉE

Mon fils n'est plus! Hé quoi! quand je lui tends les bras
Les dieux impatients ont hâté son trépas!
Quel coup me l'a ravi? quelle foudre soudaine?

THÉRAMÈNE

A peine nous sortions des portes de Trézène:
Il était sur son char; ses gardes affligés
Imitaient son silence, autour de lui rangés:
Il suivait tout pensif le chemin de Mycènes;
Sa main sur ses chevaux laissait flotter les rênes:
Ses superbes coursiers, qu'on voyait autrefois
Pleins d'une ardeur si noble obéir à sa voix,
L'oeil morne maintenant et la tête baissée,
Semblaient se conformer à sa triste pensée.
Un effroyable cri, sorti du fond des flots,
Des airs en ce moment a troublé le repos;
Et du sein de la terre une voix formidable

proceed to the linguistic detail. But in the present case, the relation of the "récit de Théramène" to *Phèdre* as a whole—and, indeed, the purpose of the play itself—have not, I feel, been clearly recognized in previous scholarship, so that the necessity of a "prestudy" seems to impose itself.

When we consider the play as a whole it will be seen that the terrible events in *Phèdre* are meant for the disillusionment of the only one of the main characters who survives: Thésée; it is on him that Phèdre's guilt and the death of the innocent Hippolyte produce their cumulative effect, by revealing to him the

---

Répond en gémissant à ce cri redoutable.
Jusqu'au fond de nos coeurs notre sang s'est glacé.
Des coursiers attentifs le crin s'est hérissé.
Cependant, sur le dos de la plaine liquide,
S'élève à gros bouillons une montagne humide :
L'onde approche, se brise, et vomit à nos yeux,
Parmi des flots d'écume, un monstre furieux.
Son front large est armé de cornes menaçantes ;
Tout son corps est couvert d'écailles jaunissantes ;
Indomptable taureau, dragon impétueux,
Sa croupe se recourbe en replis tortueux ;
Ses longs mugissements font trembler le rivage.
Le ciel avec horreur voit ce monstre sauvage ;
La terre s'en émeut, l'air en est infecté,
Le flot qui l'apporta recule épouvanté.
Tout fuit ; et, sans s'armer d'un courage inutile,
Dans le temple voisin chacun cherche un asile.
Hippolyte lui seul, digne fils d'un héros,
Arrête ses coursiers, saisit ses javelots,
Pousse au monstre, et d'un dard lancé d'une main sûre
Il lui fait dans le flanc une large blessure.
De rage et de douleur le monstre bondissant
Vient aux pieds des chevaux tomber en mugissant,
Se roule, et leur présente une gueule enflammée
Qui les couvre de feu, de sang, et de fumée.
La frayeur les emporte ; et, sourds à cette fois,
Ils ne connaissent plus ni le frein ni la voix ;
En efforts impuissants leur maitre se consume ;
Ils rougissent le mors d'une sanglante écume.
On dit qu'on a vu même, en ce désordre affreux,
Un dieu qui d'aiguillons pressait leur flanc poudreux.
A travers les rochers la peur les précipite ;
L'essieu crie et se rompt : l'intrépide Hippolyte
Voit voler en éclats tout son char fracassé ;
Dans les rênes lui-même il tombe embarrassé.
Excusez ma douleur : cette image cruelle
Sera pour moi de pleurs une source éternelle.
J'ai vu, seigneur, j'ai vu votre malheureux fils
Traîné par les chevaux que sa main a nourris.

tragic truth that the gods persecute those they seem to protect. *Phèdre* is then a baroque tragedy of *desengaño*. The "récit de Théramène" in the fifth act, parallel to the "récit de Phèdre" in the second, but intended for the King himself, has the function of driving home at last the truth of divine perfidy and human helplessness.

In the properly linguistic part of the article I take up three stylistic features of the *récit* which I show to be characteristic of Racine's style in general: the frequency of the sense-word *voir*, with its intellectual connotation ("to see" = "to witness, to un-

---

Il veut les rappeler, et sa voix les effraie;
Ils courent: tout son corps n'est bientôt qu'une plaie.
De nos cris douloureux la plaine retentit.
Leur fougue impétueuse enfin se ralentit:
Ils s'arrêtent non loin de ces tombeaux antiques
Où des rois ses aïeux sont les froides reliques.
J'y cours en soupirant, et sa garde me suit;
De son généreux sang la trace nous conduit;
Les rochers en sont teints; les ronces dégouttantes
Portent de ses cheveux les dépouilles sanglantes.
J'arrive, je l'appelle; et, me tendant la main,
Il ouvre un oeil mourant qu'il referme soudain.
"Le ciel, dit-il, m'arrache une innocente vie.
"Prends soin après ma mort de la triste Aricie.
"Cher ami, si mon père un jour désabusé
"Plaint le malheur d'un fils faussement accusé,
"Pour apaiser mon sang et mon ombre plaintive,
"Dis-lui qu'avec douceur il traite sa captive;
"Qu'il lui rende. . ." A ce mot, ce héros expiré
N'a laissé dans mes bras qu'un corps défiguré:
Triste objet où des dieux triomphe la colère,
Et que méconnaîtrait l'oeil même de son père.

THÉSÉE

O mon fils! cher espoir que je me suis ravi!
Inexorables dieux, qui m'avez trop servi!
A quels mortels regrets ma vie est réservée!

THÉRAMÈNE

La timide Aricie est alors arrivée:
Elle venait, seigneur, fuyant votre courroux,
A la face des dieux l'accepter pour époux.
Elle approche; elle voit l'herbe rouge et fumante;
Elle voit (quel objet pour les yeux d'une amante!)
Hippolyte étendu, sans forme et sans couleur.
Elle veut quelque temps douter de son malheur;
Et, ne connaissant plus ce héros qu'elle adore,
Elle voit Hippolyte, et le demande encore,
Mais, trop sûre à la fin qu'il est devant ses yeux,
Par un triste regard elle accuse les dieux;

derstand"), the "klassische Dämpfung" by which the emotional stream of narrative is interrupted by intellectual evaluations (e.g. *digne fils d'un héros*), and the paradoxical mode of expression by which Racine is wont to formulate the unnatural in nature (e.g. *le flot qui l'apporta recule épouvanté*). These three traits belong to the baroque background of Racine, in whose imagination antagonistic polar forces play: senses and intellect, emotion and intellect, anarchy and order. In other words: Racine's vision of a world in which the gods counteract their own doings, repudiate their own creation, makes itself felt in a linguistic form which, although hovering precariously on the verge of anarchy, manages always to maintain its poise.

> Et froide, gémissante, et presque inanimée,
> Aux pieds de son amant elle tombe pâmée.
> Ismène est auprès d'elle; Ismène tout en pleurs
> La rappelle à la vie, ou plutôt aux douleurs.
> Et moi, je suis venu, détestant la lumière,
> Vous dire d'un héros la volonté dernière,
> Et m'acquitter, seigneur, du malheureux emploi
> Dont son coeur expirant s'est reposé sur moi. . . .

The two most recent contributions to criticism of the "récit de Théramène" are to be found in an article of Mr. Carlos Lynes Jr., "A Defense of the 'Récit de Théramène'" (*MLN*, LIX, 387), and a note of Professor Lancaster appended to this article. Mr. Lynes takes exception to the previous statement of Professor Lancaster's (in *A History of French Dramatic Literature in the Seventeenth Century*, IV, 199) that the lengthiness and ornateness of the *récit* is to be explained by Racine's overzealous admiration of the ancients. Mr. Lynes believes that these characteristics were intended to invite "aesthetic repose" on the part of the audience. Professor Lancaster, in his answer, seems to concede the effect of "aesthetic repose," but contends that this very repose rather enhances the poignant appeal of the poetry than gives emotional relief. The debate (which is taken up again in *MLN*, LIX, 584-586, each of the two opponents blaming the other for having shifted his attitude in the course of the discussion) seems, to this somewhat puzzled *tertius gaudens*, somewhat tangential.

SINCE the time of Racine himself, critics have discussed the great length and ornate style of the "récit de Théramène" in the Fifth Act of *Phèdre*, and generations of French schoolboys have had to struggle with the problems which this passage presents. If, in this book, I feel impelled to offer my own contribution to the famous scene, it is because two American critics have recently attempted explanations which seem to me to lead in wrong directions: on the one hand they have not been "microscopical," on the other they have not been "macroscopical" enough; it is the correct combination and dosage of both approaches which, alone, can yield an insight into Racine's artistic endeavors. To posit "correctness" as a criterion may seem like begging the question; and yet any method that is able to explain more of the features extant in a work of art must be held more correct.

I shall divide this study, which will, evidently, be determined by the "Zirkelschluss," into two parts. In the first, we will proceed from the macroscopic to the microscopic, in an attempt to answer the questions: what is the design of the whole play, and how does the "récit de Théramène" fit into this whole? In the second, the procedure will be the reverse, from the microscopic to the macroscopic; we shall ask: what stylistic features characterize the *récit*, and are these features also characteristic of the whole tragedy—and, possibly, of the art of Racine in general? In this way, I hope to be able to point out, incidentally, the reason for the ornateness and lengthiness of the "récit de Théramène."

What is the design of the play? Let us begin by considering the elementary fact that, of the six characters (which does not include Ismène and Panope) in *Phèdre*, three die and three survive. All who die are guilty: Phèdre, whose guilt is evident from the beginning; Oenone, the nurse, the accomplice in her mistress's crime; and Hippolyte, whose guilt is slight but, according to Racine himself, is none the less a guilt (it is against his father's will that he loves Aricie). Of those who survive, Théramène and Aricie are blameless, while Thésée, never a figure of virtue (divided as he has always been between the labors of a hero and his less glorious erotic adventures), commits the crime, though out of blindness, of sacrificing virtue in the person of his son Hippolyte, whom he curses and sends into exile. Why, then, it may be asked, is the criminal Thésée allowed to escape unscathed? He, too, however, is crushed in the double role of victim and perpetrator of a crime which has destroyed his whole family and which he is forced to acknowledge. My interpretation is that he is spared death in order to comprehend and to acknowledge—not only his own crime and its consequences but also the perversity of the world order. The king, to whom Théramène's récit is addressed, is on the stage before us, a bewildered spectator of what can befall a royal family; he is involved in the action only by his one act of blindness; for the most part he stays in his "private loge on the stage," witnessing a drama that unfolds before him. While his son Hippolyte is destroyed by the action of the play without understanding (no god appears to explain to him the reason for his death, as in the play of Euripides, who has Hippolyte brought back before his death to be enlightened and encouraged by Artemis), and while Phèdre is destroyed with the full understanding, from the beginning, that she and her family, especially the female branch, are persecuted by Venus, Thésée must witness the destruction of his son and his wife before he is brought to see the shape of his doom. He emerges from the play as the most important character, who will, grimly, knowingly, survive his torture, and will be the living example of the lesson he has learned "dramatically." What is this lesson? Perhaps, "timeo deos et dona ferentes": the gods crush those whom they favor most. He, the protégé of the god Neptune, has been made the instrument of doom; the denouement of the action elicits his final understanding that, when he thought himself to be protected by a loving god, he was, in reality, his victim. Two gods are responsible for the devastation wrought on the family of Thésée (the destruction of the family has not been sufficiently emphasized by critics—who were misled, no doubt, by the title of the play and by Racine's failure to mention Thésée in his preface). Unlike Euripides, who allows the vengeance of Aphrodite to be counteracted by the ever-loyal Artemis, Racine presents his two gods, though working separately and by different procedures, as contributing jointly to the destruction of the family: the one by direct persecution (Venus → Phèdre), the other by "loving protection" (Neptune → Thésée)—and both together by warring against each other in the breast of Hippolyte.[1] Faced by such a conjunction of forces there is no possibility that the characters may escape; the whole tragedy, as the most crushing, the most tragic of tragedies, amounts to an accusation of the world order, and invites man's revolt against the gods.

After the unprovoked wrath of the gods has been sated, there is left to Thésée only the one gesture which his dying son had asked of him: to be kind to the guiltless Aricie. The calm of the last lines spoken by Thésée is one of conscious desperation. He has finally become a *désabusé*, as Hippolyte had predicted in his dying words; he has tasted that *desengaño* which all the Spanish moralists of Racine's time knew so well.

Since Thésée is the one for whose benefit the disillusioning events of the play are staged, we must feel him present during the whole play (the first part of the drama is full of his name, and from the beginning we look forward with suspense to his entrance in Act III), and we must seek to observe the process of his disillusionment—which begins the moment he enters the stage. Those critics who have taken exception to his "undramatic" character have not pondered the drama of enlightenment which goes on within him; it starts, as we have said, when he crosses his threshold, once again victorious through Neptune, eager to greet his wife and son—and sees first one, then the other, withdraw from him on some pretext. His suspicions are aroused, are given a focus by Oenone, and finally vent themselves when he banishes his son. At this point, though disillusioned about human relationships, he still thinks Neptune to be his ally; moreover, his grief over his son is still endurable, because coupled with anger. The report of Théramène will give him his second, his greatest shock: he will learn that Neptune has listened only too well to his impulsive prayer for revenge, and boundless desperation will overwhelm him. The final blow will come when, in the last scene, he learns from Phèdre's lips that his son was blameless,[2] and had to perish as an innocent victim of his father's commerce with the gods. Now the utter chaos and perversity of the world order stand revealed. The "récit de Théramène," as the second step in this development, is intended exclusively for the enlightenment of the king as to man's relationship to the gods, and must be studied in this light.

The picture of Hippolyte's death, "cette image cruelle" (unforgettable to Théramène: l. 1545) becomes for Thésée a picture of universal destruction. In the scene which follows our récit, Thésée, who has had time to digest its awful import, succeeds in formulating the lesson he has learned: the dubious character of divine protection, and the perversity of the cosmic scheme:

> Confus, persécuté d'un mortel souvenir,
> De l'univers entier je voudrais me bannir.
> Tout semble s'élever contre mon injustice.
> L'éclat de mon nom même augmente mon supplice.
> Moins connu des mortels, je me cacherais mieux.
> Je hais jusqu'aux soins dont m'honorent les dieux :
> Et je m'en vais pleurer leurs faveurs meurtrières,
> Sans plus les fatiguer d'inutiles prières.
> Quoi qu'ils fissent pour moi, leur funeste bonté
> Ne me saurait payer de ce qu'ils m'ont ôté.

Since the allusions to the persecution of Phèdre and her kin by Venus ("C'est Vénus toute entière à sa proie attachée,") seem to have been better understood by critics than have those to the (equally destructive) protection of Thésée by Neptune, we must study the latter more closely. It will be seen how, throughout the play, the Neptune motif combines with the Venus motif; and how the "récit de Théramène" takes up the first, while the second is dealt with in other scenes. And, as we watch the interplay of these two motifs, we will see how carefully Racine has plotted the course of the "wrath of the gods" in this tragedy of a Greek royal family.

As the play opens, Hippolyte, in the course of his conversation with Théramène, distinguishes two modes of behavior observable in his father's career, corresponding to the works of Neptune and those of Venus: on the one hand, the slaying of monsters by the "héros intrépide," on the other, his less glorious love affairs (for which Théramène excuses him, saying: "Quels courages Vénus n'a-t-elle pas domptés?"). We learn that Hippolyte has not, to his regret, equaled his father in his feats of monster-slaying; he does, however, give involuntary signs of having fallen in love—that is, of having given himself up to the power of that Venus who shares with Neptune the ascendancy over his father and who exclusively dominates Phèdre—and, through her, the whole family. Théramène, reminding Hippolyte of his earlier prowess in the service of Neptune, indicates the shift in his allegiance which has taken place (129 *seq.*):

> Avouez-le, tout change; et depuis quelques jours
> On vous voit moins souvent, orgueilleux et sauvage,
> Tantôt faire voler un char sur le rivage,
> Tantôt, *savant dans l'art par Neptune inventé,*
> *Rendre docile au frein un coursier indompté.* . . .
> Chargés d'un feu secret, vos yeux s'appesantissent.
> Il n'en faut pas douter: vous aimez, vous brûlez.

(We may compare line 991: "Quel funeste poison / L'amour a répandu sur toute sa [of the king] maison!") Hippolyte, then, has inherited his father's double nature—if on a lesser scale. When we come to the "récit de Théramène," the reader will find a parallel to the verses above, underlined by me, in the lines:

> J'ai vu, seigneur, j'ai vu votre malheureux fils
> Traîné par les chevaux que sa main a nourris.
> Il veut les rappeler, et sa voix les effraie.

Hippolyte, once the worshiper of Neptune, will at the end of the tragedy be punished for his allegiance to Venus by the god of horse-taming (there is no doubt that, in line 1538: "On dit qu'on a vu même, en ce désordre affreux, / Un Dieu qui d'aiguillons pressait leur flanc poudreux," this Racine-invented God, to whom some critics take exception, is Neptune), and will no longer be able to "faire voler un char sur le rivage," or to "rendre docile au frein un coursier indompté."³ Thus the *récit* is anticipated by the opening scene, with its reference to Neptune as the inspiration of Hippolyte's (former) accomplishments—a motif reiterated in identical terms in Act II, 559 *seq.*, when Hippolyte himself laments:

> Mon arc, mes javelots, mon char, tout m'importune;
> Je ne me souviens plus des leçons de Neptune;
> Mes seuls gémissements font retentir les bois,
> Et nos coursiers oisifs ont oublié ma voix.

As for the protection accorded by Neptune to Thésée (at least, to the "hero" Thésée), this is alluded to throughout the play. When, in Act II, we learn of rumors to the effect that Thésée is dead and has perished in the sea, in the element of Neptune ("Les flots ont englouti cet époux infidèle": 381), Hippolyte maintains stoutly: "Neptune le protège, et ce dieu tutélaire / Ne sera pas en vain imploré par mon père"; in the last words, tinged with filial pride, we can sense a tragic irony —since, later, Thésée's success with Neptune will be scored at the expense of Hippolyte's life:

> Et toi, Neptune, et toi, si jadis mon courage
> D'infâmes assassins nettoya ton rivage . . .
> Je t'implore aujourd'hui. Venge un malheureux père:
> J'abandonne ce traître à toute ta colère.

Here, it is on his prowess as a slayer of monsters that Thésée relies in his appeal to Neptune—an appeal which he is confident will be granted ("Neptune . . . M'a donné sa parole, et va l'exécuter": 1158 / ; "Neptune me la [sa perte] doit, et vous [Phèdre] serez vengée / . . . . Espérons de Neptune une prompte justice. / Je vais moi-même au pied de ses autels / Le presser d'accomplir ses serments immortels": 1178-1192). But this mood of confidence fed by desperation is shaken by the news of Oenone's suicide (I find it significant that it is in the element of Neptune that she meets her death: "Les flots pour jamais l'ont ravie à mes yeux": 1467), an event which seems to the messenger an inscrutable mystery ("On ne sait point d'où part ce dessein furieux": 1466). Has Neptune a "dessein furieux" against Thésée's household? Immediately afterwards, the king learns of Phèdre's collapse and of her desire for death, and his wrathful certitude of Hippolyte's guilt begins to crumble. With a new despair he revokes his prayer to Neptune (1483): "Ne précipite point tes funestes bienfaits, / Neptune, j'aime mieux n'être exaucé jamais" (the paradoxical phrase "funestes bienfaits" is echoed later by "faveurs meurtrières" [1693] and "funeste bonté" [1615], while the motif "j'aime mieux n'être exaucé jamais" will be strengthened at the close of the play by the line 1650 in which Thésée resolves to "expier la fureur d'un voeu que je déteste"). In the very moment when Thésée, wavering in his judgment of Hippolyte's guilt, and sensing the imminence of death which threatens his household, seeks to hold back Neptune's intervention, Théramène enters. The sight of Hippolyte's governor can only sharpen the anxiety of the father: "Théramène, est-ce toi? Qu'as tu fait de mon fils? / Je te l'ai confié dès l'âge le plus tendre"—a marvelous Racinian sentence, with its example of the "short-cut" which betrays the progress of the father's anguish and self-torture; he speaks as though he knows already what Théramène has come to tell him, and must blame the messenger for the sad news he brings. And Théramène's words confirm his darkest apprehensions: "O soins tardifs et superflus! Inutile tendresse! Hippolyte n'est plus!" Once more, *ce dieu tutélaire* has answered the prayer of his protégé. Thus we see how the Neptune motif fits into the development by which the scales are made to fall at last from Thésée's eyes.

There is a corollary motif which must be considered here, for this, also, leads up to and expands within the "récit de Théramène": the monster motif. The traditional Greek hero (a Theseus, a Heracles), aware of his divine extraction, distinguishes himself by "labors," by superhuman exploits which rid the world of monsters, that is from the infra-human bestiality which infests it and which is liable to imperil the triumph of human reason and civilization. The motif of "monster-slaying," which, indeed, permeates our whole play, is to be seen in connection with that of "the hero agreeable to Neptune." In Thésée the two are perfectly reflected, and the same might have been expected of the hero's son: this implication is not lost upon Hippolyte, when he comes to ask permission of his father to embark upon heroic enterprises: "Souffrez, si quelque monstre a pu vous échapper, / Que j'apporte à vos pieds la dépouille honorable." And it is in just this light that Hippolyte is seen by Phèdre when she first falls in love with him—according to her own words (854); Racine, with a marvelous grasp of the psychology of love, anticipating modern experience, has Phèdre pretend to see in Hippolyte a younger Thésée (thus she remains faithful to the type represented by her husband, so true is it that love is "typologically monogamic" and that matrimonial infidelity, after the passage of years, can be a form of faithfulness to the original lover!)—not, of course, the impudent lover Thésée who sacrifices to a cheap Venus, but the hero who slew *le monstre de la Crète*:

> Tel qu'on dépeint nos dieux, ou tel que je vous voi.
> Il avait votre port, vos yeux, votre langage;
> Cette noble pudeur colorait son visage,
> Lorsque de notre Crète il traversa les flots . . .

—"flots," the element of Neptune. But irony demanded that Hippolyte should not conform entirely to type: as we know, and as Phèdre was later to learn to her hurt, he has ceased to give sole allegiance to Neptune. But at the moment the mirage is complete—as Phèdre betrays her illusion by the "short-cut" of the outburst: ". . . ou tel que je vous voi" (in which the fallacy rests in the "ou"). It is another irony that later, all hope and pretense abandoned, she must ask Hippolyte to resemble his father, the monster-slayer, by slaying the monster that *she* has become: "Délivre l'univers d'un monstre qui t'irrite. . . . / Crois-moi, ce monstre affreux ne doit point t'échapper." This use of "monstre" in reference to evil human beings whose destruction is urged as a heroic deed is most significant in our play, where it frequently recurs: Aricie herself applies the term to Phèdre, whom she implores Thésée to exterminate (1443 *seq.*):

> . . . vos invincibles mains
> Ont de monstres sans nombre affranchi les humains;
> Mais tout n'est pas détruit, et vous en laissez vivre
> Un . . .

(note the powerful enjambment, reminiscent of the famous "Moi!" of Corneille's *Médée*). To Thésée, whose soul is poisoned by Oenone's slander, the innocent Hippolyte appears as a "monstre, qu'a trop longtemps épargné le tonnerre, / Reste impur des brigands dont j'ai purgé la terre" (1045)— as he had, earlier, to the tortured mind of Phèdre (384). The idea of the human monster is also implicit in Thésée's reference to his most recent conquest: "D'un perfide ennemi j'ai purgé la nature. . . . A ses monstres lui-même a servi de pâture." And, into this network of motifs fits the death scene of Hippolyte. So far as I know, no critic has noted the new significance, in Racine's play, of the sea-monster as the instrument of death. In Euripides' drama this instrument was a bull emerging from the sea to avenge Venus; Racine's sea-monster has a closer relationship to Neptune, it has been created, by an unjust god, as a tool of senseless *contrappasso* against the family of monster-slayers.

If, then, we consider Thésée primarily as the hero, the monster-slayer agreeable to Neptune, we are better able to understand what his reactions must be when he listens to Théramène's recital. As he grasps the import of the words, we are allowed to guess the course of his thoughts by the occasional outbursts which interrupt the tragic tale, and which betray not so much regret for the son he has lost as consternation over the trickery of the gods: "Dieux!"—". . . Les Dieux impatients ont hâté son trépas?"—"Inexorables Dieux, qui m'avez trop servi!" It seems to me that the criticism of Mr. Lynes is far too much concerned with the probable reactions of the public to Théramène's report; it is Thésée's reaction which is all important here—and the public watches *this*! From the general conclusion of Théramène, "des Dieux triomphe la colère," Thésée can only draw the specific implication: the "un dieu" of Théramène is Neptune to Thésée. Later, Phèdre will enter the stage and, as the king hears her confess her guilt and Hippolyte's innocence, he will realize that her doom, too, has been willed by a god ("le ciel mit dans mon sein une flamme funeste"), that, in fact, all the sufferings endured by his family have their origin in the gods. The récit, far from being a negligible part of the tragedy, is highly important; it is a high plateau which invites us to a contemplative repose before the full vista of the doomedness of man. This contemplation of the condition of man as that of a "triste objet, où des Dieux triomphe la colère" can be called lacking in dramatic value only if drama be considered exclusively as outward action—a conception which is evidently much too narrow if one remembers the choral parts of the Greek drama, especially such hymns as Ἔρως ἀνίκατε μαχᾶν. The gradual dawning upon man of his own tragic condition is, in reality, the greatest drama imaginable.[4]

Thus, those critics are quite right who relate the ornateness and lengthiness of our récit to its contemplativity; what, perhaps, they have failed to grasp is the extent of the picture we are called upon to contemplate: the condition of man under the inexorable and unjust rule of the Gods. From the crudest possible vision of reality, of blood, disorder and debris, Racine extracts, as by a kind of supreme wager, the most intellectual and poetic formulation, a transposition into the language of a compassionate and detached philosopher. Théramène belongs to that ancient theater, of which Racine says, in a passage of his preface (where commentators are wont to see only the compromise made by an artist with the moralizing Jansenists, but which may well contain the true ethical direction ascribed to dramatic poetry by Racine and, after him, by Schiller): "Leur [the ancients'] théâtre était une école où la vertu n'était pas moins bien enseignée que dans les écoles des philosophes." Théramène is a scholar in philosophy on the stage; he is, in fact, the voice of Racine. And what Sainte-Beuve once said of Racine could be said of Hippolyte's tutor: "Il a le calme de l'âme supérieure et divine au travers et au-dessus de tous les pleurs et de toutes les tendresses." The whole of this tragedy consists of transposition and indirect rendition of reality; the "récit de Théramène" is a most concentrated precipitate in the dramatic alembic of Racine. Mr. Lynes was quite close to that truth when he wrote: "As a classical dramatist Racine does not wish actual tears at all, but only intense aesthetic contemplation." But he went astray, in my opinion, when, instead of seeing in the "récit de Théramène" a reduction *in nuce* of the

general aesthetics of Racine, he attributes to the poet an intention to temper our indignation against Phèdre, whereas the
truth seems to me to be that Racine's *main* purpose was to
show us the collapse of the world order as revealed to Thésée.[5]
For Hippolyte's death is not, as Mr. Lynes would have it, to
be explained in terms of human responsibility: granted that
Phèdre was responsible for Thésée's curse, it was Neptune
who fulfilled it by sending his monster out of the blue ocean
that lapped the shores of "aimable Trézène."[6] And why did
Hippolyte's horses, a moment before so sensitive to their
master's mood that they were sharing his taciturn sadness, refuse, at the critical moment, to obey the familiar hand of their
master? The guilt of Hippolyte's death rests entirely on the
gods, and the récit is not intended so much to lessen our anger
against Phèdre as to lift us to that higher serenity in which
the bitter lesson for humanity can be received. The dying
Hippolyte himself, whose closing eyes are open to abiding
truth, formulates most clearly this same bitter lesson: "*Le
ciel* . . . m'arrache une innocente vie . . . / Cher ami, si mon
père un jour désabusé / Plaint le malheur d'un fils faussement
accusé. . . ." The victim places the responsibility for the
calamity on the Heaven that permitted the calamity to happen.

Nor is the "récit de Théramène" the only passage that
offers us an opportunity to contemplate the sorry condition of
man: the other is what might be called the "récit de Phèdre"
in Act I, Scene III, which seems to have escaped the censure
of the critics because of its lesser length (though it is equally
"ornate") and because, in this passage, it is the principal
character who is exposing her own doomed situation, so that
this can be no mere "hors-d'oeuvre." In this récit we are
shown the devastation wrought by Venus upon her victim,
which, evidently, offers a parallel to Théramène's account of
Neptune's vengeance; we witness the physical dying, more
painful than death, of a beautiful body ("Un reste de chaleur
tout prêt à s'exhaler"), which is no less moving a spectacle
of human decay than is that depicted by Théramène ("Tout
son corps n'est bientôt qu'une plaie"). Phèdre has to divulge
no sudden disastrous blow but a sequence of sufferings;

Neptune strikes swiftly, Venus works insidiously in the blood. Théramène is a messenger describing a sudden, violent incident, Phèdre is an autobiographer recounting years of suffering; she begins this biography with the words: "Mon mal vient de plus loin"—and, in fact, the malady whose course she traces had darkened the history of her family for generations. The récit of Phèdre, coming from a passionate woman who is at the same time a conscious witness of her own doomedness, excites us more; that of Théramène, who is a wise and ultimately dispassionate observer, is the more objective, making the effect of a final chorus which dismisses the audience with the truth for which they had been waiting. The two messages have converged in us. But we, the audience, must linger awhile longer, until our own understanding is echoed and corroborated by that of Thésée. When he first learns of Hippolyte's death, he may think Neptune's vengeance too violent, but not illegitimate; only in the following scene does he learn, from Phèdre, that Hippolyte was blameless. But we, whose suspicions of the gods had been aroused by Phèdre from the beginning, and who knew throughout of Hippolyte's innocence, are able to understand Théramène's reference to the accusing eyes of Aricie ("Par un triste regard elle accuse les dieux") before it is given to Thésée to grasp the full import of her accusation.

For, though we have called Phèdre's explanations to Oenone the "récit de Phèdre," she has stayed silent toward Thésée throughout the play; and this "éternel silence," which is emphasized in several passages, has served, by the intervention of the more active Oenone, to involve Hippolyte in his father's suspicions. In the paradoxical dramatic world of Racine, where the best intentions of man are hopelessly twisted by the Gods, this fatal silence had its origin in the noblest side of Phèdre's nature: it is the main instrument of the self-imposed tortures by which Racine has sought to redeem this character (we read in the preface: "Elle fait tous ses efforts pour la [la passion] surmonter. Elle aime mieux se laisser mourir que de la déclarer à personne"). The outcome is, as we know, that her pledge of silence is twice broken (Oenone, Hippolyte), with dire results in each case—

while the silence she maintains with Thésée until the final moment has equally dire results.[7] Thus, as we listen to Théramène give his passionate-dispassionate revelation of the doom weighing on man, we wonder how much longer Phèdre will be able to maintain the rule of silence toward Thésée. And when, after Théramène's recital, she finally cries out: "Non, Thésée, il faut rompre un injuste silence," we feel a vast relief to hear at last the long-repressed confession of a woman eaten up by worms of passion—a confession which testifies to the same unjust world order as that revealed by Théramène. The play can come to an end only when all the evidence of the workings of the Gods piles up before Thésée; it is Racine's procedure, motivated so skillfully, of retarding this confession that has made possible the gradual unfolding of the picture.

Before we close the chapter on the dramatic connections between the "récit de Théramène" and the play as a whole, let us stop to consider for a moment the relationship between this récit and Théramène himself; we will see that Théramène's role, in Act v, as well as the particular quality of his report, is dramatically prepared from the beginning. And, in this connection, I must question the procedure of my predecessors in criticism who are not enough "at home" in the play they discuss, who have not spent enough effort in visualizing the data and the relationships which Racine has placed at their disposal. The critic should be so familiar with the play he is studying as to be able to reconstitute the interplay between all the characters and situations, to release all the springs which the author has built into the structure of his play. To be at home in a play of Racine does not entail living in many mansions, for Racine is not Shakespeare; nevertheless, in his one-mansion edifices we must focus on many cross-relationships existing between the different characters and situations.[8] Racine has very few characters on the stage, but he exhausts all the possibilities of relationship between them; he restricts the field of vision, but he has filled it with manifold parallelograms of forces. The Théramène whom we hear speak in Act v is no mere "messenger" in the Euripidean sense; we have seen him, in the opening scene of our play, as the philosophical tutor of Hippolyte, who had the task of instructing him in the accomplishments of a ruler (among them, history with its noble or evil examples) and, at the same time, as the appointed historian of Thésée's family. We learn from Hippolyte himself how Théramène was wont to acquaint him with the events of the family history; the prince describes the eagerness with which he would listen as his tutor depicted the heroic exploits of Thésée (73 *seq.*):

> Attaché près de moi par un zèle sincère,
> Tu me contais alors l'histoire de mon père.
> Tu sais combien mon âme, attentive à ta voix,
> S'échauffait au récit de ses nobles exploits,
> Quand tu me dépeignais ce héros intrépide

—but also the regret and impatience aroused in him by the account of less glorious episodes: "Tu sais comme à regret écoutant ce discours [on Thésée's faithlessness as a lover] / Je te pressais souvent d'en abréger le cours." Here we have obvious analogies with the "récit de Théramène": in both, Théramène is the "family chronicler" and, in both, his picture of nobility is clouded by painful truths that the listener shrinks from hearing. In the récit he must tell the most tragic of truths: however much we might prefer to dwell on the beauty and heroism of the young prince, we must be made to face the wrath of the gods, and we must allow the long and ornate threnody, which has no equal on the French stage, to sink in. This is, perhaps, what Racine might have answered his critics who (in his own words) "le pressaient d'abréger le cours du récit de Théramène." It is as if Racine had anticipated, in the first scene, the criticism which his récit was to arouse.[9] The dramatist has conceived both scenes in relationship to each other, in relationship both to the character of Théramène and to the nature of his teaching. Théramène, like Racine himself, is a humanistic historiographer who can teach only in a lengthy and ornate fashion, because history is a solemn and sad spectacle which can be unveiled only by a sage who steps beyond it and speaks of it from a higher, "transposed" plane. Consequently, the question: "why did Racine make the 'récit de Théramène' so lengthy and ornate?" is asked from a point of view outside the tragedy: from the aprioristic prejudice that a play should not (evidently for the sake of *vraisemblance*) contain lengthy and ornate récits. (And, of course, the answer of Professor Lancaster: ". . . because Racine came to indulge more and more in descriptive writing from the period of *Iphigénie* on," has a slightly tautological flavor.)

We must be more modest when facing the great works of art; we must forget our critical attitudes which are, so often, only aesthetic prejudices abstracted from a routine reading which does not consider the meaning of the individual work of art. We would understand better a great masterpiece such as *Phèdre* by affirming the adage of which Professor Lancaster declares himself skeptical: "tout est au mieux dans la meilleure des tragédies." Why should we not, a priori, engage in a "critique des beautés,"[10] believing, as a working hypothesis, and until the contrary is proved, that a great masterpiece *is* perfect in all its parts? How can the average literary critic, who is so seldom a poet-critic (like Diderot or Hugo) justify his temerity in assuming as his working hypothesis: "tout n'est pas au mieux dans la meilleure des tragédies"? Does it give him comfort that he can find flaws in the masters? If, at least, these flaws were real—and not, rather, the critic's own flaws of aesthetic understanding projected back into the work he studies! To leave it to the taste of the individual reader to decide whether or not Racine was justified in inserting such a récit reveals an attitude of critical agnosticism which is at variance with the readiness to admit flaws, and which amounts to a renouncement of aesthetic canons: if there *are* flaws we must condemn them on aesthetic grounds; if the lengthy, ornate récit is out of place, it is no longer a matter of "taste" to find it so. The critic who goes so far as to raise up before us the possibility of a Racinian error, should not stop before dealing the lethal blow. If Racine has erred, we must prove it; if we cannot prove it, let us rather not suggest the possibility of error.

* *
*

After having proceeded from the whole of the play to the part, to the "récit de Théramène," which we found to reflect microcosmically the whole and to have a definite place therein, we will now reverse the procedure, asking ourselves what stylistic traits are offered by this fragment that are necessarily characteristic of the whole of the play.

1. Let us begin by considering Racine's preoccupation with the act of "seeing," which cannot fail to strike any observer of Racinian style. Twice in the récit, Théramène stresses the visual apperception of the event he has experienced: once when he mentions his own reaction to the horrid spectacle:

> Excusez ma douleur. Cette image cruelle
> Sera pour moi de pleurs une source éternelle.
> *J'ai vu, Seigneur, j'ai vu* votre malheureux fils
> Traîné par les chevaux que sa main a nourris ...

and again when he presents to us Aricie's grief on discovering the dead body of Hippolyte:

> ... *elle voit* l'herbe rouge et fumante;
> *elle voit* (quel objet pour les yeux d'une amante!)
> Hippolyte étendu, sans forme et sans couleur ...
> Et ne connaissant plus ce héros qu'elle adore,
> *Elle voit* Hippolyte et le demande encore.
> Mais trop sûre à la fin qu'il est devant ses yeux,
> Par un triste regard elle accuse les Dieux.

To Théramène the dead youth has already become a picture ("cette image cruelle"), and this crystallized image is transmitted to Thésée who, though he has not seen the "sad object" with the physical eye (and, as he is told, would have been unable to recognize it: "Triste objet . . . que méconnaîtrait l'oeil même de son père"), will be haunted evermore by what he has seen with the eyes of the soul ("De mon fils déchiré fuir la sanglante image"). This insistence on the act of seeing, whether physical or "transposed," which is not isolated in Racine, cannot fail to impress us with the importance of "sight" for Racine's *Weltanschauung* (in the literal sense of the German word): we cannot brush aside as "poetic formulae" such phrases as "l'oeil d'un père" = "un père," or the repetition of *voir* (although this is an imitation of the "anaphora" of the ancients, it must, like the many other ancient formulae borrowed by Racine, be granted a new meaning in Racine's poetic system). In the poetic world of Racine, all "things seen," all events in their matter-of-fact brutality are, for the most part, excluded: they appear only indirectly, as things spoken of. From the visible world an intellectual vision is extracted which is revealed to the public only through words: by conversation all the light of the intellect is cast upon brutal reality, so that its essence shines out before us. To present this vision, Racine must often introduce intermediate persons who lend us their eyes. In the "récit de Théramène" we are allowed to see things through the medium of a reporter who tells us "J'ai vu, j'ai vu . . . ," and who even goes so far as to impose upon us a secondary visualization: his seeing of what Aricie saw: here we have an extreme case of Racine's care in preventing the bloody scene itself from striking our senses too abruptly. Moreover, in addition to the "refraction" achieved by the use of such human intermediaries, Racine interposes still another element between us and crude reality, which is his particularly poetic and intellectual language (thus, in the case of Aricie we have two intermediary persons plus a tertiary medium: a multiplication of planes which may remind us of the baroque "mirror" technique of Velásquez).

If, now, we try to reconstruct the scene actually seen by Aricie, we will first notice that Racine, contrary to the practice of a modern naturalist,[11] does not depict directly the bloody corpse of the young hero. Even "blood" is not directly mentioned, only implied by the reference to the vestiges recognizable on the grass ("herbe rouge et fumante"). Physical blood, warm, human blood is absent—not only from the stage but from the picture in words. (Later, it is true, Thésée speaks of the "sanglante image," but the very word order shows that he has sensed not a "bloody picture" [an "image sanglante"] but a picture of carnage: the post-positional adjective does not describe physical facts but draws moral implications from the bloodshed, implying and transcending "blood."[12]) For, in this passage describing Aricie's discovery, Racine focuses our attention not on the sad object of physical vision, but on the act of seeing itself—which represents an attempt to recognize, to identify.[13] And this process of identification is presented in slow-motion: Racine prolongs for five lines Aricie's hesitancy about the identity of Hippolyte. She comes to realize that "this Hippolyte" is defined by the absence of the traits ("sans forme et sans couleur,")[14] which make him Hippolyte, "ce héros qu'elle adore." The continuity of her lover's being, which she would represent by "he" has become problematic: is this body "he"? ("elle voit Hippolyte et le demande encore"). The outer and the inner continuity are not congruous. When Aricie is finally forced to recognize that what she sees "is Hippolyte," she has cognized the destructive world order responsible for this discrepancy. And all this is to be read in her look accusing the gods.[15] Later, when the philosophical Théramène, at the close of his speech, declares that he has come to Thésée "détestant la lumière" (an expression which would, as we shall see, be appropriate also for Phèdre) we realize that his rejection of daylight[16] is equal in tragic weight to Aricie's accusing glance toward heaven.

The "récit de Phèdre" is no less "transposed" than is that of Théramène, since here Phèdre speaks of her bodily and psychological reactions, not only as a woman, but as a woman with the intellect and poetry of a Racine, capable of sifting and stylizing her emotions (incidentally, this blend with Racine is an inheritance from Seneca, whose emotional-philosophical Medea is Medea + Seneca: Medea + a philosophical poet). When Phèdre has "seen," there is involved a seeing of herself, a seeing sharpened by her critical self-judgment:

> Mon repos, mon bonheur semblait être affermi;
> Athènes me montra mon superbe ennemi.
> *Je le vis*, je rougis, je pâlis à sa vue.
> Un trouble s'éleva dans mon âme éperdue.
> *Mes yeux ne voyaient plus*, je ne pouvais parler.
> Je sentis tout mon corps et transir et brûler;
> *Je reconnus* (!) Vénus et ses feux redoutables
> J'adorais Hippolyte; et *le voyant* sans cesse . . .
> Je l'évitais partout. O comble de misère!
> *Mes yeux le retrouvaient* dans les traits de son père . . .
> *J'ai revu* l'ennemi que j'avais éloigné:
> Ma blessure trop vive aussitôt a saigné.

Ce n'est plus une ardeur dans mes veines cachée :
C'est Vénus tout entière à sa proie attachée.

Here, however, we are confronted with new implications of
the act of seeing. In Phèdre's case, the "seeing" is, in a double
sense, the tragic mainspring of her being : her sin is to have
"seen" Hippolyte, to have experienced love for him, and her
torture is to see (to cognize) that her sin is "having seen."
Phèdre's *voir* is stained with sin and knowledge of sin. The
fire of sin came through the eye (the covetous sense par excellence, according to Saint Augustine) ; it is for this reason
that Phèdre wishes henceforth to shun the light of day ("ne
plus voir le jour": note the ambiguity of *jour* = "life" and
"light of day"[15a]), and flees into the darkness of death. In her
final words she applies to herself the law of retaliation : "Déjà
je ne vois plus qu'à travers un nuage / Et le ciel et l'époux
que ma présence outrage ; / Et la mort, à mes yeux dérobant
la clarté, / Rend au jour qu'ils souillaient, toute sa pureté."
Phèdre is the incarnation of God-willed self-destruction that
comes through the eye : the eye that cognizes ; Théramène,
the spectator of tragedy, suffers only sympathetically the God-
willed destruction in the objective world.

2. In the preceding paragraphs we have had occasion to
speak of the reality-sifting quality inherent in Racine's "intellectual and poetic" language. The reader may have wondered whether the two terms are not mutually exclusive : is not
Racine, moreover, the poet of pure emotion, untrammeled by
fetters of the intellect? Is he not, better than any other poet
of his time, able to let pure feeling breathe through words
of incomparable evocatory power—"Que ces vains ornements,
que ces voiles me pèsent," and "Ariane, ma soeur, de quel
amour blessée / Vous mourûtes aux bords où vous fûtes lais-
sée"? But such lines, with their great appeal to our emotional
and acoustic imagination, have generally been isolated from
the context by modern literary critics who have gone to school
to the Romantics ; when replaced in their original context,
they appear neutralized by more intellectual expressions. For
example, the first verse quoted is followed by the lines (159-

160) : "Quelle importune main, en formant tous ces noeuds, / A pris soin sur mon front d'assembler mes cheveux?" Here the epithet *importune* implies an intellectual judgment, at variance with the rest, while the sad flute music of Phèdre's utterances is followed by the cool remark of Oenone: "Que faîtes-vous, Madame? et quel mortel ennui / Contre tout votre sang vous anime aujourd'hui?" where *mortel ennui* represents an evaluation, a diagnosis. But even when these two famous "emotional utterances" are considered in themselves, it is possible to see how the impact is softened by the expression of an intellectual judgment: in "ces vains ornements" *vains* is fraught with moral connotations (the Biblical "vanitas vanitatum"); the passage about Ariane contains a full-fledged logical demonstration underscored by repetition of the same syntactical pattern: it had been preceded by Phèdre's ejaculation: "O haine de Vénus! O fatale colère! / Dans quels égarements l'amour jeta ma mère!" (corresponding to "de quel amour blessée . . . !"), and ends with the conclusion "Puisque Vénus le veut, de ce sang déplorable / Je péris la dernière et la plus misérable." Here, underlying the exclamations, we find the logical pattern of a syllogism:

1. dans quels égarements . . . (Pasiphae was persecuted by Venus)

2. de quel amour blessée . . . (Ariane was persecuted by Venus)

3. *Consequently* (this is implied by the *puisque*), Venus persecutes all the women of the family: I am only a link in the chain.

This passage, in which the lyrical outburst is mitigated by ratiocination, is one example of what I have called, in an earlier article, "klassische Dämpfung": a continuous repression of the emotional by the intellectual. Indeed, it could be said that the alternation between these two conflicting tendencies is the most distinctive characteristic of Racine's style. As such it can be found in the speech of all his characters[17]: Racine has taught them all to speak with his voice. It is, understandably enough, especially frequent in the language of Phèdre, being a trait thoroughly consonant with her nature:

in her, boundless passion and severe analysis coincide to a remarkable degree. In Théramène's character, too, there is a comparable blend of the objective and intellectual (as historian and philosopher) with the subjective (as a compassionate friend of the God-stricken family)—though, with him, as we have said, objectivity must prevail.[18] Thus it will not be difficult to find in the "récit de Théramène" the same general tendency of tempering as that noted in the "récit de Phèdre." When, for example, he describes how he and his companions followed the bloody path that led them to the body of Hippolyte:

> De son généreux sang la trace nous conduit:
> Les rochers en sont teints; les ronces dégouttantes
> Portent de ses cheveux les dépouilles. sanglantes

he offers vivid, concrete details appealing to our imagination. And yet the emotional effect is tempered by moral interpretations: the bloody hair, stuck to the thornbushes wet with blood, become "les dépouilles." The ghastly picture is ennobled: we are asked to contemplate the remains of a hero dead in battle. Still more characteristic is "son généreux sang": the actual blood as in similar cases pointed out above, is sublimated, transposed by the epithet *généreux* into the moral sphere. Again, in the passage:

> . . . A ce mot ce héros expiré
> N'a laissé dans mes bras qu'un corps défiguré,
> Triste objet où des Dieux triomphe la colère,
> Et que méconnaîtrait l'oeil même de son père

the expression "ce héros expiré," in which the defining phrase *héros expiré* is preceded by the demonstrative, has an oratorical ring, with Ciceronian overtones. It appeals to the emotion, if you will, but to the emotion of an intellectual person. One who was still under the impact of an affecting situation would not be so able to "define" and, instead of the demonstrative, would use, perhaps, the definite article which, by referring to something as already known, allows us to remain within the situation. The "distantiating demonstrative" (as I have called it), to the contrary, suggests a point of view from outside the situation; when we say, for example, *dans ce pays* "in this country," instead of *dans notre pays* "in our country," there is effected, at least for a split second, a disinterested comparison with other countries. Similarly, the *ce* of our passage is the expression of a dispassionate historian who feels the necessity of assuring his readers that he is still dealing with the same person.

Moreover, in this same phrase *ce héros expiré*, there is another trait of style to be observed, one which had been particularly favored by Roman historians and by the Roman playwrights who dealt with historical subjects (Seneca, for example) and which has existed in French since the time of the Renaissance (cf. Lerch's treatment of this construction under the title "C'est son rêve accompli," Beiheft 42 to *ZRPh*, 1912). *Ce héros expiré* stands for *l'expiration, la mort de ce héros*—or rather, we should say that *ce héros expiré / N'a laissé dans mes bras qu'un corps défiguré* is ambiguous by intent: is it the person of the hero (who happened to be dead), or his death, which left the sad vestiges? This type of expression, which ascribes to the agent what really belongs to the resulting action, and which remains on the borderline between the abstract and the concrete, gives an intellectual, sophisticated flavor ("can a dead hero act?") to a passage which otherwise speaks so directly to the heart. Finally, the personality of Hippolyte, of that "object," is further reduced by the use of the relative adverb *où*, which seems to refer not to a person but to a locality: the object has become a "place where" the Gods have sated their anger. This *où*, of which modern symbolistic poets might have been proud, immediately renders visualization impossible: we are in No Man's Land somewhere between an object and a place, between the visible and the abstract, the emotional and the intellectual, between a picture and a definition.

In the following passage, which contains a parenthetical remark, the tendency of "Dämpfung" has found another congruous form, and one which represents a characteristic and oft-repeated pattern in Racine's verse:

Elle voit (quel objet pour les yeux d'une amante!)
Hippolyte étendu, sans forme et sans couleur.

Here we are ready to identify ourselves with the sorrowing Aricie, to see with her eyes—and Théramène-Racine decides to postpone the picture we are eager to see, perhaps in order to prepare us for the horrifying sight: that is, in order to temper our emotions. Now this parenthesis is, in its syntactical form, an exclamation, an emotional outburst (like Phèdre's "*de quelle amour* blessée . . . !"), but its contents offer a rational appraisal of the object of vision. There is in the phrase *objet pour les yeux* something definitional and intellectual; the dead youth appears as a "visual unit," framed as it were, ready to be cognized by a scrutinizing eye. The effect is obviously to place us outside the range of Aricie's feelings —since these are defined. We feel for her but not with her; we have the attitude of a sympathetic but dispassionate witness—the attitude of Théramène-Racine. In addition, the presence of the indefinite article ("les yeux d'une amante") introduces a comparison of her plight with the normal lot of lovers in general; this projection of the particular case against a framework, this invocation of a general law, is a philosophical and intellectual device, particularly characteristic of Racine (which, with him, may take on a variety of nuances: entreaty, [self-] pity, self-assertion, protestation; the latter is found in Hippolyte's last words: "plaint le malheur d'*un* fils faussement accusé").

We have to do again with an interpolation, if not with a parenthesis, in the following example:

> On dit qu'on a vu même, en ce désordre affreux,
> Un Dieu qui d'aiguillons pressait leurs flancs poudreux.

Here, all is "poetic" and "seen"—and yet, in the interpolated *en ce désordre affreux*, the events narrated are judged, a rational diagnosis is given: by means of the term "extreme" the canon of normality is brought into play. And, simply by the act of calling something "extreme," we liberate ourselves from its impact; the impression of disorder or disharmony is not allowed to dominate the scene; on the contrary, the scene is gauged and defined for us. Here, too, however, the approach is not wholly rational: in the epithet *affreux* there is con-

densed, as it were, an emotional exclamation which sums up
the whole scene: "c'était affreux!"—but, at the same time,
this epithet is neutralized by the "diagnostic" noun *désordre*.[19]
Again, we may consider the following passage, in which the
description of factual events is interrupted by a moral judgment ("digne fils d'un héros"):

> Hippolyte lui seul, digne fils d'un héros,
> Arrête ses coursiers, saisît ses javelots,
> Pousse au monstre, et d'un dard lancé d'une main sûre,
> Il lui.fait dans le flanc une large blessure.

The eye of the observer is also a moral eye: it moralizes while
it observes. Not only is the heroism of Hippolyte shown by a
description of his exploits: it is also verbally defined.

Such interpolations, which generally fill out the second
hemistich of the first line of a couplet, are generally called
"chevilles" (paddings), as if to suggest that the classical
poets of the seventeenth century were in the habit of compos-
ing, in the original draft, the first hemistich of the first line,
together with the whole second line, later to fill out the missing second hemistich of the first line. (According to this suggestion, Molière would have first written in his *Misanthrope*:
"On sait que ce pied plat. . . . Par de sales emplois s'est poussé
dans le monde," later to add "digne qu'on le confonde"). If
this analysis, which assumes a "two-installment procedure"
in poetic composition, were correct this would mean that the
intellectual element must represent an extraneous addition to
the emotional (of course, the question as to why such a
prosaic phrase was added on second thought, would be only
the more perplexing) whereas I contend that the rationalistic
interpolation was conceived *along with* the emotionally flowing sentence, and is inseparable therefrom (it would evidently
be impossible to separate the two elements in the insertion
itself: *quel objet pour les yeux d'une amante*!). It is highly
significant that, in the interpolations of Dämpfung, the classical poets put references to that stable world of moral values
toward which they most insistently strove. These reminders
of a moral and rational realm, in the midst of emotional

turmoil, exert a steadying influence; over the waves of passion there shine forth, from these "lighthouses," the tranquil beams of reason and calm.

3. Now we are ready to consider an aspect of Racine's art, the failure to recognize which has led to misunderstanding on the part of many critics, from the seventeenth century to our own time. Students of Racine are familiar with the debate between Houdar de la Motte and Boileau, in which the former attacked, the latter defended, that line of our récit in which Théramène describes the reaction of Nature to the appearance of the sea-monster: "Le flot, qui l'apporta, recule épouvanté."

According to Houdar de la Motte: "Ce vers est excessif dans la bouche de Théramène. On est choqué de voir un homme accablé de douleur, si recherché dans ses termes et si attentif à sa description."[20] To this Boileau answers: "Pouvoit-il [Racine] employer la hardiesse de sa métaphore dans une circonstance plus considérable et plus sublime que dans l'effroyable arrivée de ce monstre, ni au milieu d'une passion plus vive que celle qu'il donne à cet infortuné gouverneur d'Hippolyte?" In other words, Houdar de la Motte bases his attack on the principle of "vraisemblance," while Boileau (the translator of Longinus!) invokes "sublimity" in his defense of the passage. What the one refers to as "excessif" and the other as "hardiesse de sa métaphore" is, more specifically, the interpretation of the physical fact of a wave's ebb and flow in a sophisticated and clever manner, whereby this natural process is ascribed to the ocean's fear. Since a "précieux" expression is usually defined as "une métaphore suivie jusqu'au bout" (the classical example being Théophile de Viau's "il [le poignard] en rougit, le traître!"), or an over-extended intellectual interpretation of a physical fact, we may say that the "excess" to which the critic Houdar de la Motte objected was the preciosity of the metaphor.

But now let us place the incriminated line in its context (as the classical critics failed to do), and examine the dominant idea of the passage as a whole:

Un effroyable cri, sorti du fond des flots,
Des airs en ce moment a troublé le repos;
Et du sein de la terre une voix formidable
Répond en gémissant à ce cri redoutable.
Jusqu'au fond de nos coeurs notre sang s'est glacé.
Des coursiers attentifs le crin s'est hérissé.
Cependant, sur le dos de la plaine liquide,
S'élève à gros bouillons une montagne humide:
L'onde approche, se brise, et vomit à nos yeux,
Parmi des flots d'écume, un monstre furieux.
Son front large est armé de cornes menaçantes;
Tout son corps est couvert d'écailles jaunissantes;
Indomptable taureau, dragon impétueux,
Sa croupe se recourbe en replis tortueux;
Ses longs mugissements font trembler le rivage.
Le ciel avec horreur voit ce monstre sauvage;
La terre s'en émeut, l'air en est infecté,
Le flot qui l'apporta recule épouvanté.
Tout fuit; et, sans s'armer d'un courage inutile,
Dans le temple voisin chacun cherche un asile.

Here we are faced with the fact that Nature shrinks back
from what she has given birth to, that the monster, though a
part of Nature, is repudiated by the whole of Nature. As is
well known, the classical procedure for evoking the whole of
Nature is that of enumerating the four elements (note, in
1133, the evocation of Nature, when Hippolyte swears: "Que
la terre, le ciel, que toute la nature . . .": here, Racine has
added to the two elements mentioned by Euripides, the phrase
"toute la nature"); in our passage the four elements (the
sky, the seat of light, replaces the element of fire) respond
with fright to the frightful product of Nature—the greatest
fear being felt by the sea which gave birth to the sea-monster.
Now, if we turn to the "récit de Phèdre," we find another
example of Racinian baroque: Phèdre's address to the "soleil
. . . qui . . . rougis"—and, indeed, of the same pattern of
thought: the paradoxical fact of an ancestor who must blush
at his own progeny is of the same sort as that of Nature re-
jecting what she has brought forth.[21] Where Houdar de la

Motte saw only a witty conceit, out of place in a tragedy, and unconvincing because of its excessive *invraisemblance*, there is a deeply felt expression of what was sensed as paradox in Nature.[22] In the cases where Racine allows himself to lend human emotions to Nature, this has a functional value for the play. Indeed, the play itself is based on the comparable paradox that the Gods repudiate their creatures; they send man into the world endowed with gifts which prove to be Danaïc, and abandon him to his doom. We may remember the lines of Goethe:

> Ihr führt ins Leben uns hinein
> Und lasst den Menschen schuldig werden,
> Dann überlasst ihr ihn der Pein,
> Denn alle Schuld rächt sich auf Erden.

Racine's sensitivity to such a paradox as that of "creation and repudiation" reveals a *Weltanschauung* which is essentially baroque.

That the baroque element in Racine's art was not recognized (as such) by his contemporaries is hardly surprising. During this period, the classical ideal of reason and simplicity was accepted so implicitly in France (where it was followed so much more faithfully than was the case in Spain, Italy, England, Germany) that any tendencies which appeared to be in opposition to pure classicism were considered, by the critics, as so many flaws: aberrations from the norm. They were unable to sense in their lifetime the positive nature of such tendencies, whenever these did appear, to see them as manifestations of another artistic ideal which were integral to the work of art; instead, they were viewed only as excesses, as excrescences which could and should be pruned off. Or, if they were condoned, this was apt to be due more to an inconsistent attitude than to critical understanding (Boileau, for example, defends the line of Racine mentioned above but stoutly condemns the "clinquant du Tasse"). But, while such confusion is understandable in the classical critics, who did not have at their disposal the conception of the "baroque" which modern historians of art and literature have developed,[23] the same excuse will not hold for those of our modern historians of French seventeenth-century literature, to whom this conception has not yet penetrated and who, even after the investigations into the baroque carried on by Wölfflin, Weisbach, Walzel, etc., insist on remaining faithful to the confusion which had its *raison d'être* in circumstances of the seventeenth century.[24] Brunetière, for example, sees such tendencies as "préciosité, le boursouflé, le grotesque" only as flaws contrary to the classical ideal. And he also makes the mistake of assuming too easily that, with the triumph of classicism in seventeenth-century literature, these unfortunate tendencies were vanquished. But who can overlook the "précieux" vein in Molière, that critic of the *précieuses*? And this preciosity, of course (as well as "le boursouflé," "le grotesque") is a manifestation of the baroque.

The baroque phenomenon in the seventeenth-century art and literature must be considered in contradistinction to the (purely) classical art which preceded it: while this follows the path of the golden mean between two extremes, in an atmosphere of calm and of an equipoise easily and inevitably reached, baroque art reveals the conflict of polarities which is so acute that the final equilibrium is achieved only by a violent effort and at the expense of our tranquillity. Even when balance is attained, the vestiges of the struggle remain indelible in the work of art, so that asymmetry prevails. The conflicting forces may be worldliness and religion, sensuousness and a disillusioning recognition of the vanity of the world, passion and intellect, anarchy and authority, but in every case the victory of the second force is hard won. In such a tense atmosphere, the three "stylistic diseases" mentioned by Brunetière—each of them a distinct trend in itself —can easily flourish. In Italy, Ariosto and Tasso, in Spain, Garcilaso and Góngora represent classic and baroque poetry respectively; among the artists, Raphael represents Renaissance art as opposed to the baroque of the later Michelangelo. In France, the baroque factor, whether in art or in literature, was much less conspicuous: what a tame variant of it is offered by the preciosity and the grotesque of Théophile! Nevertheless, there are baroque elements in Corneille and Racine as well as in Molière—and most of all, in Pascal and Bossuet (the same is true of Poussin, who appears to Gide as a mitigated Rubens).

To return to our play, it is evident that *Phèdre* is the ideal type of a baroque tragedy, not only by its style, but by its basic conception (though this the historians of French literature generally do not say) : we need only consider the heroine given over to a burning passion and, at the same time, to an intellectual awareness of it which multiplies her sufferings; Thésée, the heroic monster-slayer and happy lover, powerless against those gods who seem to protect him; kingly beings, enjoying a position far above common mankind, grope in the dark of their passion or their intellectual blindness. Here we have the typically baroque theme of the great of the earth who are creatures with all the frailty, the "Kreatürlichkeit" of such (cf. Shakespeare, *Henry V* : "I think the King is but a man as I . . . all his senses have but human conditions : his ceremonies laid by, in his nakedness he appears but a man") —together with the motif of the "dream of life," whose mystery man cannot unravel. Again and again, throughout the play, the characters are involved in a struggle between conflicting forces one of which will be allowed with great difficulty to subdue the other; a resolution is always achieved (by "klassische Dämpfung"), but one feels the revolt of the senses and of the emotions. The over-all impression remains that of a Pyrrhic victory.

In this connection, it is illuminating to consider the alterations which Racine introduced in the characters inherited from Euripides. Of Phèdre he says in his preface: "Phèdre n'est ni tout à fait coupable, ni tout à fait innocente. Elle est engagée par sa destinée, et par la colère des dieux dans une passion illégitime, dont elle a horreur toute la première. . . . Lorsqu'elle est forcée de la découvrir, elle en parle avec une confusion qui fait bien voir que son crime est plutôt une punition des dieux qu'un mouvement de sa volonté. J'ai même pris soin de la rendre moins odieuse qu'elle n'est dans les tragédies des anciens, où elle se résout d'elle-même à accuser Hippolyte. J'ai crue que la calomnie avoit quelque chose de trop bas et de trop noir pour la mettre dans la bouche d'une princesse qui a d'ailleurs des sentiments si nobles et si vertueux. Cette bassesse m'a paru plus convenable à une nourrice, qui pouvoit avoir des inclinations plus serviles."

This means to imply, when interpreted in terms of modern criticism, that Racine has made the character of Phèdre more baroque: the natural nobility of a great queen is in violent contrast with her debasing passion; the play consists of the *mise en jour* (to use Racine's own expression) of the all-too-human baseness of an exalted being. This basic structure of the character Phèdre is intended to show us how love, a gift of the Gods to mankind, can become poison and debasement; by love the mighty are cast down—indeed, dehumanized. To lead us toward the heights only to precipitate us into the abyss, this is the scheme of the Gods, and the baroque poet does his utmost to preserve the sharp contrast of the two extremes—as he exposes the shame of the exalted to the eyes of the world (we may be reminded of the line "Seht wie ein König kniet!" which closes the play of Grillparzer: a sentiment typical of baroque drama wherever and whenever found). Only death, which has been hovering over the five acts of the drama, brings a resolution of the conflict. No such thought of exposing the frailty'of the mighty was uppermost in the mind of Euripides, whose Hippolyte was pure, an innocent victim of the anger of the Gods. And the reason for Racine's shift of emphasis from Hippolyte to Phèdre, a shift which has been pointed out by so enlightened a critic as Batteux, must have been that, by making Phèdre the protagonist, Racine was given the possibility of showing a princely being at its most frail ("frailty, thy name is woman" said the one who was the baroque hero par excellence): a woman in conflict between moral nobility and earthly passion.

And once the torn character of Phèdre had become the center of the play, once its theme had been changed from that of purity persecuted by the inexplicable cruelty of the Gods, to the baroque inner *Zerrissenheit* of a character within whom the God-sent monster rages, then the character of Hippolyte had to be transformed: he, too, must share in the baroque *Kreatürlichkeit* of Phèdre by assuming the role of a lover who loves against the will of his father—endowed, that is, with a flaw, however slight, in conformity with the law of the baroque stage where the limelight is cast not on ideality but on human frailty. Of Racine's innovations in this regard Batteux writes: "Phèdre criminelle, et Hippolyte vertueux, tous deux malheureux, sont mieux placés dans Euripide que dans Racine, parce qu'il est dans la nature et dans l'ordre que quand la vertu malheureuse se trouve en concurrence avec le crime malheureux, l'intérêt dominant et l'affection principale soient pour la vertu, qui n'a pas mérité son malheur, plutôt que pour le crime, qui a mérité le sien. L'objet naturel de la pitié, dit Aristote, est le malheur non mérité: d'où il suit qu'il est possible qu'Euripide ait mieux pris son sujet, relativement à l'effet de la tragédie, en subordonnant Phèdre à Hippolyte. . . . Phèdre est l'héroïne de la pièce de Racine; et c'est pour rendre son rôle plus beau et plus touchant qu'Hippolyte a été en quelque sorte dégradé. Euripide savait que les héros qu'on veut offrir à la pitié doivent être bons d'une bonté morale; Racine le savait aussi, puisqu'il donne partout l'amour de Phèdre comme l'effet de la colère de Vénus, pour la rendre moins odieuse; mais Euripide n'a eu qu'à suivre son plan simplement et sans aucun effort; Racine a eu besoin de beaucoup d'art pour suivre le sien. . . . Ne pouvant diminuer le malheur d'Hippolyte, il a fallu en diminuer la vertu, sans quoi il eût éclipsé Phèdre et emporté tout l'intérêt."[25]

Batteux has seen beautifully the dependence of Hippolyte's transformation on that of Phèdre but, imbued as he had to be with Aristotelian normative aesthetics, he could not recognize in that change the definite artistic will of Racine, so different from that of Euripides; the baroque poet who had conceived one character according to the pattern of conflict could not but shape the other accordingly. It was not apprehension lest an entirely virtuous Hippolyte eclipse Phèdre (an idea which seems to have left its imprint in Mr. Lynes' statements) which led Racine to depict Hippolyte as slightly less perfect: it was because, according to his baroque vision of the prince who is at the same time a human being, it was necessary that all the royal characters be shaken by ontologically conditioned conflicts. Phèdre "moins odieuse," Hippolyte less perfect: each represents a vision of man as a basically torn being; each of them is as baroque a creation as was Pascal's *roseau pensant.* Fénelon's and Arnauld's criticism of Racine's Hippolyte is quite beside the mark: they have failed to see the anthropological view underlying Racine's dramatic system. The lover's role assigned to Hippolyte represented no compromise with contemporary society (as has been suggested by the dubious anecdote of Racine's apology: "Qu'auraient dit nos petits-maîtres?"). In fact, Hippolyte is undermined by his pure passion for Aricie just as truly as is Phèdre by her impure passion. The gradual weakening of Hippolyte's power over his horses (which was to lead to his undoing) is parallel to the undermining of Phèdre's will-power by her consuming love. Hippolyte's love is Phèdre's passion on a minor scale; Racine presents his pessimistic judgment of love in a pure and an impure version: a total criticism which Proust will repeat.

Finally, the de-idealization of Hippolyte had to entail the creation of the ideal Aricie: this pure princess inherits the original role of Hippolyte in Euripides; and she inherits also his protecting deity, Diana. The character of Aricie was conceived not only in order to motivate the flaw in Hippolyte's character, a "super" on whom Racine could hang the label "loved by Hippolyte": it was also necessary that purity be represented in the drama. And Aricie, who stands beyond the reach of the curse which lies on the family of Thésée, is unstained by sin, unshadowed by doom.

We have begun this section by the consideration of a stylistic feature (*préciosité*) which revealed itself as a reflection of a characteristically baroque conception, and we have seen how the fabric of the play itself was shot through with baroque themes, involving the clash of polarities. Now, returning to stylistic questions, we will find, not only the feature of preciosity, which is one of the forms of the baroque in French literature, but a device which embodies the basic baroque pattern of contrasted polarities. When, for example, Phèdre's passion is described as a *flamme noire*, we are offered a paradoxical expression of the type to which the ancients gave the name *oxymoron*; such a phrase presents the impossible as possible. The flame that should bring light and life in the being called Phaedra, "the shining one," in reality brings darkness and death (Phèdre is the daughter not only of Pasiphaë, the "all-shining," but also of Minos, the god of hell, to whom, unable longer to bear the light of day, she will descend; thus she is herself an oxymoron incarnate). The fire that warms ends in the cold of death. No wonder that the poisoned love that Phèdre bears cannot warm the heart: "Je *goûtais en tremblant* ces *funèbres plaisirs*" (Act IV)—two oxymora are found in one sentence. And we may also remember the expression "funestes bienfaits" by which Thésée, filled with a presentiment of Hippolyte's death, characterizes the Danaïc gifts of the Gods. A less obvious type of oxymoron is to be seen in the line (which antagonized the unpoetic critics of Racine's time) from our récit: "Traîné par les chevaux que sa main a nourris."[26] This underscores beautifully the paradox, the *Widersinn* of life: the heroic horse-tamer is trampled by his horses. Here, just as with *flamme noire* and *funestes bienfaits*, there is the suggestion of an intolerable world order subject to the clash of polarities. And yet, by virtue of having been defined, the disharmonious is overcome: disharmony is conquered by the harmony of form.

As a final manifestation of baroque art in *Phèdre*, let us turn again to the description of the monster which is central to the récit. The motif itself was, evidently, given. What Racine has brought out most conspicuously is the element of the demoniac—if this may be defined as a death-bringing vital force. In the ancient world, the monster had its legitimate place, accepted as one of the forces of nature: in the world of Christian values, the monstrous must appear as a threat to the cosmos, sent by *natura parens* to inflict death. And this threat is felt in Racine's description, where nature, in its hideous beauty, is presented in a variety of novel forms worthy of a Baudelaire or a Flaubert:

> Cependant sur le dos de la plaine liquide
> S'élève à gros bouillons une montagne humide;
> L'onde approche, se brise, et vomit à nos yeux
> Parmi des flots d'écume, un monstre furieux.
> Son front large est armé de cornes menaçantes;
> Tout son corps est couvert d'écailles jaunissantes;

Indomptable taureau, dragon impétueux,
Sa croupe se recourbe en replis tortueux.

All in these lines is movement and action; in a momentary metamorphosis where the animate takes on the inanimate (*montagne humide*), and the reverse (*dos de la plaine*), strange shapes emerge as if painted by a Rubens or a Bosch. Those critics who have spoken of the "descriptive style" in the "récit de Théramène" should, more specifically, have spoken of the "baroque descriptive style," of the "description of the hideous and the demoniac." It is surely significant that this passage, which has always been recognized as one of the most highly descriptive to be found in Racine, is focused on the demoniac, the monstrous, the gruesome. For, what is a monster unless seen? A monster in the abstract! Since monster it had to be (because of the ancient model), it could be only a baroque monster: a monster presented in all its horrid sensuous reality.

But this anarchy of shapes and movement will be curbed by Racinian verse; the monster will be transposed into the realm of poetry. Since the matter of Théramène's story was the ugly and the destructive, the manner had to be ornate and weighty: the more exciting the events witnessed by Théramène, the more poised must be his description of it—the more of intellectual detachment, of aesthetic repose, of plastic beauty open to contemplation must we be offered. Firmly architectured alexandrines impose their measure on the ghastly vision; rhetorical patterns mold and purify crude reality. By the intellectual act of distinguishing these patterns, the emotions of the listener are held in check; while he is invited to visualize strangeness and horror, he is constantly reminded of the familiar and the traditional—for the devices used by Racine are, for the most part, highly conventional. Let us note just a few of these quite conventional features: the traditionally poetic vocabulary ("onde" for "mer," which involves the conventional device of synecdoche), chiasmus ("indomptable taureau" - "dragon furieux"), anaphoric prefixes ("se recourbe en replis"), onomatopoeia ("l'essieu *crie et* se rompt"), and finally (e.g. "monstre furieux") the classical use of "colorless" adjectives, so obnoxious to a modern critic who is apt to share the opinion of Jules Renard that " 'Ciel' dit plus que 'ciel bleu'; l'épithète tombe d'elle-même, comme une feuille morte." But the "dead" quality of such epithets is precisely what serves to establish calm and serenity. The ultimate effect of these devices is that the chaotic vital forces on the verge of explosion are stemmed, subjected to rule and form, to "klassische Dämpfung." For Racine, the baroque poet, is a French poet; he is not tempted, as a Quevedo might be, to overthrow all boundaries of form, but understands how to subject the baroque flow of vital forces to classical measure. It is true that the "récit de Théramène" is a "most baroque" piece of poetry, and its critics have been troubled by its close approach to the anarchic and the chaotic. None the less, the récit succeeds in taming the monster by style.

My three divisions devoted to the style of the "récit de Théramène" were intended to show how reality is sifted by the intellect, how the expression of emotion is attended with "klassische Dämpfung," how life is seen as a conflict between polar forces. We have also tried to show that former critics have failed to let themselves be guided by the words of the play toward its inner economy and coherence, preferring rather to establish relationships between certain unrelated details of the play and aprioristic criteria extraneous to the play. Since we have chosen to remain within the play, our procedure has been to penetrate from the periphery of the words toward the inner core. For the words of the poet are shafts leading to the innermost part of the mine, while extraneous rapprochements are dead alleys. Criticism must remain immanent to the work of art, and draw its categories therefrom.

NOTES

1. This crisscross design of divine influences is the invention of Racine: with Euripides, the chaste Hippolyte had, as his patron, the chaste Diana. Since, in Racine's version, he was not "entirely chaste," he had to be a worshiper of the patron God of his father: Neptune—and, to some extent, of Venus.

2. Blameless, of course, only insofar as concerns the pure nature of his love for Aricie (for the *fact* of this love is presented as a flaw). On the other hand, every precaution is taken by Racine to indicate that Hippolyte's listless mood, which may have caused his waning attention to the horses that he had trained, is due to this love; cf. the lines (551-552) in which Hippolyte complains that his love-longing has interfered with his once favorite sport of horse-taming (and which anticipate somewhat the lines of the "récit de Théramène": ". . . et sourds à cette fois,/Ils ne reconnaissent plus ni le frein ni la voix").

3. To these examples for the "chariot" motif there may be added lines 176-178 in Act I, when Phèdre depicts her tortured state of mind to Oenone (before giving her any explanation of her condition) by means of two images of the peace which is denied her; one of these contains precisely the motif of the chariot:

> Dieu! que ne suis-je assise à l'ombre des forêts!
> Quand pourrai-je, au travers d'une noble poussière,
> Suivre de l'oeil un char fuyant dans la carrière . . . ?

No sooner has she made this admission than she realizes that she is no longer mistress of her spirits:

> Insensée, où suis-je? et qu'ai-je dit?
> Où laissé-je égarer mes voeux et mon esprit?
> Je l'ai perdu: les Dieux m'en ont ravi l'usage.
> Oenone, la rougeur me couvre le visage.

Here we can discover the delicate working of Racine's psychology of love, of that love which restricts the field of vision and turns everything therein into a means of torture. Euripides had offered a list of possibilities which would refresh Phaedra's soul: a spring, poplars on a meadow, mountains, horseback-riding—a variety of pleasures in which to find recreation. These distractions Racine limits to one—toward which the tortured soul of Phèdre turns: she craves to be outside of turmoil, a spectator of life; she wants not to ride herself but to watch from the shadow the "noble dust" from a speeding chariot. Then, immediately, this very picture of peace is turned into poison: if she sees a race she must think of the youthful and gallant chariot-driver Hippolyte.

Here, we have been given an insight into the awakening of Phèdre's self-poisoning imagination. Racine has used restriction in the choice of the possibilities, but has intensified the efficacy of one element.

In a lecture given at the Johns Hopkins University by Dr. Richmond Lattimore of Bryn Mawr College, the speaker pointed out that the young, Amazonlike Phaedra of Euripides is presented throughout as an Out-lander, ill-acclimated to Troezene: horseback-riding was not a "lady-like" activity in the eyes of Euripides' public. In Phaedra, according to Dr.

Lattimore, Euripides has created one of his numerous characters who are ill at ease and dissatisfied with the environment in which they must live. Thus, while in Euripides, Phaedra's desire for change and recreation shows mainly her nostalgia for the activities of her native climate, in Racine, Phèdre's same desire for equestrian feats—in which Hippolytus, not she, should figure—only serves to bind her the more to her passion.

4. Batteux has excellently realized that, in Racine's fifth act, the interest shifts from Phèdre to Thésée: "Phèdre, après la scène de la rivalité, n'intéresse plus; Thésée est le seul qui reste, ou du moins qui domine sur la scène. Cette translation de l'intérêt ne se trouve pas dans la pièce grecque. Hippolyte, donné pour point de vue dès la première scène, intéresse continuement et d'une façon dominante jusqu'à son dernier soupir." But the reason for this shift is not given by Batteux: that with Racine we see an almighty and heroic king blindly and desperately groping (like another King Lear, since he is close to madness) to find where truth lies, groping with the problem of the world order. Phèdre, at the end of the tragedy is less important than is the king, before whom the whole picture must be unrolled.

5. When Mauriac, in his *Vie de Jean Racine*, says of Phèdre: "Le soleil pour elle seule, contre elle seule. Les autres humains n'existent pas. Hippolyte même n'apparaît que dans la fulguration du désir de Phèdre," he is right insofar as he means only to characterize Phèdre's monomania. This certainly is not true of the architecture of the play from an objective point of view.

6. There is, in Phèdre, a particular motif of doom attached to a location (a motif not unknown to the ancients)—especially to Trézène. The anger of the Gods brings about the situations in which the family will be destroyed by making them go to that ill-omened Trézène which, on the surface, presents itself as the *aimable Trézène*: when Hippolyte says, near the beginning of the play (28): "Et je fuirai ces lieux que je n'ose plus voir" Théramène answers: "Hé! depuis quand, Seigneur, craignez-vous la présence / De ces paisibles lieux, si chers à votre enfance?" Hippolyte counters: "Tout a changé de face / Depuis que sur ces bords les Dieux ont envoyé / La fille de Minos et de Pasiphaë." Schlegel has indicted the expression *la présence de ces lieux* ("Have you ever heard that places have a presence?"). *Pace* Schlegel, it might be stated that in this tragedy places do have a presence: we must accept the clear indication of this artistic intention by Racine. The critic, instead of indicting a striking expression, should take therefrom the clue to his understanding: a striking expression in a masterpiece cannot be due to chance, it is rather a passkey! Consider, for example, some of the allusions to the doom by which Trézène is weighed down: (267, Oenone) "Voyage infortuné! Rivage malheureux, / Fallait-il approcher de tes bords dangereux!"; (302, Phèdre) "Vaines précautions! cruelle destinée! / Par mon époux lui-même à Trézène amenée, / J'ai revu l'ennemi que j'avais éloigné"; (929, Hippolyte) "Je ne la [Phèdre] cherchais pas: / C'est vous qui sur ces bords conduisîtes ses pas. / Vous daignâtes, Seigneur, aux rives de Trézène . . ."; (953, Thésée) "Que vois-je? Quelle horreur dans ces lieux répandue / Fait fuir devant mes yeux ma famille éperdue?" The temple of faith and purity, where the wedding of Hippolyte and Aricie should have taken place, is "aux portes de Trézène" near the ancient tombs of noble

ancestors (1392). But it is precisely there ("nous sortions des portes de Trézène," says Théramène—and he repeats the words of Hippolyte ["... ou ces tombeaux / Des princes de ma race antiques sépultures"] in a minor key: "ces tombeaux antiques, / Où des rois ses aïeux sont les tristes[!] reliques") that Hippolyte is destroyed; and there, consequently, Aricie will voice her accusation of the Gods. Little wonder that Thésée will, at the end, flee "loin de ce rivage / De mon fils déchiré fuir la sanglante image." His is a cursed race on a cursed soil.

7. Racine is careful not to allow Phèdre to act directly: he makes her guilty in her thought (it is, as R. A. Schröder has pointed out in *Racine und die Humanität*, the thought, not only the deed, which makes a Christian soul guilty): just as no overt action is involved in Phèdre's love for Hippolyte, Phèdre being criminal only in her amorous thoughts, so she commits no act herself to bring about Hippolyte's death. But her evil thought ratifies Oenone's evil action.

Racine has squared the circle by making his unfortunate queen "act without acting" in the scene where she decides against her earlier impulse to reveal Hippolyte's innocence to Thésée—stung to jealousy by the king's reference to Aricie. By this act of decision she espouses, by her sin of omission, the evil adviser's sin of commission; this is the maximum of action granted her before she takes poison (her death, itself, being extremely undramatic, and the exact *contrappasso* to that insidious poison of love to which we have seen her subjected). The baroque princess, reduced to a suffering body and soul, a figure gagged and bound, as it were, must submit throughout the play to the fatality of guilt which has elected her as victim. Oenone is the evil thought of Phèdre become action; Phèdre is not allowed the outlet of direct evil action.

8. For example, in the case of Théramène and Oenone, both are mentors, both teach their royal pupils to yield to love; but Oenone encourages a criminal, Théramène a healthy, love—consequently, she must die while he is allowed to survive. Although Théramène and Oenone never meet on the stage they have been conceived in obvious parallelistic antagonism.

9. This careful preparation for an action which will develop only in the fifth act, reminds us of the parallel case in which the death of Oenone is foreshadowed in her words in Act I (*229 seq.*):

> Quoiqu'il vous [Phèdre] reste à peine une faible lumière,
> Mon âme chez les morts descendra la première.
> Mille chemins ouverts y conduisent toujours :
> Et ma juste douleur choisira les plus courts.

The commentary of the *Grands écrivains* edition, with its predilection for information concerning things extraneous to the play, gives the ancient source for the third of these lines, but fails to explain the functional value of the lines within the play: to sound the note of tragic irony.

10. Indeed, any *explication de texte*, any philological study, must start with a *critique des beautés*, with the assumption on our part of the perfection of the work to be studied and with an entire willingness to sympathy; it must be an apologia, a theodicy in a nutshell. In fact, philology has its origin in the *apologia*—of the Bible or of the classics. For philology is born from Biblical criticism and humanistic endeavors, both of them attempts to justify the *So-sein*, the "being so and not otherwise" of exemplary texts. A criticism which insists on faults is justifiable only after the

purpose of the author has been thoroughly understood and followed up in detail. The glibness with which critics, especially great German critics (Lessing, Schiller, and Schlegel), have slandered French classical drama, is only to be explained on the basis of premature judgments drawn from a quite extraneous comparison with Shakespeare.

Professor Lancaster's partial acknowledgment of the "beauty" of *Phèdre* may remind us of the similar statement of Menéndez y Pelayo on Lope's masterpiece *Fuenteovejuna*: "Hay mucho que aplaudir en esta comedia, o más bien casi todo es excelente"—a statement which has elicited the protest of a scholar of the new generation, Joaquín Casalduero (*RFH*, v, 23) who, quoting Proust's allusion to "les oeuvres d'art achevées où il n'y a pas une seule touche qui soit isolée, où chaque partie tour à tour reçoit des autres sa raison d'être comme elle leur impose la sienne" (i.e. to the "circular" quality of works of art), opposes the relativism of his predecessor in violent terms: "En su día fué esto un descubrimiento que expresaba; hoy es un lugar común que, además de no querer decir nada, denota pereza intelectual excesiva o una rigidez mental grande en quien lo emplea. No: Lope ha producido obras perfectas. . . . *Fuenteovejuna* pertenece a la clase de obras en que todo es excelente." The time is past when the critic could read a masterpiece at his ease, feeling no obligation to relate parts to whole, here approving, there disapproving, as his eudaemonistic sensibility happened to be impressed.

11. Incidentally, it may be added that the intellectual nature of Aricie's perception in this scene is not at all "unrealistic": in moments when the most terrible sights strike our vision, there comes about a crystalline lucidity in which we are most clearly aware of our mental operations: if Aricie had been the one to report on her exact impressions at the moment, she would, perhaps, have been most true to reality in saying: "Je m'approche; je vois l'herbe . . . , je vois (quel objet . . .)" etc.

12. It is true that, in the words of the dying Hippolyte as reported by Théramène, we find the line "pour apaiser mon *sang* et mon ombre plaintive." Here, however, "blood" refers not only to physical blood: it is also a metonymical periphrase for "death"—with the Biblical implication that the blood of the murdered cries out for revenge. But this suggestion of a cry of vengeance immediately gives way to an appeased sigh of a softly plaintive Vergilian, or Dantean, shadow-soul.

In *Andromaque*, also, we are offered (as Miss Hatcher will point out in her forthcoming article) a picture of a bloody corpse: i.e. when the captive heroine describes the scene her eyes beheld the night of Troy's destruction:

> Seigneur, voyez l'état où vous me réduisez.
> J'ai vu mon père mort, et nos murs embrasés;
> J'ai vu trancher les jours de ma famille entière,
> Et mon époux sanglant traîné sur la poussière,
> Son fils seul avec moi, réservé pour les fers . . . (927-931)

But this reference to a bleeding form dragged in the dust does not offer a photographic reproduction of a mutilated body to our physical vision: we are not invited to visualize physiological details. It is the husband of Andromaque (*mon époux*) who has perished, it is the last of the Trojan heroes. And this figure is shown us against the background of the burning city; the framework of the whole is the destruction of Troy, the destruction of a civilization. Moreover, the description of Hector follows upon *trancher les jours* . . . ; this portentous reference to the death of a dynasty ennobles the blood-grimed figure in the dust—in the symbolic dust of defeat.

13. With Racine, the words for "seeing" are always fraught with connotations of intellectual clarification and cognizance, as Miss Hatcher will prove; in my previous study on Racine in *Rom. Stil u. Literaturstudien*, I had ventured some tentative remarks in this connection. The preferential place given to "sight" in comparison with the other senses, as we find it in Racine, is the continuation of an Augustinian and medieval trend of thought: cognizance, love, sin all come through the sense of senses, the eye.

14. We could also point out that, to the picture offered to Aricie ("[elle vit] Hippolyte étendu, sans forme et sans couleur"), a conceptual analysis has been added: since form and color are the elements of the (Thomistic) ideal definition of beauty, this sentence must mean that Aricie saw before her a Hippolyte bereft of beauty—and, consequently, was unable to recognize him ("et ne connaissant plus ce héros qu'elle adore"). The cultured listener is no doubt supposed to know this definition of beauty in order to be able to understand the meaning of these lines.

Just how much this insistence on "intellectual seeing," which seeks to identify the object seen, is in line with what I shall call later the "baroque" *desengaño*, can be shown by a German baroque play written earlier than *Phèdre*: Gryphius' *Cardenio und Celinde*. In a passage quoted by Ernst Feise, *Journal of Eng. and Germ. Phil.*, XLIV, 188, the protagonist tells of a vision in which he saw his daemonic beloved:

> Da sah ich / und erstarrt' in ungeheurem Schrecken
> Da sah ich / und erblast! da sah ich keine Zir!
> Da sah ich / und verging / Olympen nicht vor mir!
> Ich sah ein Totenbild! / ohn Aug / ohn Lipp und Wangen
> Ohn Ader / Haut und Fleisch / gehärt mit grünen Schlangen

The traits we observed in the passage on Aricie are also found here: not only the attempt to identify the dire sight, but also the hesitancy of the "seeing" person, who dreads to acknowledge the awful reality—as well as the total *desengaño* to which this seeing leads. There is surely no relationship of dependence between Racine and Gryphius: both write within the same climate; and both have studied Seneca and have adapted his anaphoric style to their baroque purposes.

15. That Aricie does not reappear on the stage at the moment of the denouement (we hear of her in the récit and in the final lines of the play), may be motivated by the dramatic reason that the bodily presence of such a figure of light as was Aricie would have distracted attention from the main victims of the Gods. She will always be to us "la triste Aricie" who indicts divinity.

15a. An ambiguity of classical origin: "to see the light," means "to live" in the *Iliad* (18, 442).

16. Compare Hippolyte's statement, "Le jour n'est pas plus pur que le fond de mon coeur," and the following passage (line 166 *seq.*) :

> OENONE: Vous vouliez vous montrer et revoir la lumière.
>   Vous l'avouez, Madame; et prête à vous cacher,

Vous haïssez le jour que vous veniez chercher.
PHÈDRE: Noble et brillant auteur d'une triste famille. . . .
Qui peut-être rougis du trouble où tu me vois,
Soleil, je te viens voir pour la dernière fois.

for the relationship between "daylight" and "purity."

17. The serenely intellectual atmosphere that permeates the last words of Hippolyte is remarkable; we have stressed above, in the text, his clear formulation of the meaning of his death, a formulation which admits of only a slight admixture of "poetry" ("mon ombre plaintive"). It is as though Hippolyte applied "classical restraint" to his last words, and to the last moments of his existence. Even when his words are interrupted by the agony of death ("qu'il lui rende . . .") this fits into the classical pattern of "aposiopesis": there is lacking, for example, the "naturalistic" effect, depending on the truncation of a single word, as we find it in Ariosto: "nè men ti raccomando la mia *Fiordi*— / Ma dir non potè *ligi*, e qui finío." Moreover, in the unfinished words of Hippolyte, what is interrupted is not the evocation of a name that embodies the personal happiness of the lover, but the expression of an altruistic thought concerning the welfare of the other being that should live on after her lover's death.

18. Diderot, in his "Paradoxe sur le comédien," has written immortal lines which seem almost to be meant to apply to the "récit de Théramène": "Avez-vous jamais réfléchi à la différence des larmes excitées *par un événement* tragique et des larmes excitées par un récit pathétique? On entend raconter une belle chose: peu à peu la tête s'embarrasse, les entrailles s'émeuvent, et les larmes coulent. Au contraire, à l'aspect d'un accident tragique, l'objet, la sensation et l'effet se touchent; en un instant les entrailles s'émeuvent, on pousse un cri, la tête se perd, et les larmes coulent; celles-ci viennent subitement; les autres sont amenées. Voilà l'avantage d'un coup de théâtre naturel et vrai sur une scène éloquente, il opère brusquement ce que la scène fait attendre; mais l'illusion en est beaucoup plus difficile à produire; un incident faux, mal rendu, la détruit. Les accents s'imitent mieux que les mouvements, mais les mouvements frappent plus violemment.

". . . C'est lorsque la grande douleur est passée, quand l'extrême sensibilité est amortie, que l'âme est calme, qu'on se rappelle son bonheur éclipsé qu'on est capable d'apprécier la perte qu'on a faite, que la mémoire se réunit à l'imagination, l'une pour retracer, l'autre pour exagérer la douceur d'un temps passé; qu'on se possède et qu'on parle bien." Théramène is self-controlled and speaks well.

19. The "klassische Dämpfung" of Racine may have been learned from Vergil, cf. e.g. *Aeneid*, VI, 274-281:

[in the vestibule of Hell]

Luctus et ultrices posuere cubilia Curae;
pallentes habitant Morbi tristisque Senectus,
et Metus et malesuada Fames ac turpis Egestas,
terribiles visu formae, Letumque Labosque;
tum consanguineus Leti Sopor et mala mentis
Gaudia, mortiferumque adverso in limine Bellum,
ferreique Eumenidum thalami ex Discordia demens
vipereum crinem vittis innexa cruentis.

The enumeration of the two groups of monsters is, as E. Norden has pointed out in his commentary on the Sixth Book, separated by v. 277 with the interpolation *terribiles visu formae* "die einen gewissen Ruhepunkt bildet. . . . Das alles zeugt von bedachter Kunst." It must be added to these words of Norden that, by this very interpolation, the frightening description of the monsters gives way, for a moment, to a quiet *judgment* in regard to the manner in which they must appear to the eye of the spectator—and this is in line with Racine's habits. That a whole poetic attitude (not only certain devices which are derivative thereof) has been adopted from the ancients (and, necessarily, transformed) by this French classical poet is not an isolated fact: La Fontaine has learned from Horace what I have called (in *PMLA*, LIII, 393) his *suavitas*.

20. In another passage of the récit, we find intellectual criticism expressed by a play on words:

> . . . Ismène, toute en pleurs,
> La rappelle à la vie, ou plutôt aux douleurs.

The last hemistich, which indicates a paradoxically pessimistic equation "life = sorrows," is clearly an extension on the trivial phrase *rappeler à la vie*—which becomes, thereby, didactically ("plutôt") transformed into something like "call back to the sorrows (in which life consists)": this is life judged from without, not lived from within. The very self-correction which Théramène purports to impose on himself is an intellectual procedure likely to be used by an observer calm enough to pay attention to his choice of words. But to this attitude we should not, like De la Motte, attach blame.

21. This is, in fact, the situation which obtains for Phèdre also: she, too, is a monster who has been given her monstrous nature (her incestuous love) by Nature (= Venus), but is rejected by her.

22. One could ask why De la Motte did not equally object to this metaphor used by Phèdre (169):

> Noble et brillant auteur d'une triste famille,
> Toi, dont ma mère osait se vanter d'être fille,
> Qui peut-être rougis du trouble où tu me vois,
> Soleil, je te viens voir pour la dernière fois!

It could be said that the concept of a "sun that blushes" is as daring a *précieux* deviation from the normal "the sun shines," as daring an intellectual interpretation of a physical fact, as is Théophile's conception of a dagger, red with blood, blushing over its treachery.

On the other hand, the "sun" in question is also a god, and an ancestor: if Phèdre were thinking of him exclusively in that guise, the reaction of blushing from shame would be wholly congruous. Perhaps we have here a deliberate ambiguity (symbolized by the epithet *brillant*); Phèdre sees the sun both as a shining orb and as a divine being.

23. The literary historians of today, in France and elsewhere, are too prone to repeat seventeenth-century French criticism on seventeenth-century French literature. Their confidence in this criticism is due to the illusion of a homogeneous "siècle de Louis XIV," brilliant in all fields; whereas the truth is that in that epoch literature alone, not literary criticism, was outstanding. I associate myself with J. Hadamard who writes in his article "Science et monde moderne" (in the journal *Renaissance*,

1, 550) : "Le XVIIᵉ siècle a été, et particulièrement en France, un âge de décadence. . . . Il semble même que le progrès des sciences positives ait, à ce moment-là, nui aux études historiques en en détournant les esprits que, d'autre part, l'éclat de la production littéraire à la même époque éblouissait. La critique littéraire elle-même, comme le note Renan (*L'Avenir de la science*, p. 144), témoigne de la même faiblesse."

24. H. Peyre, *Rom. Rev.*, XXXI, 297, has listed a number of points of difference between the theater of Racine and that of the Greeks, according to which the former appears as a quite original creation: he fails, however, to mention the magic word "baroque."

25. Still another character had to be changed in consequence of Racine's baroque approach: the nurse Oenone. Schlegel who, on moral grounds, condemned Phèdre for putting the burden of guilt on Oenone, has not understood what is brought out excellently by W. Benjamin in his book, *Ursprung des deutschen Trauerspiels* (Berlin, 1928): that the baroque drama, which shows the rulers and princes in all their earthly glory but also in their congenital depravity as human beings, must give a preponderant part to the evil counselors who exploit the earthly power of their masters, and thereby precipitate them into the abyss of their human depravity. The kingly character of a baroque drama is sometimes extremely weak (e.g. a Herod), a pawn in the hands of his advisers, "out-Heroded" by them. What Phèdre says to Oenone, who has served her not wisely but too well (1317):

> Va-t'en, monstre exécrable . . .
> Et puisse ton supplice à jamais effrayer
> Tous ceux qui comme toi, par de lâches adresses,
> Des princes malheureux nourrissent les faiblesses,
> Les poussant au penchant où leur coeur est enclin,
> Et leur osent du crime aplanir le chemin,
> Détestables flatteurs, présent le plus funeste
> Que puisse faire aux rois la colère céleste

has also been expressed by Shakespeare, when he has his King John berate those "slaves" who serve royal failings:

> It is the curse of Kings to be attended
> By slaves that take their humors for a warrant
> To break within the bloody house of life
> And on the winking of authority
> To understand a law, to know the meaning
> Of dangerous majesty, when perchance it frowns
> More upon humor than advised respect (*King John*, IV, l. 208)

Oenone works at the behest of that blind predestination which persecutes in the great of the earth their frail humanity, their *Kreatürlichkeit* (that the kingly being is held to be noble by nature, that the adviser could more easily have "des inclinations serviles" is due not to any contempt of Racine for the lower classes but to his belief in the theocratic order of the state—an order according to which the most exalted person in the state is a "Sun King," and consequently should be ideal). On the other hand, classical drama has also furnished famous examples of good counselors; whatever the moral quality of the counselor's advice, his role is always a crucial element of baroque drama. Cf. the statement of Luis Vives in his dialogue "Regia" (1539): "Istos quos in consilium adhibet princeps, prudentissimos esse oportet, magni rerum usus et in decernendo gravitatis et moderationis summae. . . . Quia sunt oculi et aures principis atque adeo regni universi. *Et eo magis si caecus aut surdus sit rex, captus suis sensibus*, vel ob ignorantiam vel ob delicias."

26. The topos of the "horse tamed with great effort," as we have it in the line: "Rendre docile au frein un coursier indompté," is another typical theme of baroque art (one immediately remembers its frequency with Velásquez). The role given to the horses in *Phèdre* is exceptional among seventeenth-century plays (especially tragedy), if we are to believe Professor Lancaster's erudite study in *Essays in Honor of Albert Feuillerat* (Yale, 1943), p. 106. However, Professor Lancaster has failed to inquire into the reason for the infrequency of such references in seventeenth-century French tragedy (as opposed to its frequency in Spanish drama)—which reason is precisely the anti-baroque tendency of French classical tragedy. As a matter of principle, studies of this type should, in my opinion, be subordinated to categories derived from history of art and history of ideas; we should no longer follow the positivistic manner of "catalogues" (inaugurated by the German dissertation of the Stengel school: "Das Ross in den altfranzösischen Artus- und Abenteuerromanen," 1888).

4

THE STYLE OF DIDEROT

Argumentum: I had often been struck, in reading Diderot, by a rhythmic pattern in which I seemed to hear the echo of Diderot's speaking voice: a self-accentuating rhythm, suggesting that the "speaker" is swept away by a wave of passion which tends to flood all limits. This pattern (which is a feature quite at variance with classical style) is apt to appear, with varied nuances, anywhere in Diderot's writings, didactic as well as narrative (or epistolary). The conclusion seemed obvious that this rhythm was conditioned by a certain nervous temperament which, instead of being tempered by style, was allowed to energize style. Now, the historians of philosophy have long recognized that Diderot is one of the chief exponents of the eighteenth-century philosophy of mobility: while his approach is strictly empirical, there is, with him, the perpetual desire to transcend the rationally graspable. It would then appear that, in this writer, nervous system, philosophical system, and "stylistic system" are exceptionally well attuned. Moreover, given this temperament and this philosophy, we may expect to find other indications of the tendency toward mobility and "self-potentiation"—as, for example, Diderot's predilection for characters who, mimetically gifted, strive to transcend their own nature—only to fall into a kind of automatism, a mental stuttering (which was not absent from Diderot personally). Ultimately, it is in the erotic *Erlebnis* of Diderot that this urge for self-potentiation—which informs his writings and which leads, sometimes, to automatism —is grounded.

This is the only one of the articles in this collection in which I have allowed myself to attempt to penetrate to the soul not only of the author but of the man; such an approach could be legitimate only in the case of a modern author: one who enjoys the freedom permitted by the conception of the "original genius."

IDEROT himself has said of his writings (ed. Assézat, I, 177) : "Les prétendus connoisseurs en fait de style chercheront vainement à me déchiffrer," a statement which implies his own consciousness of the uniqueness of his style. Perhaps a stylistician, who must modestly confess to be only a "prétendu connoisseur en fait de style diderotique" can still, and not in vain, attempt at least to clarify the reasons for this uniqueness.

In general, stylisticians have rather shied away from Diderot, and what pronouncements they have made have been inconsequential.[1] It is amazing to see how little Lanson has to say, in his *L'art de la prose*, about the essence of Diderot's style; he judges him only from the outside, aprioristically: "Voici la prose désordonnée, tumultueuse, tour à tour bravement encanaillée, ou lyrique éperdument de M. Diderot [one may note the ironic condescension of this 'Monsieur']. Il pratique le style sensible dans toute son horreur" etc. Lanson is here simply continuing the normative genre of criticism characteristic of Sainte-Beuve who, possessed as he thought himself to be of *"le goût,"* believed he could cut Diderot in two, separating the good from the bad, Diderot's vivacity from his "exaggerations"—and who certainly did not practice, in regard to Diderot, what he declared to have learned from him: "Cette faculté de demi-métamorphose, qui est le jeu et le triomphe de la critique, et qui consiste à se mettre à la place de l'auteur et au point de vue du sujet qu'il examine, à lire tout écrit selon l'esprit qui l'a dicté" (*Causeries du Lundi*, II, 307). The critics of our day, too, fall into the a priori: H. Dieckmann, who has in recent times made the best contribution toward the unification of the seemingly contradictory opinions of Diderot (I must heartily subscribe to his statement, *Romanische Forsch.*, LII, 62: "Die fast unbestritten herrschende Auffassung von dem unbändigen und sprunghaften Denken Diderots ist einer der oberflächlichsten Irrtümer der Forschung") finds that in the majority of cases Diderot has expressed his ideas "inadequately" ("Diderot's Naturempfinden und Lebensgefühl," *Travaux du séminaire roman d'Istanbul*, I). But, surely, a judge of style, faced with what at first glance appears to him inadequate, should succeed in reaching finally a positive statement; "inadequately"[2] indicates an approach as aprioristic as is that of the dispensers of normative criticism (and, in fact, Dieckmann's is a type of normative criticism). The works of Folkierski, Gillot, and Luc list and discuss the aesthetic theories of Diderot, but what they have to say about his style is singularly shallow—witness such remarks (cited from Luc, p. 58) as: "Il écrit comme il parle. Trop mauvais artisan pour être un très grand artiste. . . . La facilité de la plume suffit. . . ." etc. Fritz Schalk, who has collected in his *Einleitung in die Encyclopädie der französischen Aufklärung* (Munich, 1936) Diderot's own programmatic utterances about his manner of writing (including his remark about its undecipherability), has refused to apply the technique of the philologian (direct observation of specific stylistic traits) by which this style could be made understandable. The best that has been written on Diderot is still, in my opinion, Groethuysen's article "La pensée de Diderot" in *La grande revue* (Nov. 15, 1913); later we shall see how our stylistic analysis squares with his interpretation of Diderot's ideas—after we shall have made some first-hand observations of our own.

Let us consider first, as a sample of Diderot's style, the (somewhat abridged) article "Jouissance," which he wrote for the *Encyclopédie* (Assézat, xv, 312):

JOUISSANCE, s.f. (Gram. et Morale). Jouir, c'est connaître, éprouver, sentir les avantages de posséder: on possède souvent sans jouir. A qui sont ces magnifiques palais? qui est-ce qui a planté ces jardins immenses? c'est le souverain: qui est-ce qui en jouit, c'est moi.

Mais laissons ces palais magnifiques que le souverain a construits pour d'autres que lui, ces jardins enchanteurs où il ne se promène jamais, et arrêtons-nous à la volupté qui perpétue la chaîne des êtres vivants, et à laquelle on a consacré le mot de *jouissance*.

Entre les objets que la nature offre de toutes parts à nos désirs, vous qui avez une âme, dites-moi, y en a-t-il un plus digne de notre poursuite, dont la possession et la *jouissancé* puissent nous rendre aussi heureux que celles de l'être qui pense et sent comme vous, qui a les mêmes idées, qui éprouve la même chaleur, les mêmes transports, qui porte ses bras tendres et délicats vers les vôtres, qui vous enlace, et dont les caresses seront suivies de l'existence d'un nouvel être qui sera semblable à l'un de vous, qui dans ses premiers mouvements vous cherchera pour vous serrer, que vous élèverez à vos côtés, que vous aimerez ensemble, qui vous protégera dans votre vieillesse, qui vous respectera en tout temps, et dont la naissance heureuse a déjà fortifié le lien qui vous unissait? . . .

La propagation des êtres est le plus grand objet de la nature. Elle y sollicite impérieusement les deux sexes, aussitôt qu'ils en ont reçu ce qu'elle leur destinait de force et de beauté. Une inquiétude vague et mélancolique les avertit du moment; leur état est mêlé de peine et de plaisir. C'est alors qu'ils écoutent leurs sens, et qu'ils portent une attention réfléchie sur eux-mêmes. Un individu se présente-t-il à un individu de la même espèce et d'un sexe différent, le sentiment de tout autre besoin est suspendu; le coeur palpite; les membres tressaillent; des images voluptueuses errent dans le cerveau; des torrents d'esprits coulent dans les nerfs, les irritent, et vont se rendre au siège d'un nouveau sens qui se déclare et qui tourmente. La vue se trouble, le délire naît; la raison, esclave de l'instinct, se borne à le servir, et la nature est satisfaite.

C'est ainsi que les choses se passaient à la naissance du monde, et qu'elles se passent encore au fond de l'antre du sauvage adulte.

Mais lorsque la femme commença à discerner, lorsqu'elle parut mettre de l'attention dans son choix, et qu'entre plusieurs hommes sur lesquels la passion promenait ses regards, il y en eut un qui les arrêta, qui put se flatter d'être préféré, qui crut porter dans un coeur qu'il estimait l'estime qu'il faisait de lui-même, et qui regarda le plaisir comme la récompense de quelque mérite; lorsque les voiles que la pudeur jeta sur les charmes laissèrent à l'imagination enflammée le pouvoir d'en disposer à son gré, les illusions les plus délicates concoururent avec le sens le plus exquis pour exagérer le bonheur; l'âme fut saisie d'un enthousiasme presque divin; deux jeunes coeurs éperdus d'amour se vouèrent l'un à l'autre pour jamais, et le ciel entendit les premiers serments indiscrets.

Combien le jour n'eut-il pas d'instants heureux, avant celui où l'âme tout entière chercha à s'élancer et à se perdre dans l'âme de l'objet aimé! On eut des *jouissances* du moment où l'on espéra.

Cependant la confiance, le temps, la nature et la liberté des caresses, amenèrent l'oubli de soi-même; on jura, après avoir éprouvé la dernière ivresse, qu'il n'y en avait aucune autre qu'on pût lui comparer; et cela se trouva vrai toutes les fois qu'on y apporta des organes sensibles et jeunes, un coeur tendre et une âme innocente, qui ne connût ni la méfiance ni le remords.[2a]

After the initial definition of the word "jouissance," we find a description of one particular case of enjoyment, sexual enjoyment, as it acts on man, this psycho-physically conditioned being, and as it serves the purpose of Nature. Although the expressions used by Diderot belong to the technical terminology of the psychology and physiology current in his time (and, for the most part, also in ours): *sens, attention réfléchie, esprits, nerfs, instincts, passion, imagination, illusions, organes sensibles*, etc., we have here a poeticized picture of the factual reality of the sexual act. Dealing as he does with an act which is not easily describable in our civilization because of the feeling it arouses of the incongruity between the positive data and their implications, Diderot had to poeticize the positive facts; let us consider the way in which this transfiguration has been achieved.

In addition to several subsidiary devices (e.g. the apostrophe addressed to man) with which I shall deal later, there is one fundamental feature to be discerned in this passage: the symbolic rendering of the rhythm of feeling by the rhythm of language—an onomatopoeic rendering of feelings which one has been in the habit of dating from Flaubert. As we follow the development of the passage quoted, we note that the rhythmical correspondance begins only with the third paragraph; in the first and second brief paragraphs we are mainly conscious of Diderot's haste to arrive at the subject matter which is so congenial to him: that erotic *jouissance* which is for him the prototype of all enjoyment (here, he has no time to discuss the "enjoyment" of art or of Nature, about which he has shown himself elsewhere so competent to speak). And his mention, in the opening paragraph, of the magnificent gardens owned (but not enjoyed) by kings, serves to enforce, by contrast, the democratic principle: "all of you (who have a soul) have at your disposal an enchanted garden in which you may enjoy the most desirable gifts of Nature."[3] And, with the first words of the third paragraph, which deals with love at the primeval stage, there is a surge of forward movement, symbolizing the rush of young lovers toward a bodily union; the accelerating sentence is given constantly new impetus by the succession of relative clauses. In the next paragraph, which describes sexual love with greater precision, the sentences become shorter, more breathless; in the fifth paragraph, in which is depicted the union of beings at a more highly civilized level, the sentences flow again: the "divine enthusiasm" begotten by this union of souls is again (though in a calmer manner than in the preceding paragraph) figured by means of urgent clauses, in which the *lorsque*'s spur the sentence onward. And finally, in the closing lines, descriptive of that stable connubium with its possibility of periodic renewal, the tension of the sentence structure relaxes.

Within a framework devoted to the historical stages of mankind, with a development so reminiscent of Rousseau (natural stage: bodily union; advanced stage of civilization: union of souls; institutionalized stage: marriage), Diderot has managed to introduce a suggestion of the sexual act itself: the perturbation of the senses, consummation, and relaxation. Most of the passage could be read as a sober piece of historical prose; only the emotional ear of the reader perceives the inner vibrations which echo the surge of erotic emotions. But in paragraph four no reader can fail to sense immediately the physiological rhythm of an erotic moment, isolated from the historical flow. And if we compare the stylistic effectiveness of the different paragraphs it is not difficult to see where Diderot's artistic sensitivity vibrates most sympathetically; the calm of the final lines is due, in part at least, to a lag of emotional interest.

Let us consider more closely the third paragraph, where we have the first example of that stylistic correspondence we have described above; here, it is not only the union of the lovers, but also the fructification of this union, which is rendered by the rhythm of the sentences. Diderot begins by addressing to all men the rhetorical question (in so many words): "Tell me, is there any enjoyment [which means possession with full consciousness of possession] so beatifying as is the enjoyment derived from that being who is your mate?" He proceeds to define this mate, this counterpart of man, in a sentence consisting of a rhythmical sequence of anaphoras and parallelistic clauses which, while dwelling on the same basic motif (of the equality of the two beings— which I have pointed out by italics), mirrors the increasing intensity of feeling and intimacy:[4]

qui pense et sent *comme*
vous,[5]

    qui a *les mêmes* idées,
    qui éprouve *la même chaleur*   [= sent comme vous
          les mêmes trans-   *a* physically]
          ports   *b* spiritually]
qui porte *ses bras* tendres et   [the epithets *tendre, délicat*
délicats vers *les vôtres*   have both a spiritual and a
                        physical connotation]

    qui *vous* enlace

And, with "et dont les caresses seront suivis de l'existence d'un nouvel être," this motif reaches its apex[6]—with which a new perspective is opened up: the existence of the new being. This being, which is dependent on the Beloved, figures now in another series of (secondary) relative clauses which are arranged in a temporal sequence depicting the growth and development of the child, and tending toward a new apex:

    qui sera semblable à l'*un de*   [the motif "comme vous" con-
vous   tinues now with the child]
    qui dans ses premiers   [the temporal sequence is indi-
mouvements *vous* cherchera   cated by "premiers"]
pour vous serrer
    que *vous* élèverez à *vos*
côtés
    que *vous* aimerez *ensemble*   [cooperation of the two]
    qui *vous* protégera dans   [physically]
votre vieillesse

qui *vous* respectera en tout temps   [morally: *en tout temps* ends the temporal sequence and makes the time-bound relationship timeless]

et dont la naissance heureuse
a déjà fortifié le lien qui *vous*
unissait[7]

With this last, we have a retrospective clause which suddenly refers us back to the moment of birth, at which the union (suggested by *enlacer*) of the lovers has been consolidated into a lasting bond (*lien*); with *déjà* and with the shift to the past tense (*a fortifié, unissait*), the line of temporal development is seen in reverse. The *dont la naissance* seals the clauses descriptive of the growing child, just as the *dont les caresses* had rounded off the lines dealing with the Beloved. And, in both sections, the repetition of the generic pronoun *vous* insists on the theme that the gift of Nature makes for an enrichment of the "vous (qui avez une âme)": wife and children are both "known possessions," enrichments and aggrandizements of the Ego of man. The *vous*-motif is willed by Nature.

The diagram I have just outlined may make a painfully rationalistic and pedantic impression upon the reader, who could be tempted to argue that, if all the effects I have pointed out were deliberately intended by Diderot, he must have been absorbed in petty measurements of sentence members. But, obviously, all the devices I have discerned are assimilated only half-consciously by the reader, and we may surmise that Diderot himself found them half-consciously.

If we turn now to the physico-psychological picture of the act of sexual union as offered in the fourth paragraph, we will find that the symbolization of thought by sentence-structure is achieved in a quite different manner. In this passage, dealing as it does with man in the stage of pure sensuality, Nature appears at the beginning and at the end as a moving force: "La propagation des êtres est le plus grand objet de la Nature"; "et la Nature est satisfaite." The underlying idea is that Nature achieves her end, the propagation of the human species, by beclouding the reason of man before the act of procreation ("... le délire naît; la raison, esclave de l'instinct, se borne à le servir, et la nature est satisfaite").[8] And the paragraph as a whole is given up to a description of this state of perturbation—which is symbolized in the rhythm of the brief, breathless staccato sentences ("le coeur palpite, les membres tressaillent"); a suggestion of haste and impatience is given also by the temporal indications: "aussitôt que," "moment," "alors" (cf. also "un individu se présente-t-il" = "immediately when ..."). The poetic art of Diderot is the greater, the more factual and scientific is his description: he clearly distinguishes, within the state of perturbation ("inquiétude vague"), the flashes of intellectual clarity ("attention réfléchie"). Out of this alternation of emotional haze and mental clarity is born a "new sense," which has been the goal toward which the preliminary fluctuations tended—and this movement toward a goal is figured by the rhythm of the sentence "des torrents d'esprits coulent dans les nerfs, les irritent, et vont se rendre au siège d'un nouveau sens qui se déclare et tourmente."[9] The climax suggested by *tourmente* is maintained throughout the following sentence—until, with the final words "et la nature est satisfaite," the tension of the sentence relaxes. The closing phrase is fraught with a double meaning: from the point of view of the lovers, it is their nature, their animal nature, which is satiated; from the teleological point of view, the goal of Nature herself has been achieved. And the *et*, which introduces the announcement of the convergence of man's and Nature's urge, is a stylistic triumph; I would call it the "*et* of culmination," in which there is the reassuring echo of a beneficent world order.

Paragraph six, which is dedicated to the civilized stage of man, is arranged so as to form three groups, the first two of them being compound sentences containing temporal clauses introduced by *lorsque*, and the third consisting of three short separate independent clauses; the two clauses "l'âme fut saisie d'un enthousiasme[10] presque divin," and "deux jeunes coeurs éperdus d'amour se vouèrent l'un à l'autre pour jamais" lead to "et le ciel[11] entendit les premiers serments indiscrets"[12] (where again we find an example of the "*et* of culmination" equally insistent on a propitious world order). Nowhere in this paragraph do we find that fragmentary sentence structure which was used so felicitously in the preceding passage to render the state of emotional perturbation. The two compound sentences at the beginning are of the accelerating type we noted in paragraph three; in the last three clauses, the movement somewhat slackens, to suggest the calm, the lasting joy, of the quasi-mystic union. In reading this prose, which is addressed as well to the ear as to the mind, one will find one's voice rising steadily and uninterruptedly until the final terrace is reached—to correspond with the movement of the souls toward Heaven. For, in this paragraph, the divine emotion of the lovers inspires them to call upon Heaven as their witness and protector—in contrast to the preceding passage, in which the purely fleshly union was presided over by Nature. Indeed, the whole sixth paragraph appears as a transposition of the fourth on a higher plane. The development of monogamic marriage is a decisive step in the history of civilization: it is a mark of the progress from the state of Nature to the civilized state; and therefore, in this paragraph, the temporal aspect is stressed: by *lorsque*, and by the historical past tense; in paragraphs three and four we find the present: sexuality is an a-temporal phenomenon of man's nature. And it is also true that this decisive step of monogamy was taken when man became conscious of time: "deux jeunes coeurs se vouèrent l'un à l'autre *pour jamais*"; les *premiers* serments indiscrets . . ."; "combien le jour n'eut il pas d'*instants* heureux, avant celui où l'âme tout entière chercha à s'élancer et à se perdre. . . . On eut des jouissances *du moment* où l'on espèra." The time-consciousness which leads to the "mystic" union is itself a result of the development of man in time (we may assume that the Augustinian idea that time is engendered by the immortal divine soul of man is not quite absent from this passage).

And here, for the first time, Diderot deals with the stages leading up to the choice of a mate (indeed, only in the state of civilization can there be a question of individual choice), and with the additional factors by which love, on this higher level, is complicated (here, not before, we have a suggestion of what Stendhal was later to call "crystallization de

l'amour") ; now, instead of the blindness and automatism of
the pure sex urge, as pictured in paragraph four, mental de-
liberation is presented: the woman weighs the objective merits
of her suitors—and it is important to note that, in the civilized
stage, it is woman who takes the initiative (in this paragraph
it is her mate who is described in dependent clauses). In this
way the drama of hope and fear enters to complicate love. The
second historical factor which Diderot mentions as contributing to the refinement of amorous sensibility is, inter-
estingly enough, the clothed state of the lovers; by this
avenue, not only suspense but illusion becomes possible. (The
awkwardness of such a blunt juxtaposition of technical and
spiritual cultural history: the weighing of individual merits —
the wearing of clothes, cannot be denied). This reference to
the illusionary effect of clothing is almost the only allusion
to the bodily to be found in this paragraph; another may be
seen in "après avoir éprouvé la dernière ivresse"—where,
however, the erotic ecstasy is represented as a thing already
past; in both cases the sensuous is brought in only indirectly.

But while there can be little doubt that the type of love
described in this paragraph is presented as a higher form of
the sexual relationship, it is indicative of Diderot's own natural preferences that it is here that, for the first time, a critical note enters; the note of disillusionment is unmistakable in
Diderot's statement that the illusions made possible by
civilization tend to "*exagérer* le bonheur" (must not "illusion"
lead to disillusionment?) ; again, the delights of the "mystic"
union are qualified as "un enthusiasme *presque* divin," while
"l'âme tout entière *chercha* à s'élancer" suggests something
quite different from the note of pure and uninhibited rapture
which vibrates in the preceding paragraph.

And the rational element which had already been presented,
in paragraph six, as a factor in the "love of two souls," becomes predominant in the last paragraph, dealing with the
institutionalization of love: here the lovers are shown as
rather soberly comparing the enjoyments of love with other
pleasures, as calculating the possibilities of renewal within
an established union—a union which will require some sacrifice of the individual's self, an "oubli de soi-même" which one

cannot help contrasting with that concentration upon enjoyment ("attention réfléchie sur eux-mêmes"), upon the aggrandizement of the ego, which was stressed in paragraph four. And so it is fitting that the impersonal and gnomic *on* (which made its first appearance at the end of paragraph seven) should be used exclusively in the final paragraph. No longer are we given a picture of "les deux sexes" or of "deux jeunes coeurs" who rush to embrace: it is the colorless *on* which figures in the generalizations about marriage which Diderot offers. Indeed, here, it is the institution of marriage which is the protagonist, to which the individual must pay tribute; the *organes sensibles*, the *coeur tendre*, the *âme innocente* are now simply the preconditions for marriage which it is man's duty to fulfill.[18]

Throughout this article we have found an "innervation" of language by emotion, a translation into rhythm of emotions[14] —and the predominant emotion is that of a dynamic accelerating self-expansion, self-potentiation. This rhythmic translation, this innervation of language, seems to appear mainly in two forms: there is the breathless, tense, cramped "style coupé" which was prominent in paragraph four, and the freer flow of the longer periods, which was in evidence in the other passages. It was the first type, with its suggestion of automatism, which was used in the description of the most sensuous aspects of connubium: indeed, it is the rhythm of orgasm itself.[15] And, whenever it appears, it may be taken as a sure indication that the phenomenon described (or, the description itself!) is felt by Diderot as a physical, nervous experience.[16] In contrast, the more flowing rhythm seems to denote a state of enthusiasm in which body and soul are fused in a more harmonious expansion.

The passage we have just chosen for our first orientation in the style of Diderot describes, variously, the psychophysical harmony of a sexual relationship in which body and soul are in unison and which serves Nature, society, and Heaven. But Diderot, with his gift of psycho-physical innervation of language, was equally able to adapt his style to the description of disharmony. Let us choose, as an extreme case of disharmony, an example of perversion, as it is found in the scene of the homosexual Mother Superior in *La re-ligieuse*, in whom emotional unsteadiness, hypocrisy, and natural kindness are inextricably mixed. After having finally succeeded in drawing out of the young nun, Suzanne, the account of the hardships and persecutions she had endured in the convent where she had previously been established, she gives vent to her mingled emotions in the following words (as reported by Suzanne in a memorandum addressed to a certain marquis before whom she wishes to justify herself) : " 'Les méchantes créatures! Les horribles créatures! Il n'y a que dans les couvents où l'humanité puisse s'éteindre à ce point. . . . Heureusement je suis douce; j'aime toutes mes religieuses; elles ont pris, les unes plus, les autres moins, de mon caractère, et toutes elles s'aiment entre elles. Mais comment cette faible santé a-t-elle pu résister à tant de tourments? Comment tous ces petits membres n'ont-ils pas été brisés? Comment toute cette machine délicate n'a-t-elle pas été détruite? Comment l'éclat de ces yeux n'est-il pas éteint dans les larmes? Les cruelles! Serrer ces bras avec des cordes!' Et elle les baisait. 'Arracher la plainte et le gémissement à cette bouche!' Et elle la baisait. 'Condamner ce visage charmant et serein à se couvrir sans cesse des nuages de la tristesse!' Et elle le baisait. 'Faner les roses de ces joues!' Et elle les flattait de la main et les baisait. 'Déparer cette tête! arracher ces cheveux! charger ce front de souci!' Et elle baisait ma tête, mon front, mes cheveux. 'Oser entourer ce cou d'une corde, et déchirer ces épaules avec des pointes aigües!' Et elle écartait mon linge de cou et de tête; elle entr'ouvrait le haut de ma robe; mes cheveux tombaient épars sur mes épaules découvertes; ma poitrine était à demi-nue, et ses baisers se répandaient sur mon cou, sur mes épaules découvertes et sur ma poitrine à deminue."

This passage begins smoothly enough, with no hint of anything shocking or even startling. The Mother Superior's opening words have the lulling quality of platitudes; Diderot has prepared us for them by previous statements as to the conditions prevailing in convents ("Ah! monsieur, les méchantes créatures que des femmes recluses. . . !" had been said earlier by Suzanne herself [p. 75], while her former Mother Su-

perior had remarked to her [p. 68] : "Entre toutes ces créatures que vous voyez autour de moi, si dociles, si innocentes,
si douces, eh bien! mon enfant, il n'y en a presque pas une,
non, presque pas une, dont je ne puisse faire une bête
féroce"). And, as the Mother Superior begins her series of
pitying exclamations over the violence visited upon the body
of the nun, we seem to be following a familiar path: we had
already been given Suzanne's own detailed account, which
the Mother Superior is evidently here reproducing factually,
if with embellishments. It is only gradually that we realize
that what is unfolding before us is no repetition but a ghastly
parody. Even the first caresses might be accepted as manifestations of genuine (if highly sentimental) compassion—
but we soon become aware that this is the working of an
automatism which cannot stop.

It is also evident that we are offered here the picture of a
nature working on two planes simultaneously; we realize that
we must constantly distinguish between words and deeds.
The Mother Superior would convince Suzanne by her words
that she is moved by a mellow Christian spirit, by an abhor-
rence of inhumane acts; but her own acts reveal themselves
more and more clearly as manifestations of a selfish sexual
love which would exploit the same young body that had been
so cruelly tortured. At first, of course, there is only one
track: in the opening lines (from "les cruelles! . . ." to ". . .
les cruelles!") her reactions are purely verbal, as she recapit-
ulates the total injury done to "cette machine délicate." But
when she begins to list separately the details of Suzanne's
torture, limb by limb, she accompanies this account with
gestures—as if restaging the painful incidents in a "contrappasso" of love. But we sense with horror that we are witnessing, instead, a new assault on the nun's body. And surely
Diderot means to stress the parallelism of the two criminal
procedures: each limb that had been tortured is now violated
by caresses (even the detail of the "cheveux épars" reappears), to the accompaniment of soft words of compassion.[17]

The double track which is so evident in the behavior of the
Mother Superior bears witness, obviously, to a basic split in

her personality: in one part of her being, as manifested in her speech, she desires to appear (and, perhaps, even to be) purely compassionate; in another part of her being, which reveals itself in her gestures, the covetous will of the body rules. In her acts she is moved from below, she behaves, that is "hypo-critically" (Gr. ὑπόκρισις "thinking from below"); Diderot knew that bodily perversion is necessarily linked with hypocrisy.

We spoke earlier of the suggestion of automatism in this passage. It is interesting to see to what pains Diderot goes to enforce this impression. The most obvious trait is the fact that each anatomical reference is accompanied, without fail, by a gesture. But the automatism is present not only in this mechanical coupling of speech and gesture: it can be seen also in the speech considered in itself, and in the gestures (and the manner in which they are reported). As for the words of the Mother Superior, these consist of a sequence of conventional, sentimental expressions—which constitute, as it were, a variant of the "blason," in which, according to tradition, each member of the beloved body is praised in turn; in her recital, accompanied by gestures, we have a grotesque reminder of the origin of this literary genre, which grew up out of the religious practice of the *exercitium spirituale* which requires the believer to visualize every stage of Christ's bodily suffering; with the perverted Mother Superior, this becomes an *exercitium corporale*, in which the visualization becomes enactment. And the law of this genre is the law of automatism: once the first step is taken the process must run its course. In our passage the monotony of the process is reflected in the invariability of construction: the sequence of infinitives, the anaphoric repetition, first of exclamatory questions (*comment . . . .*), then of demonstrative pronouns.

And the same dulling monotony of construction appears, to an extreme degree, in the refrain which announces each succeeding gesture (which is always the same: a kiss that becomes increasingly more revelatory and more menacing): "et elle le[s] baisait." The repetition of this formula has a hypnotic effect—which is enhanced by the fact that it is the victim herself who is speaking, and whose words thus seem to

reflect the hypnotic state[18] induced in her by the evil automatism of the Mother Superior (earlier Diderot had referred
to the "contagion" which had spread from the malady of this
woman). An important stylistic element of the refrain is the
conjunction *et*, which seems to me to represent a parody of the
sublime "fiat lux *et* lux facta est."[19] In the Biblical expression
we have the suggestion of a "divine automatism," as it were,
according to which a wish is inevitably followed by its ful-
fillment; thus, by means of this pattern, a vicious realization
of desire is presented as if it were a natural, a sanctioned consequence. In the case of "serrer ces bras. . . ! . . . et elle les
baisait," obviously, the desire which is realized has not been
expressed in words. But the accompanying gestures reveal the
true meaning of the Mother Superior's words—which, in
themselves, could be ambiguous. Little by little, it has become
evident that her speech, in which she intended to convey a
generous sympathy, has become infected with the selfish
possessiveness of her physical acts. Words-and-gestures form
an inseparable couple, and from the moment the sequence of
these couples is begun, the physical dynamism of the gesture[20]
endows them with a mechanical, accelerating movement, a
movement toward the abyss—until, finally, words cease entirely and sensuality is rampant: "Ces baisers se répandaient. . . ."

Can we recognize in this passage, as we were able to do in
the article on "jouissance," a rhythmical reproduction of the
subject matter? It is evident that here we have to do with the
mechanical repetition of two alternating rhythmical patterns:
the high-flown, sentimentally poetic language of the exclamations ("faner les roses . . . !"), and the emotionless, factual
refrain, "et elle le baisait"—which has obviously an ironical
flavor. We have to do with two rhythms, one of which mocks
the other. In each of the couples formed by these two jarring
patterns, as in the passage as a whole, there is reflected the
split personality of the hypocritical pervert.

At the same time it is true that this passage, with its
description of words and gestures, is but one overflow of
emotion, continuously increasing until the climax of uninhibited, overt, vicious love-making is reached—a stream of

feelings which tend to flood all dams. And the words chosen by Diderot echo this urge of self-potentiation on the part of an individual who wants to break her chains and to experience unfettered exaltation; they also reveal the ominous presence of the mechanism behind the foolish enterprise. Recapitulating our finds in the two passages quoted from Diderot, we see in both the same motif of self-potentiation—though complicated and retarded in the second case by inhibition—a motif which we may state to be basic to Diderot's *Lebensgefühl*. His most effective or conspicuous passages, those in which one feels the vibrations of Diderot's own nature,[21] will always be those which describe the emotional movement of an individual "hors de lui-même."

In both examples above, the emotion has been one of sexual passion; our discussion so far may have given the impression that Diderot is given mainly to such descriptions. As a matter of fact, I am convinced that the sexual act, with its power of expanding the individual, is the *Grunderlebnis* for Diderot (from Diderot's time to our own, his critics have mentioned his overflowing sensuousness, his indulgence in the *graveleux*, etc.) and that he is at his best in achieving what we have called the "innervation of language by emotion" when he has to translate into language the vibration of the senses. But his "innervation" has a wider range: he is able to translate rhythmically the "vibrations" of imagination—though here, too, the sensuous origin, even the sexual origin, of the emotional pattern may be discerned. That it is not the reverse process which has taken place, I infer not only from the well-known sensualistic approach of Diderot's philosophy, but also from the more general consideration that, in linguistics, the concrete precedes the abstract: the "etymology" of a stylistic pattern must be found in that situation which is closest to concrete, to sensuous, reality. It was just such reality which prevailed in the two previous passages, where we have found the close congruity of style and reality; whatever of similarity we may find in other, less obviously sensuous, passages must be considered as a secondary application of patterns based primarily on the sexual.

I shall choose for comment here one from many comparable

passages in Diderot's *Le neveu de Rameau*; in my citation I
have adopted a somewhat clearer distinction between narration and speech than is to be found in the Assézat edition
(v, 399) : "Puis il se remit à chanter l'ouverture des 'Indes
galantes' et l'air 'Profonds abîmes' [of Rameau the uncle],
et il ajoutait : Le quelque chose qui est là et qui me parle me
dit : Rameau, tu voudrais bien avoir fait ces deux morceaux-
là ; si tu avais fait ces morceaux-là, tu en ferais bien deux
autres ; et quand tu en aurais fait un certain nombre, on te
jouerait, on te chanterait partout. Quand tu marcherais, tu
aurais la tête droite, ta conscience te rendrait témoignage à
toi-même de ton propre mérite, les autres te désigneroient du
doigt, on dirait : C'est lui qui a fait les jolies gavottes (et il
chantait les gavottes : Puis avec l'air d'un homme touché qui
nage dans la joie et qui en a les yeux humides, il ajoutait en se
frottant les mains :) Tu aurais une bonne maison (il en
mesurait l'étendue avec ses bras,) un bon lit (et il s'y étendait
nonchalament,) de bons vins (qu'il goûtait en faisant claquer
la langue contre son palais,) un bon équipage (et il levait le
pied pour y monter), de jolies femmes (à qui il prenait déjà
la gorge et qu'il regardait voluptueusement) ; cent faquins te
viendraient encenser tous les jours (et il croyait les voir
autour de lui : il voyait Pelissot, Poinsinet . . . il les entendait,
il se rengorgeait, les approuvait, leur souriait, les dédaignait,
les méprisait, les chassait, les rappelait ; puis il continuait :) Et
c'est ainsi que l'on te dirait le matin que tu es un grand
homme ; tu lirais dans l'histoire des Trois Siècles que tu es un
grand homme, tu serais convaincu le soir que tu es un grand
homme, et le grand homme Rameau s'endormirait au doux
murmure de l'éloge qui retentirait dans son oreille même en
dormant, il aurait l'air satisfait : sa poitrine se dilaterait,
s'élèverait, s'abaisserait avec aisance, il ronflerait comme un
grand homme . . . (Et en parlant ainsi, il se laissait aller
mollement sur une banquette ; il fermait les yeux, et il imitait
le sommeil heureux qu'il imaginait. Après avoir goûté quel-
ques instants la douceur de ce repos, il se réveillait, étendait
les bras, bâillait, se frottait les yeux, et cherchait autour de
lui ses adulateurs insipides)."

If, in the case of the Mother Superior of *La religieuse*, the

intended significance of the words was given a lie by the
gestures, which represented the peremptory will of the body,
here, the gestures merely execute what the words outspokenly
imply. But in both cases it is true that the words unleash
gestures by which they are expanded, by which they are pro-
longed and multiplied, as it were: the gestures are the potentiation afforded by the body in reaction to the thoughts expressed by the words. Again, in the previous passage, we had
occasion to point out the suggestion of automatism present
in the description of the emotional development; this ended
with a picture of the machine triumphant; we were not shown
the moment after, when the machinery runs down—though it
was only too obvious that such emotional tension must end in
self-annihilation. In the paragraph just quoted from *Le
neveu*, we are also given the picture of a machinery in accelerating motion, but this does finally break down before our
eyes.[22] We see a character who starts with a hypothetical situation ("If I had composed the two arias of my uncle") which
he elaborates upon at greater and greater length, accompanying each new fiction with appropriate, vivid gestures, until he
is finally exhausted by the physical and emotional energy he
has expended. These gestures, called into being by the vivacity
of his imagination, begin by being only accessory embellishments,[23] whose meaning and whose validity is determined exactly by the meaning and validity of the words. In the course
of the elaboration, however, to the extent that the words de-
part further and further from reality, the gestures become
more and more impassioned and evocative, they come more
and more to constitute a reality in themselves—and as such
they react upon the speaker himself, who ends by being convinced by his own gestures: the passage ends with the nephew
completely seduced by his own imaginative pantomime.

In this incident Diderot has summed up the character of
the nephew—as in the nephew himself he has symbolized the
paradox of artistic existence; this whole dialogue is a pendant
to the *Paradoxe sur le comédien*. The nephew is gifted with
extraordinary powers of expression which seek immediate
form, but the very talents which enable him to find so easily
and so quickly an appropriate form are ultimately responsible

for his failure to embody his artistic gifts in a form that is permanent and has objective reality. The nephew is presented as a performer, an imitator, instead of as creator (he sings well the airs of his uncle, which he could never have composed). Diderot was well aware that every creative artist must be first of all an imitator—just as every imitator, every performer, has the possibility of being creative,[24] in his way, if he can distinguish between the two planes. The tragedy of the nephew lies in his inability to make this distinction: as he listens to himself singing the arias his uncle has composed, he has the sensation of being a creator like his uncle, of being a "grand homme" ready made, with all the practical consequences that would follow therefrom.[25]

The philosopher, who cares only to discern truth is, according to Diderot's statements in *Le neveu*, by nature unmimical, and is thereby preserved from the danger which threatens every artist. It could be said that, in this dialogue, Diderot the philosopher is instituting a trial against his own artistic sensitivity, with all its expressive, impersonating, pantomimic, caricaturing, satirical elements.

As we read this treatment of a being who becomes the victim of his heated imagination, we could be reminded of episodes in Rabelais where a fantastic spinner of tales has been duped by his own fabrications: for example, that of Picrochole and his advisers who conquer the world in their dreams and are henceforth able to speak of the conquest in the past tense. And yet, when we read Rabelais' account we are only amused; it makes no impact on our nervous system. But no one, I believe, can read this description of the nephew without sharing something of the nervous anguish of the author Diderot who, in this dialogue as a whole, is so deeply concerned with the problem of artistic activity: the paradox that the artist, by his enthusiasm for reproducing reality, may falsify all reality including his own, the paradox that hypervitality leads ultimately to self-destruction. And, indeed, it is a diminutive death that we witness in this passage. As we see the self-exhausted body slump before us in a half-fictitious sleep, there is a suggestion of physical decay.

And Diderot has been able to render by the rhythm of his

style the process by which hypervitality leads to self-destruction. In the first part of the passage we find the devices of
gradation and increase and expansion, which are already
familiar to us and which indicate a heightening of emotion
(as the "machine" picks up speed): as the nephew's fanciful
construction is built higher and higher, the rhythm of his
speech is accelerated until, with "le grand homme" the apex
is reached and the decline sets in: at first "le grand homme,"
repeated, maintains the high point, but then, by virtue of this
repetition, this "perseveration" of automatism,[26] what had
been a stimulant becomes a soporific, as the dreamed-of state
(expressed by a sequence of conditional tenses) yields to the
reality of exhaustion. The same curve of movement is to be
seen in the language describing the gestures: we may note the
accelerating *déjà*, and the string of imperfects following upon
each other pell-mell, depicting the progress of self-infatuation ("il croyait voir - il voyait . . . - il les entendait"), with
all the contradictions of his momentary moods ("les chassait,
les rappelait," etc.).[27] In the final gestures that accompany his
awakening, the planes of reality and irreality are so confused
that we hardly know whether it is the exhausted, bemused
actor or the *grand homme* he thinks he has become, who is
gesticulating. Here, just as in the passage describing the
Mother Superior, the gestures "take over": in the first case
they serve to reveal the true meaning latent in ambiguous
words; in the second, they have the effect of establishing an
artificial reality out of hypothetical words. In both cases alike
the movement is generated by the dynamism of the gestures—
the actual bodily force which Diderot has made us feel by
language.

We have said that the self-destruction brought about by
excessive expressivity was seen by Diderot as a danger to
which any artistic nature is exposed, and about which he was
particularly apprehensive in his own case. It is true that
numerous passages can be found (as quoted in Schalk's
article) in which Diderot praises his own "désordre toujours
nouveau" and states with apparent nonchalance: "je jette mes
idées sur le papier et elles deviennent ce qu'elles peuvent"; he
also quotes appreciatively Montaigne's self-description: "ou

par la résistance d'un aultre, ou par la propre chaleur de ma narration, je grossis et enfle mon subject par voix, mouvements, vigueur et force de paroles, et encore par extension et amplification, non sans interest de la vérité naifve. . . . La parole vifve et bruyante, comme est la mienne ordinaire, s'emporte volontiers à l'hyperbole." But it must not be overlooked that Diderot was aware of the threat to any true representation of reality inherent in the "realistic" gifts of "grossissement," "extension," "amplification." It is for this reason that, in the *Paradoxe sur le comédien*,[28] and in the *Rêve de D'Alembert*, he develops the thesis that the great artist (as well as the great scientist) should strive to be cool-minded and rational, instead of giving way to his emotions, and that he expresses his distrust of the tears coming from the nervous system, the "entrailles" of the actor—a distrust Montaigne would have calmly smiled away. Montaigne, who was as little nervous over the problem of reality as was Rabelais, never doubted that he was pursuing a positive course to the goal of the "vérité naifve"; and, though he may have harbored many doubts and even fears, he knew the nature of his feelings as unquestionable and precisely definable realities. With Diderot we have an existential doubt as to the reality of the artistic existence; he is torn between feverish enthusiasm and despair as he sees the consequences of artistic sensitivity in its contact with life. It is as if he has created the nephew out of the doubtful material of his own artistic nature, as a gesture of rejection and condemnation.[29]

In this scene, we must believe that Diderot's condemnation of expressivity is absolute: we are given a vivid picture of decomposition with no suggestion of any higher principle in whose service the enthusiasm is exerted—an enthusiasm inspired by self-infatuation and by a concern for worldly advantage. Later on in the dialogue, when he comes to talk of the new musical trends in contemporary opera, the nephew is again caught up in a rapture that leads to a collapse of his being. But, in this case, his enthusiasm serves the noble purpose of championing the cause of the new music; accordingly, the reactions of Diderot himself (which he did not trouble to express in the earlier scene) are mingled: "Admirais-je? Oui, j'admirais. Étais-je touché de pitié? j'étais touché de pitié; mais une teinte de ridicule était fondue dans ces sentiments et les dénaturait."[30]

It is in this same scene that Diderot, who figures in the dialogue as MOI, asks his own creation how it could be that a person of such taste and such powers of discrimination in music could be so lacking in moral sensitivity.[31] And he has the nephew answer that his musical sensitivity has necessarily entailed the underdevelopment of his moral fiber. In this answer, which Diderot, as MOI, does not contest, the amorality of an artist is presented as a necessary concomitant of the "sensitive," expressive, artistic temperament. Goethe, in the notes to his translation of *Le neveu*, sums up this figure as a characterless adulator, an opportunist capable of any crime and deserving our contempt and hatred (the only touch of stability and dignity being revealed in his serious, disinterested discussion of musicological problems).[32] What Goethe has failed to see is the fact that the characterlessness of the nephew is only a consequence of his artistic mutability[33]— which is the primary factor of his being. It is difficult to understand that Goethe the artist should have failed to discover in this dialogue Diderot's concern with the moral paradox involved in all artistry,[34] the amorality which stems from the artistic impulse itself, the shamelessness of the performer (which prompted, in our times, the tenor Gigli to offer himself immediately to the Allied authorities occupying Rome, with the words: "I have sung for Mussolini and for the Germans —and now I will sing for you"). But, at the same time, the easy espousal of the opportunities of the moment can also lead to actions which, in another person, would be accepted as evidence of great character. The nephew does not always act as a parasite, an opportunist: he is capable of at least an occasional outburst of generous indignation which will cost him an opportunity for easy living—and which he prefers to sacrifice rather than give up the opportunity of shaming his host by an appeal to standards of "un peu de goût, un peu d'esprit, un peu de raison." The nephew belongs to the line of the "grands vauriens" (to use the epithet which Diderot applies to him elsewhere in the dialogue) who enact "la pantomime des gueux" in French literature: Renard the Fox, Panurge, *Mascarillus fourbum imperator*, Sganarelle, Gil Blas, Figaro; he is of those who let themselves live "au jour le jour," giving evidence of intelligence and of a critical, skeptical spirit: near-artists, serving as catalytic agents in an inert society, virtuosos of intellectual mobility who can stir up thinking in their fellow men. In the nephew we have the *raw material* of an artist and we see the conflicts which his artistic nature must bring upon him in a bourgeois society: essentially bourgeois in the enjoyments he desires, he is able to criticize the narrowness of bourgeois society. Diderot has posited the problem of the bourgeois artist with a clarity unequaled by the Romantics.

I have found it necessary to expatiate at such length on the basic idea underlying the *Neveu de Rameau* because, in my opinion, this had not been fully understood by the critics, and also because it is this idea (i.e. the paradox involved in the enthusiasm of a "sensitive" musician) which determines the rhythmic patterns of the long monologues of the nephew which make up the main bulk of this work. Let us now return to the second of our two pendant scenes, to the one in which the nephew, as he impersonates his musical ideal, is shown moving on a higher level, and in which Diderot's language manages to record this change of altitude. Here the nephew's fury of enthusiasm is described as having the dimensions and the connotations of a cosmic upheaval. Here, too, traces of physical disintegration are portrayed: saliva drips from his mouth as he speaks and, at the end of a seizure of gesticulation, he falls into a coma of exhaustion, from which he awakens with a start, wild-eyed, staring at imaginary bystanders. As Diderot reports the scene: "Mais vous vous seriez échappé en éclats de rire à la manière dont il contrefaisait les différents instruments; avec des joues renflées et bouffies, et un son rauque et sombre, il rendait les cors et les bassons; il prenait un son éclatant et nasillard pour les hautbois; précipitant sa voix avec une rapidité incroyable pour les instruments à corde dont il cherchait les sons les plus approchés; il sifflait les petites flûtes, il roucoulait les traversières; criant, chantant, se démenant comme un forcené, faisant lui seul les danseurs, les danseuses, les chanteurs, les chanteuses, tout un orchestre, tout un théâtre lyrique, et se divisant en vingt rôles divers; courant, s'arrêtant avec l'air d'un énergumène, étincelant des yeux, écumant de la bouche.

". . . Que ne lui vis-je pas faire? Il pleurait, il riait, il soupirait, il regardait ou attendri, ou tranquille, ou furieux; c'était une femme qui se pâme de douleur, c'était un malheureux livré à tout son désespoir; un temple qui s'élève; des oiseaux qui se taisent au soleil couchant; des eaux ou qui murmurent dans un lieu solitaire et frais, ou qui descendent en torrent du haut des montagnes; un orage, une tempête, la plainte de ceux qui vont périr, mêlée au sifflement des vents, au fracas du tonnerre. C'était la nuit avec ses ténèbres, c'était l'ombre et le silence, car le silence même se peint par des sons. Sa tête était tout à fait perdue.

"Épuisé de fatigue, tel qu'un homme qui sort d'un profond sommeil ou d'une longue distraction, il resta immobile, stupide, étonné; il tournait ses regards autour de lui comme un homme égaré qui cherche à reconnaître le lieu où il se trouve; il attendait le retour de ses forces et de ses esprits; il essuyait machinalement son visage. Semblable à celui qui verrait à son réveil son lit environné d'un grand nombre de personnes dans un entier oubli ou dans une profonde ignorance de ce qu'il a fait, il s'écria dans le premier moment: 'Eh bien, messieurs, qu'est-ce qu'il y a?... D'où viennent vos ris et votre surprise? Qu'est-ce qu'il y a?...' Ensuite il ajouta: 'Voilà ce qu'on doit appeler de la musique et un musicien!' "

Here, the self-potentiation of the nephew which leads to exhaustion is, as we have said before, in the service of the noble cause of true (that is, in his way of thinking, expressive) music and, consequently, Diderot has insisted more on the creative aspects of the enthusiast's cosmic expansion than on its mechanistic aspects. Here, no words are reported, no gesture is specifically described, so that we cannot follow any development of automatism in the nephew's emotional state. The narrative of Diderot falls into three parts: the first describes the strange sounds uttered by the nephew (with the corresponding postures); in the second, these are interpreted; and only in the third does Diderot concentrate our attention on the physical state of the nephew. The nephew, instead of speaking, lends his voice to imitating an orchestra, becoming himself a living vocal instrument, and impersonating a Wagnerian-like *Gesamtkunstwerk*; when the meaning of this (imitated) orchestra is revealed, we recognize it as a world orchestra, echoing the music of the universe. The corybantic rapture which seizes the nephew is comparable to that invasion of the priest of Dionysos by his god, to that self-identification of the imitator with the cosmic force invading him, which, according to Nietzsche, has led to the birth of tragedy.

In the first paragraph quoted, we witness in the movement of the period the self-acceleration and self-potentiation of language which corresponds to the expansion and self-multiplication of the protagonist himself ("faisant lui seul les danseurs, les danseuses, les chanteurs, les chanteuses; tout un orchestre, tout un théâtre lyrique . . ."); in the second, the human and the natural forces unleashed by world harmony are given their full range and gradually subside, returning to that "music of silence" ("le silence même se peint par des sons") which already the Pythagoreans had discovered: the crescendo in which vague tumultuous forces make themselves heard ("une femme . . . un malheureux . . . un temple . . . des oiseaux . . . des eaux . . . un orage, une tempête") yields to a decrescendo in which quieter and more familiar elements emerge: "la nuit avec ses ténèbres . . . l'ombre et le silence"; this descent from the apex of "un temple qui s'élève" has been already suggested by "des eaux . . . qui descendent en torrent du haut des montagnes." The music of silence to which all music returns (as to the dominant in *Abt Vogler*) is the symbol of subsiding cosmic forces—and of the exhaustion of the "énergumène." In the third paragraph we witness the blankness of the nephew's mind as he awakens from his coma ("il resta immobile, stupide, étonné"—three epithets asyndetically juxtaposed, which sustain the mood of stupefaction). The idea of automatism is faintly suggested by *machinalement*;[35] but even in this description of collapse, the machine is not made to swallow up the man—who is able to conclude his "demonstration" with the words: "Voilà ce qu'on doit appeler de la musique et un musicien!" (here is stated the problematic connection between expressive music and expressive musicianship), and to proceed immediately to further discussion. Self-potentiation by music is allowed for a moment to dominate in the being of this Protean actor-of-himself. Later, the nephew will again turn to grimaces and become again a mechanical "pagodah" ("Quand elle [Nature] fagota son [Rameau the Elder's] neveu, elle fit la grimace, et puis la grimace, et puis la grimace encore. Et en disant ces mots, il faisait toutes sortes de grimaces du visage: c'était le mépris, le dédain, l'ironie, et il semblait pétrir entre ses doigts un morceau de pâte, et sourire aux formes qu'il lui donnait; cela fait, il jeta la pagode hétéroclite loin de lui et dit: 'C'est ainsi qu'elle me fit et qu'elle me jeta à côté d'autres pagodes. . . .' ").[36] But in our passage no mechanism is allowed to seize our attention; rhythm is lost in meaning.[37]

This passage of *Le neveu de Rameau*, which describes the invasion by creative enthusiasm, is not isolated in Diderot's work—where we can find depicted various degrees of creative exaltation. At a low rung of the ladder (not far above the place assignable to the first description of the nephew), we may place the following passage from *Sur les femmes*, in which is presented the hysteria of the visionary Karsch: "Lorsque la Prusienne Karsch lève son oeil vers le ciel enflammé d'éclairs, elle voit Dieu dans le nuage. . . . Cependant la recluse dans sa cellule se sent élever dans les airs; son âme se répand dans le sein de la Divinité; son essence se mêle à l'essence divine; elle se pâme; elle se meurt; sa poitrine s'élève et s'abaisse avec rapidité; ses compagnes, attroupées autour d'elle, coupent les lacets de son vêtement. . . . La nuit vient; elle entend les choeurs célestes; sa voix s'unit à leurs concerts. Ensuite elle redescend sur la terre; elle parle de joies ineffables; on l'écoute: elle est convaincue."

Here we have a development through a nervous state toward heavenly peace and a final return to the earth. It is particularly interesting that the "style coupé," the style of nervousness, prevails even when the mystic's heavenly vision is recorded: there is not the musical flow which would be consonant with the celestial concerts she is supposed to hear—probably because Diderot himself could not hear the heavenly

concerts that Raphael's Saint Cecilia chanted in her heart as
well as he was able to hear the music of the nephew's orchestra.

In the next example we have a description of the poet being visited by enthusiasm. While this has much in common
with the second vision of the nephew, we are spared here the
description of the state of physical collapse: that painful
awakening of the creative poetic genius from his trance, from
the Saturnine process of self-consumption: "L'enthousiasme
naît d'un objet de la nature. Si l'esprit l'a vu sous des aspects
frappants et divers, il en est occupé, agité, tourmenté. L'imagination s'échauffe; la passion s'émeute. On est successivement
étonné, attendri, indigné, courroucé. . . . Le poète sent le
moment de l'enthousiasme; c'est après qu'il a médité. Il s'annonce en lui par un frémissement qui part de sa poitrine, et
qui passe, d'une manière délicieuse et rapide, jusqu'aux ex-
trémités de son corps. Bientôt ce n'est plus un frémissement;
c'est une chaleur forte et permanente qui l'embrasse, le fait
haleter, qui le consume, qui le tue, mais qui donne l'âme, la
vie à tout ce qu'il touche. Si cette chaleur s'accroissait encore,
les spectres se multiplieraient devant lui. Sa passion s'élèverait
presque au degré de la fureur. Il ne connaîtrait de soulage-
ment qu'à verser au dehors un torrent d'idées qui se pressent,
se heurtent et se chassent."

But, on the other hand, it is even more impregnated with
that "physical rhythm" (as was also the description of the
mystic's enthusiasm) which we noted in the article on "jouissance."[88] H. Dieckmann, in his article on "genius," has pointed
out the importance for the history of ideas of this passage
which, instead of giving, in the manner of the seventeenth
century, a pompous, rhetorical definition of the genius, describes critically an inner experience of Diderot himself: "the
nature, the origin, the importance of the genius find their congruous expression, because Diderot is capable of attaining the
same degree of inner tension and intensity which he tries to
describe." But Dieckmann has failed to note the stylistic
kinship of the paragraph on the creative experience of genius
with that on sexual experience—a kinship which allows us to
recognize the inner parentage between Diderot's feeling of

the creative in art and that of the creative in Nature. In this connection we may quote Rilke's remarks (*Briefe an einen jungen Dichter*, p. 20) on R. Dehmel (whose life program was "brünstig leben und dichten"), in which Rilke points out the identity of the artistic and the sexual act: "Und tatsächlich liegt ja künstlerisches Erleben so unglaublich nahe am geschlechtlichen, an seinem Weh und an seiner Lust, dass die beiden Erscheinungen eigentlich nur verschiedene Formen einer und derselben Sehnsucht und Seligkeit sind. Und wenn man statt Brunst Geschlecht sagen dürfte, Geschlecht im grossen, weiten, reinen, durch keinen Kirchenirrtum verdächtigten Sinne, so wäre seine Kunst sehr gross und unendlich wichtig. Seine dichterische Kraft ist gross und wie ein Urtrieb stark, sie hat eigene rücksichtslose Rhythmen in sich und bricht wie aus Bergen aus ihm heraus."

In all the preceding descriptions of "states of being," the subject described has been swept away by his emotions, the usual pattern (whether using the "style coupé" or the more flowing rhythm) being that of exaltation followed by deflation. In the following dialogue (from the *Rêve de D'Alembert*), too, the movements of rise and fall may be discerned:

MLLE. DE L'ESPINASSE: Il m'a semblé plusieurs fois en rêve—

BORDEU: Et aux malades dans une attaque de goutte—

MLLE. DE L'E.: Que je devenais immense.

B.: Que leur pied touchait au ciel de leur lit.

MLLE. DE L'E.: Que mes bras et mes jambes s'allongeaient à l'infini, que le reste de mon corps prenait un volume proportionné; que l'Encélade de la fable n'était qu'un pygmée; que l'Amphitrite d'Ovide, dont les longs bras allaient former une ceinture immense à la terre, n'était qu'une naine en comparaison de moi, et que j'escaladais le ciel et que j'enlaçais les deux hémisphères.

B.: Fort bien. Et moi j'ai connu une femme en qui le phénomène s'exécutait en sens contraire.

MLLE. DE L'E.: Quoi! elle se rapetissait par degrés, et rentrait en elle-même?

B.: Au point de se sentir aussi menue qu'une aiguille: elle

voyait, elle entendait, elle raisonmait, elle jugeait; elle avait un effroi mortel de se perdre; elle frémissait à l'approche des moindres objets; elle n'osait bouger de sa place.

When the feeling of expansion prevails in the speakers, the sentences have a free, uninterrupted flow, both partners seeming to sing a duet on the theme of expansion into the infinite; when that of contraction prevails, the "style coupé" is used (*fort bien* and *quoi*! are jerky interruptions of the flow; the asyndetons depict the perturbation caused by the "contraction").

There is, however, an important difference between this passage and all the others which we have considered: the speakers (the physician Bordeu and the intellectual Mlle. de l'Espinasse) are not emotionally shaken; they are giving an objective description of certain psycho-physical states observable in cases of dreams and illness. In spite of the fact that extraordinarily morbid or fantastic experiences are being described, we may read the description without a feeling of strain, for it was not written by Diderot out of nervous tension. We see from this that Diderot was capable of objectivizing the finds to which his subjective, sensitive nature gave him the clue. And, in this way, it became possible to render in an artistic style the scientific data which, with specialists, would be treated in a dry, factual manner: the sciences are relieved of their compartmentalization and isolation and become accessible to the art of style. Diderot is, perhaps, a "demi-poète," as Sainte-Beuve has said; but, truer to truth seems to me the statement that he was a "thinker-poet," a thinker who felt in himself the urge to translate his thoughts into poetic prose. That capacity, which characterized Diderot, of giving "gesticulating" expression to everything he thinks, becomes a way of conquering the new realm of science for literature.

* *
*

And now, in order to round out the picture of Diderot and to place him in his time, I may quote here some comments from Groethuysen's article, which should not surprise us after the acquaintance we have made with Diderot's style. Groethuysen recognizes a drama going on in Diderot's mind, involving the clash of two antagonistic forces: Diderot's mobility and his respect for scientific data.

In regard to his mobility, Groethuysen remarks: "[Ce qu'on désigne au XVIIIᵉ siècle comme esprit] Ce n'est plus cette vérité simple et ingénue du XVIIᵉ siècle . . . , qui consiste à bien définir et à bien peindre, à mettre de l'ordre et de la clarté dans les idées que l'homme du XVIIIᵉ siècle recherchera. . . . C'est une liberté nouvelle que l'homme acquiert . . . l'esprit au XVIIIᵉ siècle restitue en quelque sorte à la pensée sa mobilité spontanée. Diderot est le philosophe de cette liberté nouvelle dont jouit l'esprit qui s'abandonne à son propre mouvement, à sa vie, sans être entravé par le souci d'une objectivité qui lui imposerait des formes déterminées. Voyez la marche d'une conversation, voyez les circuits qu'on y fait: les rêves d'un malade ne sont pas plus hétéroclites. Cependant comme il n'y a rien de décousu dans la tête d'un homme qui rêve, ni dans celle d'un fou, tout se tient aussi dans la conversation.³⁹ . . . Pour lui, la pensée vraiment comprise ne saurait être détachée du penseur. . . . Au XVIIᵉ siècle la valeur de la pensée se mesurait sur l'objectivité qui en forme le contenu. . . . Au XVIIIᵉ siècle, on insiste sur l'originalité de la pensée, sur les tournures d'esprit, sur les différentes manières d'envisager les choses. . . . Aussi Diderot n'ira-t-il plus à la recherche de l'expression finie et achevée. . . . Autour de l'idée qui n'est qu'esquissée se grouperont les idées accessoires flottantes et variables. . . . Le langage reflètera le jeu des pensées se cherchant, se retrouvant, se fuyant et ne pouvant jamais se saisir complètement. C'est ainsi que l'esprit, dans des formes nuancées et multiples, devient conscient de sa vie mobile. Si ensuite il se tourne vers le monde des phénomènes et des apparences, les aspects toujours changeants sous lesquels la vie se présente à lui paraissent comme une projection de sa propre mobilité. . . . Ainsi Diderot trouve en face de soi un monde qui, vu l'instabilité de ses changements, vu la multiplicité des interprétations possibles . . . , semble ne pouvoir opposer aucune résistance au libre essor des facultés de l'esprit."⁴⁰

Groethuysen then proceeds to state that Diderot, this representative of instability, sought and found the counterbalance of a firmly resistant reality opposing him, in the exact scientific research of his century, which consisted in cataloguing and circumscribing facts, in observation and experimentation; in this way the philosopher of the "esprit de finesse" becomes the forerunner of modern positivism. Both aspects of Diderot's mind, his emotional mobility and his urge to assimilate the solid facts of science, appear in his articles written for the *Encyclopedia*. We are dealing here only with the artistic style of Diderot (a style whose origin we discovered in a sample article from the scientific *Encyclopedia*!) not with his scientific writing proper—with the exception, perhaps, of the passage from the *Rêve de D'Alembert*, where we were able to show the penetration of artistic style into scientific prose.

In the passage just quoted textually from Groethuysen, that critic suggests that Diderot, the philosopher of the mobility of the mind, was bound to have a style of mobility;[41] he seems, however, to think of Diderot's language rather as conveying to the reader the "jeux des idées," as reflecting patterns of thought; Diderot's style evidently appears to him as "intellectually conditioned," revealing the ballet of ideas in the costume of words. I have attempted to show by my demonstration in detail that the style of mobility found with Diderot consists in the close adherence of his language to his thought, by way of a sort of inborn mimicry—that his style is an irruption of the *physiological* rhythm of speech into writing. It is for this reason that Diderot must dialogize, monologize, harangue, taunt, apostrophize—apostrophize not only persons but even his own subject-matter. Thought converts itself immediately into the flesh of speech and, with Diderot, speech means "allonger les bras" in a desire to leave behind one's ego and to expand toward a fellow being; it means a conversation with a partner, in which the dialectic in Diderot's nature is brought out by dialogue. Even in the *Encyclopedia* he harangues when we might expect him only to inform (cf. the beginning of the article "jouissance"). For Diderot, there was no bookish teaching, there was only flexible, alive, mobile speech, functioning for the self-liberation of the individual. Not only did Diderot reveal the thinker behind the thought, he revealed the speaker behind the thinker—the speaker, in the main, being himself. What best survives in Diderot's works (in the field of belles-lettres) is the creation of that type of "homme sensible" which he was himself and which he has embodied in a series of characters: Jacques le fataliste, le neveu de Rameau, Hardouin (in "Est-il bon? est-il méchant?")—characters who are satisfied to "live their attitude" of mobility toward the world, to express the mobility of their thinking, and their craving to free themselves from the limitations imposed upon them by their own nature.[42] Thus we are able to see, in Diderot's writings, the speaker Diderot in life-size before us, with his *Neveu*-like verbal orchestra—the virtuoso, a very orchestrator of his thought:[43] it is out of the laws of his nature that, in the *Neveu*, he is able to describe the swelling orchestration of an idea, as a scene of self-annihilation.

The phenomenon of Diderot the energumen is ultimately the manifestation of the dynamism of the self-propelled motion, the self-ignition, of a frenzied mind.[44] In that parody of the nephew which was a parody of himself, Diderot has declared the autonomy of expressivity, the dionysiac delirium which enjoys no god but itself (not without reason did Diderot praise the "gourde sacrée" of Rabelais' priestess Bacbuc—in *Jacques le fataliste*). Diderot has experienced to the bitter end the self-annihilation of the self-igniting mind; but we must be grateful that he has written the satire of it, warning of the danger of expressivity when it severs its ties with Logos. It is the absence of the feeling for the divine (which Meister has already pointed out: Diderot's nature is "riche, fertile, abondante en germes de toute espèce, douce et sauvage, simple et majestueuse, bonne et sublime, mais sans aucun principe dominant, sans maître et sans Dieu") which has made possible that autonomy of expressivity and that bodily mimicry of thought by speech which leads to the disintegration of thought: when the Spirit of God no longer bloweth whither it listeth, man feels his thought autonomous, and speech, no longer subdued to Logos, becomes predominantly a matter of the body, subject to automatism: something felt in one's veins and nerves (Dante felt things in his veins—including the supernatural—but these obeyed the supernatural). Diderot has discovered and expressed most vividly the Charybdis of automatism to which the emotional human soul, which would avoid the Scylla of dry rationalism, may fall victim; with his deep respect for natural law, he had to realize the limits and the frustration which the natural organization of man ultimately imposes on man: the frenzied singer paralyzes his vocal cords.

The feverish staccato style was invented by Diderot because he was deaf to the legato of the divine melody. And, just as the recession of the divine made possible, in a manner unequaled before Diderot, the description of the sexual mechanism, so the description of the bodily, physiological, mechanical side of thought was a new achievement, bought at the price of firm canons imposed by the divine. But, by his self-excommunication, Diderot was enabled to discover new paths for poetry, which, in the nineteenth century, have been followed by great poets (regardless of their religious attitude). For example, the element of the dionysiac which Diderot could claim to have rediscovered, lives gloriously in Hugo's poem Le Satyre (in "Légende des Siècles").[45] To invert a line from this same poem ("On fait du ténébreux avec du radieux"), it could be said, in reference to Hugo's poetry which was prefigured by Diderot: "on fait du radieux avec du ténébreux."

The philosophy of mobility as well as its expression by bodily mobility, by "mimicry," was not possible before the eighteenth century:[46] not before this period of the "original genius" could we have the impersonation of language by way of the writer's biological nature—and the ensuing possibility for the reader or stylistician to penetrate into the biological web of the writer's nature by a study of his style. And, when we find in a writer the cohabitation of this philosophy of mobility with this mobile style, an insoluble problem arises: we will probably never be able to disentangle the manner of expression from the manner of thinking or to decide which of the two came first: whether Diderot's natural mimicry (and his stylistic orchestration of it) conditioned his philosophy or whether the philosophy of his period penetrated his bloodstream and colored his style. The nerves and the philosophy of a time appear here so inextricably intermingled in the person of one man that analysis must simply abdicate —at least in our present state of knowledge about man's dependence on Nature.

Having come to the end of this article, I ask myself, in all humility, why no previous critic, so far as I know, has been able to formulate clearly the particular Diderotian essence. We seem to have here an example of the situation described by Henry James in *The Figure in the Carpet*: clues to the writer's general artistic intention have been given the critics in "every page and line and letter. The thing's as concrete there as a bird in a cage, a bait on a hook, a piece of cheese in a mouse-trap. It's stuck into every volume as your foot is stuck into your shoe. It governs every line, it chooses every word, it dots every *i*, it places every comma"—and, nevertheless, the critics have not seen the figure in the carpet which repeats itself, with all its circumvolutions, in the work before their eyes! It may be that the very prodigality of the evidence has blinded the critics, who are accustomed to searching for hidden clues.

NOTES

1. A study such as *Diderot's Imagery* by Eric M. Steel (New York, 1941), which is patterned on similar works dealing with the imagery of Shakespeare or Donne, proceeds by applying to Diderot the ready-made concept of "imagery," illustrating this by means of quantitative comparisons (in the *Rêve de D'Alembert* the percentage of similes is greater than in the *Lettre sur les aveugles*) which entail an overevaluation of the raw material on which the author draws (do Diderot's similes involve more birds or more flowers?). I should like to set down as a rule for all the generations of dissertation-writers to come: *never start writing on a subject of literary history unless you have made a particular observation of your own on this subject!* If you have been struck by a certain quality of Diderot's imagery, then write on this imagery—but not if you have only thought coldly, in the abstract: "Diderot is missing from the list of those whose imagery has been covered; why not fill in the gap?"

Imagery should be considered not *per se*, but according to the particular function that the author ascribes to it in his different works. There is, for example, practically no imagery in *Le neveu de Rameau*, Mr. Steel tells us. But why? (I would explain this as due to the fact that, in this work, the central device chosen by Diderot to render the central theme [mental mobility] was that of rhythm.) Conversely, in the *Rêve de D'Alembert,* this device is quite frequent: the two basic images are those of the spider-web and the cluster of bees—the latter, as Dieckmann has shown, borrowed from the physician Bordeu, who is also the protagonist of the *Rêve*. It is because Diderot is concerned in this dialogue with the seemingly frail or loose, but none the less stable, configurations in Nature, that he has chosen these two similes (and no others).

Quite a different function is to be assigned to the imagery of Diderot's *Entretien d'un philosophe avec la Maréchale,* in which the rational, arithmetical mind of the Maréchale, that positivistic Catholic, expresses itself in numbers and quantities—as, for example:

"Que gagnez-vous donc à ne pas croire?" [the philosopher counters: "Est-ce qu'on croit, parce qu'il y a quelque chose à gagner?"]

"La raison d'intérêt ne gâte rien aux affaires de ce monde ni de l'autre" [the Assézat edition remarks correctly: "la raison d'intérêt, sur laquelle roule presque toute son argumentation"]

". . . le mal, ce sera ce qui a plus d'inconvénients que d'avantages; et le bien, au contraire, ce qui a plus d'avantages que d'inconvénients" [in the utilitarian definition of moral concepts the quantity of usefulness is the dominant factor]

Thus, it is not surprising to find, in her conversation, images borrowed from the world of business:

"J'avoue que je prête à Dieu à la petite semaine"

"Mais oui : on peut faire l'usure avec Dieu tant qu'on veut ; on ne le ruine pas. Je sais bien que cela n'est pas délicat, mais qu'-importe ? Comme le point est d'attraper le ciel, ou d'adresse ou de force, il faut tout porter en ligne de compte, ne négliger aucun profit"

"Hélas ! nous aurons beau faire, notre mise sera toujours bien mesquine en comparaison de la rentrée que nous faisons. Et vous n'attendez rien, vous ?"

"petit à petit, cela fait somme"

[the philosopher counters: "Pour moi, je mets à fonds perdu"]

[this is the reaction of the Maréchale to the concession by the philosopher of some minor bad actions prevented by religion—a reaction couched in the language of the French bourgeois who, all his lifetime, makes "de petites épargnes"]

Here, then, imagery has a characterizing value; the type of metaphor used by the Maréchale (and, incidentally, by the philosopher who would disprove her arguments) is congenital with her turn of mind. Diderot is here illustrating (to an excessive degree, perhaps) the truth of the Latin dictum: *oratio vultus animi*. (Unless I am mistaken, this dialogue is not mentioned in Mr. Steel's dissertation.)

We have again a different use of imagery in the *Regrets sur ma vieille robe de chambre*, in which the device is intended as a reflection of a playful arbitrary attempt on the part of the writer to endow with life the objects surrounding him, to treat them as human beings, as friends or sweethearts. The problem of this essay is concerned precisely with our attachment to the things of our environment, an attachment which tends to take on quasi-human value; it is a problem quite in line with the general eighteenth-century tendency which cherished the cozy intimacy of the "intérieur," in contrast to that of the seventeenth century, "le grand siècle," in which the abstract, the monumental, the "public" was so greatly appreciated. In this masterpiece of Diderot's, the varying intensity of the personifications corresponds to the hesitancy or boldness of the author to recognize the human character of things. At the beginning, Diderot plays upon the ambiguity of the personal pronoun *elle*—it is only in line 14 that we understand that it represents not an animated being (as would be suggested by *sa complainte, le flanc*) but Diderot's old dressing gown (a garment which, since the time of Descartes, has been suggestive of the bachelor philosopher) : "Pourquoi ne l'avoir pas gardée? Elle était faite à moi ; j'étais fait à elle. . . . Il n'y avait aucun besoin auquel sa complaisance ne se prêtât. . . . L'encre épaissie refusait-elle de couler de ma plume, elle présentait le flanc. . . . Sous son abri, je ne redoutais ni la maladresse d'un valet, ni la mienne. . . . J'étais le maître absolu de ma vieille robe de chambre ; je suis devenu l'esclave de la nouvelle." Then comes the simile: "Le vieillard passionné qui s'est livré, pieds et poings liés, aux caprices, à la merci d'une jeune folle, dit depuis le matin jusqu'au soir : Où est ma bonne, ma vieille gouvernante ?"

A human relationship is further indicated in the following passage, in which a masculine variant to the simile is introduced: "Une nouvelle gouvernante stérile qui succède dans un presbytère, la femme qui entre dans la maison d'un veuf, le ministre qui remplace un ministre disgracié, ce prélat moliniste qui s'empare du diocèse d'un prélat janséniste, ne causent pas plus de trouble que l'écarlate intruse en a causé chez moi." (This "scarlet intruder" becomes later on an "impérieuse," a "somptueuse écarlate.")

At the end, Diderot reassures us that his acquisitive sense has not gotten the mastery over him: he is able to give away a prized possession; but when he speaks of giving up "Laïs," he refers to this painting as to a mistress: "Ne craignez pas que la fureur d'entasser de belles choses me prenne. Les amis que j'avais, je les ai; et le nombre n'en est pas augmenté. J'ai Laïs, mais Laïs ne m'a pas. Heureux entre ses bras, je suis prêt à la céder à celui que j'aimerai et qu'elle rendrait plus heureux que moi. Et pour vous dire mon secret à l'oreille, cette Laïs, qui se vend si cher aux autres, ne m'a rien coûté."

It is because Diderot wished to suggest the intimate, almost personal relationship which ties us to cherished objects, that he had recourse to the images just cited—which serve to illustrate a personal way of seeing which he has recognized in himself.

I must repeat that we should observe stylistic procedures by taking the concrete work of art as the point of departure, not some a priori standpoint outside of the work. We must decipher the "hieroglyphs," as Diderot has called the discoveries of poets (the "expressions énergiques," "le beau propos," etc.) in the *hic et nunc* of the works where they are found.

2. Dieckmann's term "inadequately" is surprising. According to him, there were different strata in Diderot's being, the deepest of which is rarely revealed in his style. As an example of a rare case in which the reader is allowed a glimpse into Diderot's *Seinsgefühl* (that is, in which Diderot expresses himself "adequately"), Dieckmann quotes a letter from Diderot's private correspondence in which ideas are expressed which are quite aberrant from the usual tendencies of the Encyclopedists: "Les sensations douces, lorsqu'elles sont continues, calment, sans qu'on s'en aperçoive, les mouvements les plus violents. On ne se défend pas de cette paix de la nature qui règne sans cesse autour de soi. On s'en défend d'autant moins qu'elle agit imperceptiblement. Ce n'est point une éloquence qu'on entende, c'est une persuasion qu'on respire; c'est un exemple auquel on se conforme par une pente naturelle à se mettre à l'unisson avec tout ce qu'on voit. L'immobilité des arbres nous arrête; l'étendue d'une plaine égare nos yeux et notre âme; le bruit égal et monotone des eaux nous endort. . . . Toutes les douleurs finissent par être lentes et mélancoliques. Les querelles dans les champs ont un aspect plus hideux que dans les carrefours des villes; c'est comme un cri perçant dans le silence et l'obscurité de la nuit; c'est un contraste de guerre avec l'image d'une paix générale. . . . Ici d'instinct, on s'assied, on se repose, on regarde sans voir, on abandonne son coeur, son âme, son esprit, ses sens à la liberté; c'est à dire qu'on ne fait rien pour être au ton de tous les êtres. Ils sont, et l'on est. Tout est utile, tout sert, tout concourt, tout est bon, on n'est rien sans y tâcher. Est bien mal né, est bien méchant, est profondément pervers, celui qui médite le mal au milieu des champs. Il lutte contre l'impulsion de la nature entière qui lui répète à voix basse et sans cesse, qui lui murmure à l'oreille: demeure en repos, demeure en repos, reste comme tout ce qui t'environne dure comme tout ce qui t'environne, jouis douce-

ment comme tout ce qui t'environne, laisse aller les heures, les journées, les années, comme tout ce qui t'environne, et passe comme tout ce qui t'environne; voilà la leçon continue de la nature."

Dieckmann considers as quite exceptional in attitude and expression, Diderot's remarks about harmony in Nature: "So wenig achtet Diderot auf die fasslichen Sinneseindrücke, dass er den Höreindruck mit dem Seheindruck vertauscht: in Einklang mit allem was man *sieht*? Auch die Wendung: 'pour être au ton de tous les êtres' ist nicht klanglich gemeint, sondern bezeichnet das Ineinsfühlen mit dem Sein der Dinge." I feel that Mr. Dieckmann would not have found this passage exceptional had he been able to locate it in the history of ideas. The definition of the "peace of Nature" here attempted is in exact accordance with Rousseau (e.g. in the *Nouvelle Héloïse*) and with other thinkers of the eighteenth century: "peace in Nature" with them was related (as I shall show elsewhere) to the idea of "world harmony" as elaborated by the ancients (Plato, Cicero, Plotinus, etc.), by Augustine, and by Renaissance and Baroque writers; that Diderot was familiar with the Renaissance idea of world harmony (as expressed by Marsilio Ficino, etc.) is proven by his frequent simile in which he compares the resonance which one thought awakens in another with the vibrations imparted to the other strings of an instrument when one string is plucked. Now, for the ancients, harmony was as well a term of psychology and moral teaching as of music and natural philosophy: thus, in the passage from Diderot, the acoustic expressions ("se mettre à l'unisson," "être au ton") are illustrative at the same time of moral peace and of the peace of Nature, just as was the case in ancient literature. "Peace" is "the good," it is "love" (in "tout sert, tout concourt, tout est bon," the reminiscence of *concurrere* belongs to a traditional pattern which also included *consonantia, concordia,* etc.) ; it is spontaneous achievement ("imperceptiblement," "sans y toucher"), it is "musical harmony" and "world harmony" ("tous les êtres . . ."). "Strife" is "the wicked," strife is "hatred" ("méchant," "pervers") ; it is conscious machination ("méditer le mal") ; it is musical disharmony ("un cri perçant"). The gentle fusion of the perceptions of the particular senses into one self-contained *Stimmung* is a manifestation of peace and harmony. Thus Diderot is here continuing a two-thousand-year-old Platonic-Augustinian tradition. He manages, however, to give this his own personal touch; and I feel that Dieckmann has failed to sense the Diderotian ring in this passage—by which the thought is translated into rhythm: the extinction of consciousness in man, as he is lulled to sleep by Nature, and the cradling silence of Nature, could not have been expressed more musically; the sentences (much more so than in the *Rêverie* of Rousseau, who is rather given to formulating definitions) have the "monotonous" effect of dulling all sharp discordances—until we come to the lullaby which Nature sings to man: "demeure en repos, demeure en repos," with the repetition of "comme tout ce qui t'environne." This lullaby of Nature, incidentally, is not basically different in its pattern from the lullaby with which the nephew of Rameau puts himself to sleep (the refrain "le grand homme Rameau") : so constant in Diderot is the acoustic rendering of feelings! Far from sharing Dieckmann's idea that Diderot "pays no heed" to the data of the particular senses, I must state that Diderot shows his sensitivity to the acoustic as such by his translation of feelings into rhythm.

2a. Diderot's analysis of eroticism has evidently influenced the passage in Friedrich Schlegel's *Lucinde* where the repetition of the sexual act is defined as a combination of the determined and the undetermined (*Bestimmtes-Unbestimmtes*). Cf. also *ibidem* the *reizende romantische Unordnung* ascribed to eroticism. With Schlegel as a link, we may see a continuous line extending from Diderot's sensualism to that of Heine and Nietzsche.

3. This feeling for the direct accessibility of the enchanted garden of natural love could be called the "rococo" element in Diderot's attitude toward love, a feeling which includes some elements of the Enlightenment together with a remnant of French *gauloiserie*: by the eighteenth century, Tasso's paradise of sensuous love, which had been the prerogative of princes, had passed to all men as a gift from Nature. This mixture of the rococo with features of the Enlightenment has not been taken into account by Sainte-Beuve, who quotes with disapproval the passages of Diderot's *Salon* (x, 365) on the young painter Loutherbourg: "Courage, jeune homme, tu as été plus loin qu'il ne l'est permis à ton âge. . . . Tu as une compagne charmante, qui doit te fixer. Ne quitte ton atelier que pour aller consulter la nature. Habite les champs avec elle. Va voir le ciel se lever et se coucher. . . . Vois les herbes brillantes des gouttes de la rosée. . . . Quitte ton lit de grand matin, malgré la femme jeune et charmante près de laquelle tu reposes. Devance le retour du soleil. . . . Cet astre commence à peine sa carrière; ta compagne charmante a les yeux encore fermés; bientôt un de ses bras te cherchera à son côté. Hâte-toi de revenir. La tendresse conjugale t'appelle. Le spectacle de la nature animée t'attend."

Sainte-Beuve, while appreciating the description of the landscape "tout humectée de rosée et de lumière," finds unwarranted and indecent the allusions to the *compagne*, of which he quotes only two. It is in the name of "le goût" that he disapproves of this picture of "ce coin entr'ouvert de l'alcôve maritale"; he finds in Diderot's style "un déshabillé libre et bourgeois." Thus Sainte-Beuve is content to apply the purely normative judgment of "taste" instead of attempting historically to understand the taste and the thought-behind-the-taste of Diderot and his time. The thought, indicated in the last sentence of the passage just quoted, is evidently the same as that of the article "Jouissance": woman is animated nature, she belongs to nature as truly as do the landscapes depicted by the young artist. The taste revealed by these lines is that of the rococo, that sense of the immediate accessibility to man of the enchanted garden of sensuous love, of that "action génitale, si naturelle, si nécessaire et si juste" (as Diderot says in an apologia for the verb *foutre*, vi, 222). Diderot, like Watteau or Fragonard, wants us to feel how close to man Nature has put the rosy-fingered Eos, how easy she has made the Embarcation for Cythera. The sensuous picture offered by Diderot of the marital alcove is indeed "bourgeois," but it is, strangely enough, also Homeric, since one of the tenets of Diderot's creed is that the sexual freedom of the Homeric gods should be accessible to every bourgeois. Sainte-Beuve's repugnance, which is easily shared by a modern reader, can be explained by the fact that we no longer feel the "pathos" of sexual emancipation.

4. This passage appears to be an enlargement of the statement contained in Diderot's essay *Sur les femmes*, in which he blames Thomas for

not having spoken (in his "Essai sur le caractère, les moeurs et l'esprit des femmes") ". . . avec plus d'intérêt et de chaleur du seul être de la nature qui nous rende sentiment pour sentiment, et qui soit heureux du bonheur qu'il nous fait." "Mais il a voulu que son livre ne fût d'aucun sexe; et il n'y a malheureusement que trop bien réussi. C'est un hermaphrodite qui n'a ni le nerf de l'homme ni la mollesse de la femme." Diderot has evidently brought to the article "Jouissance" that "warmth" of style which he found missing in Thomas and which seemed to him required by the subject matter; it is his general tendency to write of a subject in a style which corresponds to it artistically, in a style that not only explains but represents it: "Il ne suffit pas de parler des femmes, et d'en parler bien, monsieur Thomas, faites encore que j'en voie."

5. One sees that this *vous* is no longer the indefinite "vous qui avez une âme," addressed indiscriminately to all men with feeling, but a dual ("vous deux") descriptive of "the couple": a general dual, however, since all mankind falls into couples. It is significant that when Diderot taunts the "homme pervers" who might object to his description of sexuality, he addresses him as "tu" ("Tais-toi, malheureux . . .") as if in order to isolate him in his perversion from the loving community of men.

6. The same "ritornello" development may be seen in the sentence from the "Neveu de Rameau" which defines the triumph and downfall of the musician Rameau (the Elder):

ce musicien célèbre

> qui nous a délivrés du plain-chant de Lulli . . .

> qui a tant écrit de visions inintelligibles sur la théorie de la musique où lui ni personne n'entendait jamais rien,

> et de qui nous avons un certain nombre d'opéras où il y a de l'harmonie, des bouts de chants . . .

> et qui, après avoir enterré *le Florentin* [= Lully], sera enterré par les virtuoses florentins, ce qu'il pressentait. . . .

7. I foresee objections to my attempt to find an organic meaning in certain linguistic traits; one could argue that, since there are many cases of accumulated *qui*-sentences in Diderot which do not depict productivity and potentiation, I am consequently not justified in finding this meaning expressed by them when the passage happens to deal with productivity and potentiation. But whenever one deals with the problem of expressivity of language, "expression" can be stated only when meaning and linguistic form converge: Grammont has often explained that *tic-tac* is a "mot expressif" (an onomatopoeia) because, in it, sound and meaning are conjoined, while *tactique*, while offering the same sound clusters, is not expressive because nothing in the concept of "tactics" asks for imitation by sound.

In *Les bijoux indiscrets*, we have a similar sentence which depicts, by means of accelerated rhythm (here, it is noun clauses, not relative clauses, that are involved) the progress of (psychological) possession of the Beloved (IV, 310): "Je voudrais qu'elle approuvât mes soins, qu'elle ne m'éconduisit pas par des mines, qu'elle m'apprît une bonne fois si je lui plais; qu'elle m'instruisit elle-même du moyen de lui plaire davantage; qu'elle ne me celât point les progrès que je ferais dans son coeur; qu'elle n'écoutât que moi, n'eût des yeux que pour moi, ne pensât, ne rêvât que moi, ne fût occupée que de moi, ne fit rien qui ne tendît à m'en convaincre; et que cédant un jour à mes transports, je visse clairement que je dois tout à mon amour et au sien. Quel triomphe! et qu'un homme est heureux de posséder une telle femme!" Trahard remarks: "Quand Amisadar parle, on croit entendre déjà Diderot s'adressant à Sophie Vollard." And, indeed, we do hear the same note of "possessiveness" in the following lines from one of Diderot's letters to Sophie (Trahard, p. 113)—which should, incidentally, be added to the dossier of "jouissance": "Il se répand sur tout votre corps un frémissement délicieux, tout vous annonce un amour infiniment plus grand, tout vous y convie: et vous ne voulez pas mourir et faire mourir de plaisir! Vous vous refusez à un moment qui a bien aussi son délire: celui où cet homme, vain d'avoir possédé cet objet qu'il prise plus que l'univers entier, en répand un torrent de larmes!"

The same basic sentence pattern prevails when Diderot imagines his union with Sophie after death—which, owing to his atomistic ideas, becomes a meeting of molecules: "O ma Sophie, il me resterait donc un espoir de vous toucher, de vous sentir, de vous aimer, de vous chercher [acceleration, striving toward the union], de m'unir, de me confondre avec vous quand nous ne serons plus [apex of mystic union], s'il y avait pour nos principes une loi d'affinité, s'il nous était réservé de composer un être commun, si je devais dans la suite des siècles refaire un tout avec vous, si les molécules de votre amant dissous avaient à s'agiter, à s'émouvoir et à rechercher les vôtres éparses dans la nature [in the hypothetic sentences the same movement of union starts once more toward a broad apotheosis]."

8. Here, for the first time, we find a rhythm which will recur many times in our paper: this "style coupé" (the term Diderot himself applied, in a laudatory vein, to Seneca's writing), which is produced by a sequence of short sentences, gives a mechanical effect—which is never likely to be achieved with the longer periods, however artificially they may be contrived. And this must imply a correspondent automatism in the organic process described: Diderot seems to have been sensitive to the inherent mechanism of the body when it is left free to act on its own level.

9. Here we have a discreet formulation, in which factual details are avoided, of that narrowing of consciousness during the sexual act which Diderot felt no qualms about describing in his letter to Sophie (Ledieu, p. 95): "Mais n'est-ce pas une chose bien bizarre que le songe n'offre presque jamais à mon imagination que l'espace étroit et nécessaire à la volupté, rien autour de cela; un étui de chair et puis c'est tout." In the article on "jouissance" there can be no sudden stop like "et puis c'est tout," since, here, Diderot is concerned not only with the egotistic feelings of the individual, but the continuing ebb and flow of Nature. This "et puis c'est tout" is revelatory of Diderot's basically unregenerate nature, the absence of the divine in his sexual *Grunderlebnis*, which has made possible Diderot's revoltingly coarse descriptions of the mechanics of the

sexual, in which there is not the slightest attempt at poeticization (cf. the letter quoted by Ledieu, p. 116).

10. The word "enthusiasm," as used here of the sexual enjoyment—not, for example, of the exaltation of the poet, the philosopher—need not astonish the reader. It will become evident in the course of my article that Diderot shares the Platonic conception (of which he gives his own version) of that θεία μανία "divine fury" which is present alike in the prophet, the *mystes*, the poet, and the lover. It is characteristic of Diderot's sensualistic approach that, when he applies the word *enthusiasm* to love, it is to sexual love.

11. Here, where Diderot associates "le ciel" with monogamy, we must translate this as "Heaven"—in contrast to the passage in the "Supplément au voyage de Bougainville," where it is evidently "the sky" (i.e. Nature) that is meant: that ever-changing background which would seem to re-quire the mutability of human relationships; it is this passage which has inspired Musset's "Souvenir": "[Marriage is] Contraire à la loi générale des êtres; rien en effet te paraît-il plus insensé qu'un précepte qui proscrit le changement qui est en nous, qui commande une constance qui n'y peut être, et qui viole la Nature et la liberté du mâle et de la femelle en les enchaînant pour jamais l'un à l'autre . . . ; qu'un serment d'immutabilité de deux êtres de chair, à la face d'un ciel qui n'est pas un instant le même?"

In fact, the variability of the natural background is the framework of the whole dialogue: this begins and ends with a discussion of the incon-stant weather, which changes during the dialogue. This symbolism must have been deeply present to Diderot's mind, for (as Chinard points out in his Introduction to the "Supplément," p. 47), the same framework of variable Nature is used for his "Sur l'inconséquences du jugement publique et de nos actions particulières," written during the same period.

12. Autobiographical confirmation of this recollective moment of Dide-rot's thought may be found in a passage of his letter to Sophie, quoted by Ledieu, p. 76: "Ce fut une chose si douce que le premier aveu, qu'on ne se lassa point d'y revenir. Ce fut une chose si douce que le premier moment, qu'on alla toujours le recherchant. On serre toujours contre son sein celui qu'on aime, et l'art d'écrire n'est que l'art d'allonger les bras." The writ-ing of a love letter becomes a caressing of the past.

But, when I chose the motto of this chapter, I wished to suggest a wider meaning for Diderot's statement: writing in general is an erotic act for Diderot, an act that tends to integrate him into what is creative and self-potentiating in Nature.

13. In the mention of the poisoning factors of mistrust and remorse (which have no power on young, healthy, innocent, Arcadian beings), we may see, without betraying Diderot's thought, an allusion to the influ-ence of Christianity, which has injected these unwholesome elements into natural sexual life (compare Diderot's references, in the "Supplément au voyage de Bougainville," to "crainte," "châtiment," "remords," which reactions he attributes to the marital policy of the Church).

14. This does not mean that traditional elements are lacking in his style. For example, the aphorism, repeatedly used in our passage, is a centuries-old device; again, such a phrase as "les voiles que jeta la pudeur sur les charmes" derives from sensuous French poetry and represents a

style which had been current in prose from "Le grand Cyrus" to "Le temple de Gnide"; the superlatives "les illusions les plus délicates," "le sens le plus exquis" are a traditional encomiastic device in "ideal" descriptions of Arcadian idyls. But the sentence rhythm to which these traditional elements are subjected, is new.

That Diderot had a clear conception of "rhythm" as an artistic factor in poetry and prose, and in speech, is shown by his remarks (XI, 268): "Qu'est-ce donc que le rhythme? C'est un choix particulier d'expressions; c'est une certaine distribution de syllabes . . . ou un enchaînement de petites onomatopées analogues aux idées qu'on a, et dont on est fortement occupé . . . , à la nature, au caractère, au mouvement des actions qu'on se propose de rendre. . . . Il est inspiré par un goût naturel, par la mobilité de l'âme, par la sensibilité. C'est l'image même de l'âme rendue par les inflexions de la voix . . . sans la facilité de trouver ce chant, cette espèce de musique, on n'écrit ni en vers ni en prose: je doute même qu'on parle bien. Sans l'habitude de la sentir ou de la rendre, on ne sait pas lire; et qui est-ce qui sait lire? . . . C'est elle qui prête aux écrits une grâce toujours nouvelle. . . . Ce n'est pas à l'oreille seulement, c'est à l'âme d'où elle est émanée, que la véritable harmonie s'adresse. . . . Ce ne sont pas les idées qui coûtent; c'est le ton qui leur convient."

15. Though there is poeticization in Diderot's treatment of the sexual theme, there is no real poetry: the poeticization consists of an avoidance of mentioning technical facts—which are, only too obviously, uppermost in the mind of the author. Thibaudet, in his article "Langage, littérature et sensualité" (*Nouvelle revue française*, XXXVII, 716), remarks that the eighteenth century is "le siècle de la périphrase érotique," that it had lost the Racinian, the Vergilian power of poetic alchemy whereby brute reality is transmuted. He quotes a passage from the *Aeneid* descriptive of the love of Mars and Venus, and comments: "Chacun de ces mots, le long de ce vers *qui digitos habet* frappe une touche, et cette touche déclenche quelque chose dans une mémoire organique, dans un passé de la sensation. L'homme fait des fouilles dans cette mémoire, dans ce passé, dans cette culture de la sensation qui lui donne aussi une sensation de culture."

16. Compare his physiological description, containing expressions reminiscent of his sexual *Grunderlebnis*, of the way in which he reacts to a virtuous action (letter to Sophie Volland of the 18th of October, 1760): ". . . celui [le spectacle] de l'équité me remplit d'une douceur et d'un enthousiasme où la vie, s'il fallait la perdre, ne me tiendrait à rien; alors il me semble que mon coeur s'étend au dedans de moi, qu'il nage; je ne sais quelle sensation délicieuse et subite me parcourt partout; j'aime à respirer; il s'excite à toute la surface de mon corps comme un frémissement, c'est surtout au haut du front, à l'origine des cheveux, qu'il se fait sentir; et puis les symptômes de l'admiration et du plaisir viennent se mêler sur mon visage avec ceux de la joie, et mes yeux se remplissent de pleurs."

17. Anyone, when reading this description must experience a slight shudder of repulsion—which is surely not alone due to the perversity of the Mother Superior. We feel that the glance of the author himself lingers unduly on the "charmes" of the young nun, as he savors her Greuze-like décolleté ("à deminue"). There is some undigested, unrefined, unassuaged sensuality in Diderot that allows him to abuse the privilege

of an author. And if we think that we get this impression of Diderot's enjoyment through the words of the nun herself, we must realize that this creature of Diderot's is made to appear conscious of her own seductive powers; that she has been infected by her creator's sensuality.

18. If this interpretation is true, there is obviously a lack of realism to be noted: Diderot would be making the nun relive the moment of hypnotism, from which she must have recovered when she writes her account.

19. As another parodistic example of this *et*, compare the following passage from *La religieuse*, in which the archdeacon extracts a "renunciation of Satan" from the innocent nun:

> Il me dit ensuite: "Faites un acte de foi" et je le fis.
> "Faites un acte d'amour" et je le fis.
> "Faites un acte d'espérance" et je le fis.
> "Faites un acte de charité" et je le fis.

In the following example the original suggestion of miraculous creation is better preserved: "[l'esprit observateur] c'est une machine rare qui dit: 'cela réussira' et cela réussit; 'cela ne réussira pas' et cela ne réussit pas; 'cela est vrai' ou 'cela est faux' et cela se trouve comme il l'a dit. Il se remarque et dans les grandes choses et dans les petites. Cette sorte d'esprit prophétique [!] n'est pas le même dans toutes les conditions de la vie; chaque état a le sien."

20. The imposition of a pattern on a character's gestures has been anticipated in the scene of the young nun's ordination by her first Mother Superior. While, here, there is no suggestion of perversion, an ironical touch is given by paralleling the ritual gestures of the ordination with the steps of a dance: [the Mother Superior inspects the young nun after she has taken the veil] "Elle me composa la tête, les pieds, les mains, la taille, le bras; ce fut presque une leçon de Marcel [a famous dancing-master of the time] sur les grâces monastiques: car chaque état a les siennes."

21. That, quite against my usual approach, I am here justified in dragging into the discussion of a work of art the character of the artist, becomes clear from the fact that Diderot was given to depicting his characters according to himself. We may compare, for example, the following self-portrait, in which he shows the influence of his temperament on his way of speaking (it is this passage with which Lanson, after Sainte-Beuve, opens the chapter on Diderot): "La tête d'un Langrois est sur ses épaules comme un coq au haut d'une clocher; elle n'est jamais fixe dans un point; et si elle revient à celui qu'elle a quitté, ce n'est pas pour s'y arrêter. Avec une rapidité surprenante dans les mouvements, dans les désirs, dans les projets, dans les fantaisies, dans les idées, il a le parler lent. Pour moi, je suis de mon pays; seulement le séjour de la capitale et l'application assidue m'ont un peu corrigé" with the portrait of the Mother Superior in *La religieuse*: "C'est une petite femme toute ronde, cependant prompte et vive dans ses mouvements: sa tête n'est jamais assise sur ses épaules; ... ses yeux, dont l'un, c'est le droit, est plus haut et plus grand que l'autre, sont pleins de feu et distraits; quand elle marche, elle jette ses bras en avant et arrière. Veut-elle parler? elle ouvre la bouche, avant que d'avoir arrangé ses idées; aussi bégaye-t-elle un peu ... ; elle est alternativement compatissante et dure; sa figure décomposée marque tout le décousu de son esprit et toute l'inégalité de son caractère. ..." It is from her creator

Diderot that she has taken her chameleonesque mobility and her speech which cannot keep up with the rapidity of her mind.

22. In other passages of our dialogue, the nephew's tirade will end in self-interruption, when he feels that he has reached the realm of the inexpressible: e.g. p. 396 (after offering many hypothetical enumerations): "vous riez? mais laissez-moi dire . . ."; p. 404 (after a sequence of *moi*'s that tend to glorify his personality): "moi! moi enfin! j'irais! . . . Tenez, monsieur, cela ne se peut. . . ." In such cases Diderot means to signify that hypervitality and hyperexpressivity are bound to end in inarticulateness.

23. That Diderot had an eye for the gesture that functions as a complement and a completion of words must be explained not only by the discovery, achieved in the psychology of his time, of the psycho-physical unity of the human body, but also by his own fundamental desire for self-fulfillment, for achievement of psycho-physical unity. This trait is rather extraordinary in a French thinker, since the French, in general, tend toward the subjugation of body and gesture to mind and word; it is more characteristic of the Mediterranean type, with whom word and gesture are one—if, indeed, the gesture does not take precedence over the words, which merely follow the acting. Given the function assigned by Diderot to gestures among other expressive means, it is not surprising that he should have chosen for his *Neveu* a protagonist who is a born actor, a "Schauspieler seiner selbst," as Nietzsche would have put it.

It is not only the foolish nephew whose gesticulations Diderot finds it interesting to describe; he does the same in the case of the scientist D'Alembert (in *Le rêve de D'Alembert*, II, 124): ". . . je suis bien un, je n'en saurais douter (en disant cela, il se tâtait partout)." Here we have a case of "penser avec les mains," a procedure which appealed instinctively to Diderot; to think about the unity of man would immediately have bodily consequences and bodily evidence. Again (*ibid.* 131): "Il avait imité avec sa main droite le tube d'un microscope, et avec sa gauche, je crois, l'orifice d'un vase. Il regardait dans le vase par ce tube, et il disait. . . ." D'Alembert, the intuitive scientist, being as "fou" as was the nephew, must be presented with gesticulations of his own.

24. It is no accident that the dionysiac nephew was a musician. That the dionysiac expresses itself directly in music was, incidentally, Diderot's own experience: compare his remark to Falconet, quoted by Trahard, that he and other creative minds often hear "flutes."

25. We may be reminded here of Diderot's definition of the "imitator" (quoted by Dieckmann): "La nature pousse l'homme de génie, l'homme de génie pousse l'imitateur. . . . Le génie attire fortement à lui tout ce qui se trouve dans la sphère de son activité, qui s'en exalte outre mesure. L'imitateur n'attire point, il est attiré; il s'aimante par le contact avec l'aimant, mais il n'est pas l'aimant."

26. Diderot has discovered the efficacy of the prose refrain in narrative; before him, there existed only the refrain in poetry—with the exception of its use in conversation, as in Molière's "Et Tartufe?" or "Que diable allait-il faire dans cette galère?" (which, likewise, indicate a mechanism prevailing in a character). The prose refrain is predicated on the reader's capacity to distinguish it from the poetic refrain, which suggests not the imposition of a mechanism upon reality that disturbs its natural flow,

but the recurrence of natural, of eternal laws: "Mais où sont les neiges d'antan?" (a cosmic mechanism, perhaps—as we have spoken of the "divine mechanism" of *Fiat lux. Et lux facta est*).

We find the same criticism of a mechanism by a mechanical refrain in the "lullaby" with which Diderot represents the timorous, conventional mind of a jurist as putting itself to sleep ("Entretien d'un père avec ses enfants"): "Les juges s'en tiennent strictement à la loi, comme mon père et le père Bouin; et font bien. Les juges ferment, en pareils cas, les yeux sur les circonstances, comme mon père et le père Bouin, par l'effroi des inconvénients qui s'ensuivraient; et font bien. Ils sacrifient quelquefois contre le témoignage même de leur conscience, comme mon père et le père Bouin, l'intérêt du malheureux et du fripon . . . ; et font bien. Ils redoutent, comme mon père et le père Bouin, de prononcer un arrêt équitable dans un cas déterminé, mais funeste dans mille autres . . . ; et font bien."

With Diderot, the use of the "refrain" to suggest automatism seems to appear only in descriptions of heightened emotion, when the person concerned loses his mental balance and is caught up in the machinery of feeling.

But in our contemporary literature this device is quite often used to reproduce the mechanical aspect of quite routine thought processes of the "stream of consciousness." In the passage below from Marquand's *So Little Time* (p. 399), there is also to be found the suggestion that the character is obsessed by the automatic aspect of everyday life itself: "He [Jeffrey, the playwright] did not know why he should be sensitive about appearing financially before Milton Cooke. After all, he did not have implicit confidence in Milton's judgment, and yet he depended upon Milton because Milton was in the Standard Bank and knew about such things. What was more, Madge [Jeffrey's wife] always depended on Milton, because Milton was what she described as a 'man of business.' . . . Besides, Milton was a friend—they had been in the same class at Harvard. Jeffrey had never known about this until Milton had told him one day, shortly after he began looking at Madge's things, and shortly after that Milton had asked him to lunch at the Harvard Club. . . . Shortly after that, Milton had asked him to his apartment for a quiet little dinner, and while Madge and Laura, Milton's wife, talked in the other room, Milton had told Jeffrey what a headache everything was on Wall Street. There might have been a time, Milton said, when one man, with reasonable intelligence, could supervise his own savings, but now it was getting to be more and more of a science. . . . Milton was talking about the S.W.C., and about a scandal that had broken downtown, and Milton had known the man very well. No one had been as surprised as Milton. . . . Milton was always sure that nothing would come up but, then, you never could tell. Milton seemed to have a dusty sort of immortality. He made Jeffrey feel that he might die, but that somehow Milton never would, since estates and investment lists must go on forever. Milton was reaching into the briefcase again, his fingers moving adroitly through the papers. . . . Jeffrey smiled. 'And if I die on the way,' he said, 'just call up Milton.' . . . Madge never liked to joke about death. But then, that was what Milton was there for, because Madge knew that Milton, or someone like Milton, would live forever."

In this passage, it is obvious that "Milton" has become a prose refrain (almost never is the pronoun "he" allowed to take the place of the name), representing the mechanical thinking of Jeffrey and Madge who are haunted by the thought of Milton-the-Institution with his "dusty sort of immortality," and of the precedence over individual life which financial arrangements have in their world. Since the passage is mainly given up to the "style indirect libre" ("Milton was always sure that nothing would come up, but then, you never could tell"), the oft-repeated "Milton" must be the magic name that the two money-impressed characters have continually on their lips or on their minds: such a sentence as "yet he depended upon Milton because Milton was in the Standard Bank" is only a transposition of Jeffrey's thought: "I must depend on Milton because Milton. . . ."

27. It is interesting to see how Diderot gives to stage-directions a stylistic movement, a literary flavor of their own. Indeed, we must not think of them simply as factual stage-directions; we should read the passage as a whole, as Diderot must have conceived it, giving to the description of gestures and the rendering of words, alike, their proper acoustic value. (For example, the repetitious rhyming flexional endings in *-ait* are no overdose of "style" on the part of Diderot, but the organic expression of his inner "mechanism of enthusiasm.")

28. There are critics, such as J. Reinach, for example, who are astonished that Diderot should champion the cause of cool reason against turbulent sensitivity: this means that they have recognized only one pole in Diderot's basically paradoxical or dialectical nature: the man who could weep about an artistic creation of his own (*La religieuse*)—as later Balzac was to do—sensed the danger of absorption by his capacities of impersonation, and felt keenly the advantages of calm and economy of effort. Mr. Dieckmann has rightly written: "The *Paradoxe sur le comédien* is, in truth, a polemic of Diderot's against himself, an antagonism between his extremely sensitive and his rationalistic tendencies."

29. How close, in Diderot's opinion, the nephew is to the real genius is shown by the following passage in which a famous mathematician is described (quoted by Dieckmann from XI, 125): "Celui-ci est un imitateur sublime de nature; voyez ce qu'il sait exécuter . . . admirez son ouvrage étonnant; eh bien, il n'a pas sitôt déposé l'instrument de son métier, qu'il est fou. Ce poète que la sagesse parait inspirer et dont les écrits sont remplis de sentences à graver en lettres d'or, dans un instant ne sait plus ce qu'il fait; il est fou. Cet orateur qui s'empare de nos âmes et de nos esprits, qui en dispose à son gré, descendu de la chaire, il n'est plus maître de lui; il est fou. . . . Heureux, cent fois heureux, m'écriai-je encore, M. Baliveau, capitoul de Toulouse! C'est M. Baliveau qui boit bien, qui mange bien, qui digère bien, qui dort bien. . . . M. Baliveau est un homme fait pour son bonheur et pour le malheur des autres. Son neveu, M. de l'Empirée, tout au contraire." (Baliveau and M. de l'Empirée are characters in Piron's *La métromanie*.)

30. To express it in the words of Diderot himself, as found elsewhere in the dialogue: "Je n'estime pas ces originaux-là. . . . Ils m'arrêtent une fois l'an parce . . . qu'ils rompent cette fastidieuse uniformité que notre éducation, nos conventions de société, nos bienséances d'usages ont introduite . . . c'est un grain de levain qui fermente. . . . Il secoue, agite, il fait

approuver ou blâmer; il fait sortir la vérité, il fait connaître les gens de bien, il démasque les coquins, . . . c'est alors que l'homme de bon sens écoute et démêle son monde."

Or, in the absolutely concordant observations on "sensibilité" to be found in the *Paradoxe sur le comédien*, which sound like a description of the nephew (and which Trahard was right in placing at the beginning of his discussion of this character) : "La sensibilité . . . est, ce me semble, cette disposition compagne de la faiblesse des organes, suite de la mobilité du diaphragme, de la vivacité de l'imagination, de la délicatesse des nerfs qui incline à compatir, à frissonner, à admirer, à craindre, à secourir, à fuir, à crier, à perdre la raison, à exagérer, à mépriser, à dédaigner, à n'avoir aucune idée précise du vrai, du bon et du beau, à être injuste, à être fou."

Diderot, that "homme de bon sens," may perhaps have listened oftener than he would admit to the stimulating fool that existed in himself. The union of the stimulating fool with the epicurean and opportunistic "average man" ("je suis l'apôtre de la familiarité et de l'aisance," says the nephew) in all these *vauriens* is a typically French blend: the German type (e.g. Michael Kohlhaus) and the Spanish (e.g. Don Quijote) are not epicureans but stoics. Falstaff, perhaps, comes very close to the French figures, only that his belly does not make him fit for dynamicism. It would appear that the period of the French bourgeois, whose desires tend toward the preservation of an unquestioned, mediocre, material welfare, has engendered a revolutionary type which is critical of this same bourgeoisie.

31. In fact, the nephew's self-characterization: "Vous savez que je suis un ignorant, un sot, un fou, un impertinent, un paresseux, ce que nos Bourguignons appellent un fieffé truand, un escroc, un gourmand . . ."; "j'étais leur petit Rameau, leur joli Rameau, leur Rameau le fou, l'impertinent, l'ignorant, le paresseux, le gourmand, le bouffon, la grosse bête" is derived from Marot's enumeration of derogatory epithets (in his characterization of the "valet de Gascogne," another in the series of the French "grands vauriens")—which culminates in the indulgent conclusion "au demourant le meilleur fils du monde." This same indulgent attitude was also characteristic of the milieu in which the nephew moved.

It is interesting to read the description of Diderot himself, drawn up according to Marot's pattern, as given by a contemporary: cf. Trahard, II, 60.

32. When Goethe calls the nephew a "nicht ganz talentloser, phantastisch-praktischer Musikus" he has blurred the real paradox in this character: it is of no great moment whether he has talent or not, whether he is fantastic or practical; what truly matters is the basic paradox which he consistently illustrates. In the portion of the dialogue which has pleased Goethe the most, the nephew makes himself the advocate of that new music of Duni and the Bouffons, which Diderot himself felt to be the right music (as is shown by the approving remarks of MOI), the music which characterizes and expresses human nature, instead of stylizing it into a uniform, evenly flowing *bel canto*. But, while the nephew, as musical critic, knows true values—as a performer of this expressive music he is shown to be utterly lacking in restraint and coordination. Here Diderot has the nephew become the mouthpiece of his own (musical) ideals, while

behaving like a clown as he enacts these ideals. Thus the reactions of Diderot the philosopher, who watches, along with us, the ridiculous spectacle of this performer playing an orchestra of imaginary instruments, who finally collapses under the stress of emotion, are divided between admiration and derisive pity. Expressive art must not be performed expressively: this truth, which is expounded in the *Paradoxe sur le comédien*, is here illustrated by the deterrent example of the nephew, who is chosen because, unlike his uncle the creative artist, he is only performer and imitator. He is the uncreative musician; we see him beat his brains, knock his forehead, searching for a creative idea; when none is forthcoming, he finds a new gesture: with his hand over his heart he exclaims: "je sens, oui, je sens." He is an embodiment of "le paradoxe du musicien sensible."

33. Nor is there lacking autobiographical confirmation of Diderot's fear of being unable to cope with reality and of being overpowered by his imitative mobility (Ledieu, p. 139) : "Grimm m'a dit plusieurs fois que j'avais été fait pour un autre monde. . . . ce qu'il y a de certain, c'est qu'il y a bientôt cinquante ans que je suis étranger dans celui-ci, que je vis d'une vie imitative, qui n'est pas la mienne, et que je suis comme un chien qui apprend à marcher sur deux pattes. De là une démarche tantôt originale, tantôt gauche."

34. This failure may be explained, perhaps, by the fact that Diderot, in the nephew has presented the artistic nature *in corpore vili*; and Goethe, the translator and interpreter of Cellini, was wont to predicate the artistic nature only on genuine artistic achievements. Sainte-Beuve remains even further behind understanding, since he confesses that he can see in the dialogue only less than Goethe. And he does what un-understanding critics will always do: blame the author for what they have not understood: "Ce sont des idées qui se sont enivrées et qui se sont mises à courir les unes après les autres." But these ideas originated in a potent brain which Sainte-Beuve has failed to understand.

Daniel Mornet in his article "La véritable signification du Neveu de Rameau" (*Revue des deux mondes* [1927], p. 889), distinguishes three elements in our dialogue: (1) a realistic element, the description of the "physiognomy" and "pantomime" of Jean-François Rameau, who was a historical personage; (2) a polemic or satire against the moral prostitution prevalent among writers of the time; (3) a forceful demonstration of the moral consequences of Diderot's own philosophy—which, according to Mornet, was a materialistic one. Accordingly, to begin with (1), the description of the nephew's pantomime would be relegated to the biographical datum of the historical Rameau (while, according to Mornet, the actual features and behavior of the historical Rameau have been greatly embellished, this represents a "dramatic and poetic realism" on the part of Diderot, who sees this figure "à travers son imagination échauffée"). To this I would answer that what Mornet considers as artistic embellishments added by Diderot onto the historical features of Jean-François Rameau ("rehaussées, diversifiées, amusées d'une vie frénétique et sans aucun doute surnaturelle") are rather the core of the artistic character: it is the "vie frénétique" that Diderot has embodied in a person whom he borrowed from contemporary history for illustrative purposes. And one must wonder at the psychological awkwardness of the critic which can conceive of supernatural gifts as an "amusing" embellishment!

As for the two morals of this dialogue (points 2 and 3), neither is basic, it seems to me: there is really only one problem, that of the "vie frénétique": a problem which unfolds before us dialectically and dramatically —and which is never solved (as little as the problem of "Est-il bon, est-il méchant?" is solved). By Mornet's three-fold classification, the unity of the problem is dissolved and its poignancy diluted.

Moreover, though Mornet makes much of the satirical intention of this dialogue (he stresses the fact that Le neveu de Rameau has the subtitle "Satire"), that is, in my opinion, only secondary: the nephew is not exclusively the butt of satire; admiration forms part of the medley of feelings with which Diderot views him (and he is declared by his creator to be "better than most; for he is, at least, no hypocrite"). As for the satiric light cast on contemporary (especially on literary) mores, it could be said that this gives us, so to speak, only a by-pleasure—as we listen to the nephew fulminate against the bourgeois world, whose pleasures he does not disdain.

According to G. Rohlfs, who was kind enough to send me an offprint of a short note of his in Arch. f. neuere Sprachen, CLXXXII, 137, E. R. Curtius has published an article on Le neveu de Rameau in which he seeks to refute the thesis of Mornet, and sees in the work of Diderot a satire patterned on Horace's Seventh—that paraphrase of the Stoic teaching "only the wise man is free; the fool is a slave." I am quite willing to agree that this Stoic and Horatian idea is present in Diderot's "satire"; I am not in a position to state whether Curtius is satisfied with thus cataloguing our work or whether he has pointed out the relationship of the Neveu with the inner rhythm of Diderot himself.

The idea of the corpus vile of the artist will be taken up later by Nietzsche who, when portraying the artist—that "über alle Massen sinnlicher und eitler Affe"—was wont to exemplify with the actor (and saw the "Schauspieler seiner selbst" in the artist Wagner). Again, Thomas Mann insists that the raw material of the actor is apishness ("affisch - komödiantisch") and that of the epic narrator, swaggering ("das Aufschneiderische"): cf. his speech on Wassermann in "Die Forderung des Tages." And Thomas Mann's character Felix Krull, the "confidence man," is only another version of Diderot's nephew with all his eagerness to act, to simulate, to masquerade, to consider himself an artist superior to the rest of mankind, and with his profession of anti-bourgeois feelings and immoralism: Thomas Mann's protagonist has imbibed in early youth the teaching of his god-father that Phidias was a thief: "Eine auffallende Mischung. Aber so sind die Leute. Sie wollen wohl das Talent, welches doch an und für sich eine Sonderbarkeit ist. Aber die Sonderbarkeiten, die sonst noch damit verbunden—und vielleicht notwendig damit verbunden—sind, die wollen sie nicht und verweigern ihnen jedes Verständnis."

35. We must stress here the word "machinalement" which is a neologism for Diderot's time: machinal is first attested with Voltaire in 1731, when he speaks of Peter the Great's phobia against water. While the seventeenth century reader (because of Descartes' celestial mechanics) had held such terms as machine (du monde), used in reference to the cosmic structure, in high esteem, the use of this word in a human reference, had no such lofty reference (Mme. de Sévigné: "Nos pauvres machines sont sujettes à bien des misères"). The texts cited by Littré concerning machinal for the

eighteenth century mention, for example, those "terreurs machinales" stemming from our human nature (from which education should free us), or express uneasiness over the "accord machinal" characteristic of the regimented Swiss army.

With Diderot, on the contrary, the best actions of man may sometimes be "automatic": it is "machinalement" that one of the two "Amis de Bourbonne" receives the blow intended for the other. The "spirit of observation" characteristic of the genius able to prophesy results without having to calculate them (IV, 26) is a "machine rare." In the *Paradoxe sur le comédien* the perfect comedian appears as the one who subjects himself to the automatism of a "mannequin" (the famous actress Clairon espouses in her acting "l'âme d'un grand mannequin qui l'enveloppe"). The great actor in general makes use of the "grimace pathétique," the "singerie sublime." The great comedian, the courtesan, the "flatterer by profession" (here, Diderot must have thought of the nephew) are "pantins" moved by the thread of their master. The very fact that Diderot can see automatism in the highest and in the lowest activities alike, shows that he is not, in principle, suspicious of automatism; it becomes alarming (though none the less a fascinating phenomenon for the observation of a scientist) only when the machinery is uncontrolled, with no engineer at the throttle.

36. The nephew whom Diderot describes as given to automatism has himself a keen eye for the automatism of others: the hypochondriac to whom he has hired himself as entertainer is described (p. 430) as a *pagodah* with a thread attached to his chin, who moves his jaws like an automaton; a "bégueule" who poses as an intellectual is described (p. 431) by a sequence of *item . . . item* which give the effect of a mechanism. The person who sees comic automatism everywhere must needs have something of the automaton in himself—as was, of course, the case with Diderot.

37. It is remarkable that, with Diderot, speech never deteriorates into psittacism or inarticulateness, as is the case with some modern writers—for example, Céline. Diderot describes the dionysiac in a language which renders it faithfully, but by means of an always grammatically correct French: indeed, a quite formal order may sometimes be observed, as, in our passage, the use of *ou . . . ou*: "il regardait *ou* attendri, *ou* tranquille, *ou* furieux . . . des eaux *ou* qui murmurent . . . *ou* qui descendent." This pattern, by means of which the contradictory parts of the subject matter are organized into the logical form of the alternative, has come (along with *et . . . et*) to be considered pedantic in modern French.

It is true that there can be found in Diderot's writings one type of "incoherent" syntax: the syncope represented by such examples as the following, where parallel actions are involved: (letter to Sophie of November 10, 1760) ". . . mon marivaudage, car je marivaude, Marivaux sans le savoir, *et moi le sachant*"; (*La religieuse*, v, 157): "Il acheva de me confier de sa vie, *moi de la mienne*, une infinité de circonstances qui formaient entre lui et moi autant de points de contact et de ressemblance." Compare also, from *Le neveu* (v, 391): "Je serais mieux entre Diogène et Phryne. Je suis affronté comme l'un, et je fréquente volontiers chez les autres" [*les autres*] = Phryne and the other courtesans?]; this example is the only one of the three which has been commented upon by the editors of the Assézat edition.

38. It must not, however, be forgotten that when Diderot insists on the bodily manifestations of the enthusiasm of the genius he is only reviving the bodily experience of the θεία μανία which had already been defined by antiquity (according to the Aristotelians, the poetic frenzy was even conditioned by bodily illness) and which the theoreticians of the Renaissance had taken pleasure in describing: "deus, ecce deus jam corpora fatigat, / altius insinuat venis, penitusque per artus / deditur atque faces saevas sub pectore versat. / Nec se jam capit acer agens calor igneaque intus / vis saevit totoque agitat se corpore numen" (Vida, cf. R. Meissner, *Festschrift f. Oskar Walzel*, p. 37). Shakespeare's line "the poet's eye, in a fine frenzy rolling" is a well-known bodily description of the *furor poeticus*. Diderot has transferred the traditional description of the θεία μανία to his own, characteristically eighteenth-century conception of the genius, and has made this description graphic by his personal gift of "innervation of style." Also in line with ancient thought is the equality of treatment which Diderot gives to "the lunatic, the lover, and the poet."

39. This statement is very important for the understanding of the conduct of the dialogue in Diderot's writings. Since, for Diderot, the conversation of a fool is no more and no less coherent than is any human conversation, and reflects the totality of life—why not depict conversation (and life) in general by that of a fool? With this theory, all the tricks and ticks of the nephew which Diderot brings into such relief are justified: not only his extravagant style and gestures, but also, for example, his habit of carrying on a conversation with himself, of interpolating a speech, and even a dialogue, within a speech (pp. 405, 446); here we witness a multiplication of levels and a demonstration of the power and vitality of human speech. Even genuine artists, in Diderot's opinion, can permit themselves a like freedom of interpolation; in his *Paradoxe sur le comédien*, Diderot's partner in the dialogue relates admiringly how two comedians playing Molière's *Dépit amoureux* interpolated a domestic quarrel between the lines of the play (in such a case we would have a tertiary interpolation: quarrel between the actors - their playing of Molière - the dialogue with Diderot). Again, in the *Rêve de D'Alembert*, Mlle. de l'Espinasse reads to Dr. Bordeu the notes she has taken down of the delirious words of her friend D'Alembert, who evidently was under the illusion of speaking to a fellow philosopher; the primary dialogue (between D'Alembert and the philosopher) is fitted into that between l'Espinasse and Bordeu. In *Jacques le fataliste* we have the innkeeper who speaks alternately as a story-teller and as an innkeeper. And the same *dédoublement* can be discerned with Diderot himself: he may introduce the public as speaker (e.g. in his "Ceci n'est pas un conte"), or he may address his own subject matter or the protagonists of his tale: the first takes place in his *Regrets sur ma vieille robe de chambre* (on which Sainte-Beuve has frowned: "l'apostrophe me gâte le naturel"), the second, in the article "Jouissance" and in the essay *Sur les femmes*.

Again, since a dream, like the conversation of a fool, is no more and no less coherent than conversation in general, and reflects the totality of life, Diderot can, in *Le rêve de D'Alembert*," entrust a discussion of the totality of life to a conversation on a dream—the conversation and the dream having equal validity. We learn in this dialogue how a discovery has come to the scientist in his sleep: to D'Alembert, who had recently noticed a spider in the center of its web, the same pattern reappears in his dream, where he sees the organization of the unit called man as a network of sensations centered around one point. The conclusions which Bordeu and Mlle. de l'Espinasse develop logically from the incoherent words spoken by D'Alembert in his sleep, the latter has discovered as a consequence of his physiologically conditioned state of mind. After he has waked up, he listens rather passively to the logical exposition of the two partners who now tell him what he had already elaborated, subconsciously. We have here a bifurcation of the scientist's nature: the instinctive, intuitive (physiological) part of D'Alembert speaks out of his dream; the rational, theoretical part is expressed by the two partners. Here, Diderot has given dramatic expression to a saying of his (quoted by Schalk, p. 135, from the *Encyclopédie*): "Le génie porte naturellement son flambeau, et l'esprit qui ne suit pas avec la même vitesse reste en arrière et tâtonne dans les ténèbres"; we may also compare the sentiment expressed in a letter to Sophie (Ledieu, p. 91) which must have been written at the time of the *Rêve*: "Heureux celui qui a reçu de la nature une âme sensible et mobile! . . . C'est son coeur qui lie ses idées. . . . Cela tient du délire et ce n'est point du délire; cela tient du rêve et ce n'est point le rêve; ce sont les fils du réseau [the simile of the spider] qui commandent à leur origine; le maître se résout à la condition d'interprète."

Thus D'Alembert the theoretician must go to school to his intuition.

40. Paul Valéry, in his article on Montesquieu (in *Variété*, II) has come to approximately the same conclusions regarding the characteristics of the eighteenth century: this was, for him, the period of "the beginning of the end of a social arrangement," when the existing order was still enjoyed though, at the same time, there was a longing for freedom and disorder—which was afforded by the criticism of the existing order: "Alors, entre l'ordre et le désordre, règne un moment délicieux. . . . C'est l'heure de la jouissance et de la consommation générale. . . . Une flamme encore féerique, qui se développera en incendie, s'élève et court sur la face du monde. Elle éclaire bizarrement la danse des principes et des ressources. Les moeurs, les patrimoines fondent. Les mystères et les trésors se font vapeurs. Le respect se dissipe, et toutes les chaînes s'ammollissent dans cette ardeur de vie et de mort qui va croître jusqu'au délire."

41. Since it is true that the mobility we have observed in Diderot's writing belongs to a general tendency of eighteenth-century philosophy, it might be wondered if what has been pointed out as peculiar to Diderot may not also be observed in the writings of his contemporaries. And yet, even with a writer who was so akin intellectually and temperamentally to Diderot as was La Mettrie (the two were not friends, perhaps because of this very similarity), it is possible to see how "mobility" takes on an aspect quite different from that which we have noted with Diderot. For example, in La Mettrie's writing, nowhere have I found any indication that the rhythm of his periods is informed by his basic concept of the mechanical in man. What seems to me most conspicuous in his style is a certain "spirit of rapidity," the self-enjoyment of an imagination which delights in darting ahead unhampered; in the "exaggerations" of his descriptions there is a lightness of touch, a freedom of movement, which contrasts with the tension and exhaustion which Diderot's efforts so often seem to cost him. This "freedom" of expression is well illustrated in the two examples

below dealing with the play of the imagination: "Par elle [imagination], par son pinceau flatteur, le froid squelette de la raison prend des chairs vives et vermeilles; par elle, les sciences fleurissent, les arts s'embellissent, les bois parlent, les échos soupirent, tout prend vie par les corps inanimés ... elle ne marche pas seulement à la suite des grâces et des beaux arts, elle ne peint pas seulement la nature, elle peut aussi la mesurer. Elle raisonne, juge, pénètre, compare ... approfondit. ... Plus on exerce l'imagination ou le plus maigre génie, plus il prend pour ainsi dire d'embonpoint; plus il s'agrandit, devient nerveux, robuste, vaste et capable de penser."

In this continuous, effortless crescendo, the phrase "prend des chairs vives" is immediately expanded to ". . . vermeilles," and a little later to "prendre de l'embonpoint"; the imagination of the author himself delights in immediate expansion. La Mettrie must have been describing his own imagination when, a little farther on, he remarks: "Voyez cet *oiseau sur la branche*[!], il semble toujours prêt à s'envoler; l'imagination est de même. Toujours emportée par le tourbillon du sang et des esprits; une onde fait une trace, effacée par celle qui suit; l'âme court après, souvent en vain: il faut qu'elle s'attende à regretter ce qu'elle n'a pas assez vite saisi et fixé: et c'est ainsi que l'imagination, véritable image du temps, se détruit et se renouvelle sans cesse."

It is true that, in the following passage, he recommends the bridling of imagination; but he seems to have experienced none of Diderot's anguish over the destructive power of a too fertile imagination. There was a basic gaiety in his nature which preserved him from the existential fear by which Diderot was haunted; as Frederick the Great wrote at La Mettrie's death: "M. de La Mettrie était né avec un fond de gaîté naturelle intarissable; il avait l'esprit vif et l'imagination si féconde, qu'elle faisait croître des fleurs dans le terrain aride de la médecine."

42. It is by reference to Diderot's conception of the necessity of mobility, when the human mind is faced with reality, that we can best explain *Jacques le fataliste*, this replica of the *Don Quijote* novel, whose basic plot is built upon the principle of the interruption and correction which reality forces upon minds which have rigid convictions (e.g. the fatalistic Jacques) or proclivities (e.g. Jacques' master who, with his craving for "stories," would subject life to the fixed experiences of the past). In this book, the speeches of the characters are regularly interrupted by situations which ask for appropriate deeds; human speech, with its "fixing function," is shown as a factor which prevents man from coping with reality. The basic narrative device used by Diderot in this work is that of interruption of the speaker: the innkeeper, at the most dramatic stages of her story of the Marquis des Arcis and Mme. de La Pommeraye finds herself beset by trivial solicitations ("Madame? Madame? Madame?" - ". . . je vous ai défendu de m'appeler; appelez mon mari" - "Il est absent" - "Messieurs, je vous demande pardon, je suis à vous dans un moment")—a graphic demonstration of the exactingness of life that breaks up crystallized speech.

43. Needless to say, the critics who complain about the fragmentariness of Diderot's work (e.g. Sainte-Beuve, Reinach, etc.) forget that this fragmentariness is conditioned by the style of mobility which made Diderot see things in flashes and, also, was responsible for his indifference to publishing his writings—which he may have dismissed as momentary out-

bursts. Diderot was more interested in performance than in achievement, more interested in activity than in acts.

Another fallacy of the critics is to judge Diderot contradictory and inconclusive because of this same mobility of mind and style. It is true that the movement of Diderot's writing seems to follow no straight line, but moves in circles. Nevertheless, this gyration takes place around the same set of problems. And the problem of the mobility of the mind can be made understandable only by an artistic process in which it is reflected. The nature of the problem treated by Diderot has unfortunately led the critics to see inconsistency in his apperceptive mind.

It is also easy to answer the objections about the absence of "creative imagination" in Diderot ("creative imagination" being identified with the invention of plots) and to justify those digressions in Diderot's "novels" which arouse Reinach, for example, to such impatience. In order to illustrate the mobility of the mind, Diderot multiplies anecdotes and digressions; a ready-made plot would have subordinated the freedom of the mind to an external inorganic order. Reinach states of *Le neveu de Rameau* that it is a fireworks of which nothing remains but a momentary impression. But since the dialogue in question is concerned with the fireworks of the human mind, how could this be depicted save by "momentary impressions"?

44. That human speech in itself has a self-igniting force (we say in common speech that a person "warms up" to his own words) is well known. But Diderot has found a "linguistic mechanism" whereby to render it: the use of the accelerating noun-clauses introduced by an anaphoric *que*. The following passage pictures the increasing firmness of speech and of conviction on the part of the speaker ("Entretiens d'un père avec ses enfants") : "Le docteur Bissei, après un moment d'incertitude, répondit ferme qu'il le [a murderer] guérirait ; *qu*'il oublierait le nom du malade, pour ne s'occuper que du caractère de la maladie ; *que* c'était la seule chose dont il fût permis de connaître ; *qu*'il faisait un pas au delà, bientôt il ne saurait plus où s'arrêter ; *que* ce serait abandonner la vie des hommes à la merci de l'ignorance, des passions, du préjugé, si l'ordonnance devait être précédée de l'examen de la vie et des moeurs du malade."

Or, again, the speech may become more heated and vivacious the less truth there is to the words ("Entretien d'un philosophe avec la Maréchale") : "Elle me répondit que c'était une chose d'usage [to show one's décolleté] . . . *qu*'il ne fallait pas se vêtir ridiculement. . . ; *qu*'elle se laissait habiller pas sa couturière. . . ; *que* c'était la fantaisie de son mari. . . ." Or when the words describe idle dreams (*La religieuse*) "[the hopes of a nun are:] qu'on trouvera les portes ouvertes, un jour ; *que* les hommes reviendront de l'extravagance d'enfermer dans des sépulcres de jeunes créatures toutes vivants, et *que* les couvents seront abolis ; *que* le feu prendra à la maison ; *que* les murs de la clôture tomberont ; *que* quelqu'un les secourra. Toutes ces suppositions roulent par la tête."

Finally, the speech may consist "only of words," of gossip (and it is this variant of the *que*-clause which has led, in certain Romance dialects, to a fixed form suggesting rumor, gossip, etc.). In the following example the gossipy nature of the Mother Superior's conversation is also indicated by zeugma (*demander* is out of place after the first clause; the Mother Superior may not have distinguished, by her voice, between question and statement: she simply wants to rattle away) : "Elle [la supérieure] me demande comment je me portais; *que* l'office avait été bien long aujourd'hui; *que* j'avais un peu toussé; *que* je lui paraissais indisposée. . . ."

45. I have nowhere seen any reference to this rapprochement—which seems obvious to me. Mornet only remarks, by way of illustrating the opinion of the realistic school of commentators: "Jean-François Rameau— serait [sic] une sorte de faune non point mythologique, mais bien 'vivant.'"

46. The contagious quality of Diderot's mimicking style can be seen in its influence on Goethe, the translator of *Le neveu de Rameau*: in a note appended to this translation, in which he sums up the ideal characteristics of the French writer as embodied in Voltaire, we find a long list of qualities from which I detach only the following enumeration: "Leichtigkeit, Lebhaftigkeit, Feinheit, Brillantes, Saillantes, Petillantes, Pikantes, Delikates, Ingeniöses"—which surely sounds like an imitation of the prose of Diderot.

And the same stylistic contagion acts on Hofmannsthal when he defines Diderot's *Neveu* as an impersonation of life with all its contradictions (*Gesamm. Werke* III, 133): "Diderot, für den die Welt existierte, Diderot, der den Narziss Rameau schrieb, der die Gestalt schuf, die von Leben trieft und von Wirklichkeit strotzt und von mehr als Wirklichkeit funkelt, diesen Schwätzer Narziss Rameau, diesen Denker, diesen Schmarotzer, diesen im Innern unbestechlichen Richter der Menschen, diesen Lumpen, diese verführerische Seele von einem Menschen . . . für einige . . . spaziert er noch immer umher . . . und redet, redet, redet, und indem er redet, und klatscht und philosophiert und Komödie spielt und einen dicken Bankier kopiert und eine kleine Dirne kopiert und bellt wie ein Hund und dazwischen das Menschliche schmerzlich höhnt wie Hamlet und darüber lächelt wie ein Weiser Griechenlands—unter diesem strömt von seinen wulstigen feuchten Lippen, strömt von seiner nicht sonderlich edlen Stirn ein Etwas, das die Luft erfüllt, das Fetzen von Lebensmöglichkeiten herumstreut in allen Ecken, Fetzen von Liebe, Hass, Verachtung, Zärtlichkeit, Glanz, Jammer, Dirnenhaftigkeit, Reinheit, Gottähnlichkeit, jammervoller Verlassenheit . . . Leben, Leben, Leben. Welch eine französische Kreatur, welch eine menschliche Kreatur, welch eine zeitlose Kreatur, welch eine nicht wieder zu vergessende Kreatur!" It is as though the German poet could not speak of the *Neveu* without falling into Diderot's "automatism of enthusiasm."

5

INTERPRETATION OF AN ODE
BY PAUL CLAUDEL

Argumentum: One stanza (the first) from one poem ("La Muse qui est la Grâce"), belonging to a series of six "Grandes Odes," is singled out from the whole work of Claudel for stylistic interpretation—a stanza of unusual length (covering several pages) in which the author seems to set forth the purpose of the ode(s), and which, at first sight, appears oppressively dense and opaque. The linguistic detail which, here, served as the point of departure was the repetition of the epithet "grand," found five times in the selection. The five lines in which it occurs were found, when analyzed logically, to offer a skeleton outline of the author's program; when observed from the lyrical point of view, they revealed an ever-increasing intensity and breadth. This suggested that theme and rhythm must be considered together: the theme is that of gradual ascension and triumph (a two-fold triumph: that of man over Nature, and that of the poet struggling to conquer his subject), and this forward and onward movement is incarnated in the ever-ascending waves of the rhythm—as in the verbal motif-work. But, as one begins to follow the course of the poem, one sees that this ascending movement makes its way against an adverse current: the poet's expressions of determination and confidence in his solemn purpose are counterbalanced in the first part of the poem: we find successive outbursts (gradually diminishing) of petulance, which reveal a conflict in the poet (such devices as the repetition of "Laisse-moi . . ." !), as well as occasional shifts of tone from the lofty to the trivial and jocular. Both of these are due to the influence (from which the poet has not yet been able quite to free himself) of the pagan Muse, to whom he had formerly paid allegiance. Thus the whole stanza reveals itself as expressing a struggle between pagan and Christian forces in the breast of the poet—a struggle which informs also the other odes of the collection, and which is inherent in any attempt on the part of a modern Christian poet who would write in the form of an ancient ode. And, with this, we are brought to a comparison of

Claudel's Christian ode with the paganistic ode of Ronsard: where the latter failed, Claudel has succeeded in resolving the ever-present paradox underlying the reception by a modern artist of an ancient form. Whereas a literary historian, interested in his categories, may easily speak of "Christian vs. pagan poetry," this *versus*, this sign of a historical struggle of cultures, is reenacted in Claudel's soul and is embodied in the linguistic form of his poem.

> *"O grammarien dans mes vers!*
> *Ne cherche point le chemin, cherche le centre!"*
> *(Cinq Grandes Odes, 1)*

THE passage below is taken from the fourth ode in the collection *Cinq grandes odes suivies d'un processional pour saluer le siècle nouveau* (Paris, 1913), which deals, with variations, with the task of the Catholic poet in our modern world. Ode IV "La Muse qui est la Grâce" was written at Tientsin in 1907. The passage we shall consider is Strophe 1 of the ode, which is constructed according to a Ronsardian or Pindaric scheme: after an introduction there follow three "strophes" with their respective "antistrophes" (the first containing the words of the poet, the latter those of the Muse), and the poem ends with an "epode" which, like the introduction, reveals to us the feelings of the poet.[1] To this ode Claudel has prefixed the following "argument" (in which I have introduced references to the metrical divisions): "[introduction] Invasion de l'ivresse poétique. [strophes and antistrophes I-III]. Dialogue du poète avec la Muse qui devient peu à peu la Grâce. Il essaye de la refouler, il lui demande de la laisser à son devoir humain, à la place de son âme il lui offre l'univers entier qu'il va recréer par l'intelligence et la parole. En vain, c'est à lui personnellement que la Muse qui est la Grâce ne cesse de s'adresser! C'est la joie divine qu'elle lui rappelle et son devoir de sanctification personnelle.— [epode] Mais le poète se bouche les oreilles et se retourne vers la terre. Suprême évocation de l'amour charnel et humain." Here follows the text of Strophe 1:

—O Muse, il sera temps de dormir un autre jour! Mais puis-
que cette grande nuit tout entière est à nous,
Et que je suis un peu ivre en sorte qu'un autre mot parfois
Vient à la place du vrai, à la façon que tu aimes,
Laisse-moi avoir explication avec toi,
Laisse-moi te refouler dans cette strophe; avant que tu ne   5
reviennes sur moi comme une vague avec un cri félin!
Va-t-en de moi un peu! laisse-moi faire ce que je veux un peu!
Car, quoique je fasse et si que je le fasse de mon mieux,
Bientôt je vois un oeil se lever sur moi en silence comme vers
quelqu'un qui feint.
Laisse-moi être nécessaire! laisse-moi remplir fortement une
place reconnue et approuvée,
Comme un constructeur de chemins de fer, on sait qu'il ne sert   10
pas à rien, comme un fondateur de syndicats!
Qu'un jeune homme avec son menton orné d'un flocon jaunâ-
tre,
Fasse des vers, on sourit seulement.
J'attendais que l'âge me délivrât des fureurs de cet esprit
bachique.
Mais, loin que j'immole le bouc, à ce rire qui gagne des
couches plus profondes
Il me faut trouver que je ne fais plus sa part.   15
Du moins laisse-moi faire de ce papier ce que je veux et le
remplir avec un art studieux,
Ma tâche, comme ceux-là qui en ont une.
Ainsi le scribe égyptien recensait de sa pointe minutieuse les
tributs, et les parts de butin, et les files de dix captifs
attachés,
Et les mesures de blé que l'on porte à la meule banale, et les
barques à la douane.
Ainsi l'antique sculpteur avec sa tignasse rougie à la chaux   20
attrapé à sa borne de basalte noir avec la massette et le
ciseau,
Et de temps en temps il souffle sur ses caractères pareils à
des clous entrecroisés pour ôter la poussière et se recule
avec contentement.
Et je voudrais compasser un grand poème plus clair que la

lune qui brille avec sérénité sur la campagne dans la semaine de la moisson,

Et tracer une grande Voie triomphale au travers de la Terre,

Au lieu de courir comme je peux la main sur l'échine de ce quadrupède ailé qui m'entraîne, dans sa course cassée qui est à moitié aile et bond !

25 Laisse-moi chanter les oeuvres des hommes et que chacun retrouve dans mes vers ces choses qui lui sont connues,

Comme de haut on a plaisir à reconnaître sa maison, et la gare, et la mairie, et ce bonhomme avec son chapeau de paille, mais l'espace autour de soi est immense !

Car à quoi sert l'écrivain, si ce n'est à tenir des comptes ?

Que ce soit les siens ou d'un magasin de chaussures, ou de l'humanité tout entière.

Ne t'indigne pas ! ô soeur de la noire Pythie qui broie la feuille de laurier entre ses mâchoires resserrées par le trisme prophétique et un filet de salive verte coule du coin de sa bouche !

30 Ne me blesse point avec ce trait de tes yeux !

O géante ! ne te lève pas avec cet air de liberté sublime !

O vent sur le désert ! ô ma bien aimée pareille aux quadriges de Pharaon !

Comme l'antique poète parlait de la part des dieux privés de présence,

Et moi je dis qu'il n'est rien dans la nature qui soit fait sans dessein et propos à l'homme adressé,

35 Et comme lumière pour l'oeil et le son pour l'oreille, ainsi toute chose pour l'analyse de l'intelligence,

Continuée avec l'intelligence qui la

Refait de l'élément qu'elle récupère,

Que ce soit la pioche qui le dégage, ou le pan du prospecteur et l'amalgame de mercure,

Ou le savant, la plume à la main, ou le tricot des métiers, ou la charrue.

40 Et je puis parler, continu avec toute chose muette,

Parole qui est à sa place intelligence et volonté.

Je chanterai le grand poème de l'homme soustrait au hasard !

Ce que les gens ont fait autour de moi avec le canon qui ouvre les vieux Empires,

Avec le canot démontable qui remonte l'Aruwhimi, avec
    l'expédition polaire qui prend des observations magné-
    tiques,
Avec les batteries de hauts-fourneaux qui digèrent le minerai,   45
    avec les frénétiques villes haletantes et tricotantes, (et ça
    et là une anse bleue de la rivière dans la campagne solen-
    nelle),
Avec les ports tout bordés intérieurement de pinces et d'an-
    tennes et le transatlantique qui signale au loin dans le
    brouillard,
Avec la locomotive qu'on attelle à son convoi, et le canal qui
    se remplit quand la fille de l'Ingénieur-en-chef du bout de
    son doigt sur le coup-de-poing fait sauter à la fois la double
    digue,
Je le ferai avec un poème qui ne sera plus l'aventure d'Ulysse
    parmi les Lestrygons et les Cyclopes, mais la connaissance
    de la Terre,
Le grand poème de l'homme enfin par delà les causes secondes
    réconcilié aux forces éternelles,
La grande Voie triomphale au travers de la Terre réconciliée   50
    pour que l'homme soustrait au hasard s'y avance!

Strophe I opens after the poet has already been invaded by
the poetic frenzy, and when he is ready to formulate the task
he feels to be incumbent upon him; this strophe, in which
this formulation is developed, is addressed to the Muse,
whose answer, given only in Antistrophe I, sets up a conflict
which rages throughout the poem: viz. the question of the
estrangement of the poet from the earth. Though we isolate
this one strophe of one ode, the notes will provide the connections with the other parts of the ode and the other odes
of the collection.

An artistic unit such as this, startling as it must have appeared when first printed, is hardly less baffling to us today:
it offers the form of a sphere, whose unbroken surface seems
to yield no likely point of attack. For, whatever particular
part we may choose to concentrate upon, we are intimidated
from the start by the thought that this will always be only
a particular part, and that such concentration may impair our

understanding of the unity and cohesiveness of the work of art. But, if we think of this globe as a sun-ball, and of the particular points as sunbeams, we may be sure that, just as from any particular sunbeam we may infer the live force which sends forth all the sunbeams, so we will be able to penetrate from any peripheral point of the work of art to its core. It is my firm belief, corroborated by the experience of many exercises practiced in seminars with my students, where I chose to start from any particular point suggested by one of the group, that any one good observation will, when sufficiently deepened, infallibly lead to the center of the work of art. There are no preferential vantage points (such as the "ideas," the structure, of the poem, etc.) with which we are obliged to start: any well-observed item can become a vantage-point and, however arbitrarily chosen, must, if rightly developed, ultimately lose its arbitrariness.

Let us decide to start with the language of the poem—which, in itself, offers various aspects: the poet's syntactical license, his blend of popular and learned words,[2] etc. I shall deal first with Claudel's technique of "word-motifs," where the possibilities are still greater: I could start from any single one of the leading words indicated in the title of this collection, or in the title of our ode ("Muse," "Grâce," "odes," "saluer," "siècle nouveau")—all of which are repeated or paraphrased in our strophe. I choose to start with the epithet "grand" in the title "Cinq grandes odes . . . ," an epithet which suggests that level of poetic sublimity which is traditionally associated with the ode, and which distinguishes Claudel's ode from the lighter Anacreontic variety with which in France the genre has traditionally been confused since the time of the Pléiade. The epithet "grand" occurs six times:[3]

(1) O Muse! . . . puisque cette grande nuit tout entière est à nous

(22) Et je voudrai compasser un grand poème

(23) Et tracer une grande Voie triomphale au travers de la Terre

(42) Je chanterai le grand poème de l'homme soustrait au hasard!

(49) Le grand poème de l'homme enfin par delà les causes
secondes réconcilié aux forces éternelles

(50) La grande Voie triomphale au travers de la Terre
réconciliée pour que l'homme soustrait au hasard
s'y avance!

Three things are great: the night of inspiration (1), the poem
envisaged (22, 42, 49), and the progress of man (23, 49, 50)
—which shall be the subject of this poem. The purposeful-
ness and precision of Claudel's use of "grand," as illustrated
by these six passages,[4] is evident and could suggest that the
passages themselves have prominence in the architecture of
our strophe; and, upon examination, this turns out to be the
case. The first passage sets the background of the composition of our strophe (while also connected with the Introduction descriptive of the invasion of poetic frenzy); in the last
(which is the final line of the strophe) we are offered the
program of Claudel's poem—his *arma virumque cano*, which
he builds up for us piecemeal in the preceding four lines: we
see first a triumphal way traversing the earth, then man freed
from the accidental and, finally, the convergence of both
motifs in a triumphant apotheosis.[5] We could also speak of
five motifs contained in this program and which are basic
to the strophe: "homme" (11), "voie triomphale," "terre"
(23), "l'homme," "soustrait au hasard" (42)—several of
which we find repeated or paraphrased in these same six passages.

These six versets can be immediately reduced to four (1;
22-23; 42; 49-50), giving us three subdivisions of the
strophe which we may be allowed to call "stanzas"—although
no such indication is given by the printed arrangement. In
the upward progression of this strophe the lines we have
isolated represent plateaux breaking our climb toward the
peak whence we can envisage the final panorama of Claudel's
vision. Or if, remembering the surging flow of our poem,
which from the start engulfs us like an ocean, we may be
allowed to change our metaphor, these high ridges which
loom above the rest of the lines are so many crests of onrush-
ing waves, the last of which seems to prolong itself beyond

the limits of our strophe—whose final word is "avance!"[6] We may, perhaps, conjecture that by this rolling upward and onward of word-floods and word-waves, Claudel means to figure the progression and ascension of man in his conquest of Nature; not only will the poem tell of progress, it will, itself, vibrate with the rhythm of a progress which carries us along in its forward movement—an idea become poetic activity. Here we are reminded of the poetry of Péguy in which we find the same process of gradual expansion toward a climax (though with Péguy each climax leads immediately, without recession, to a new height). What Claudel and Péguy have in common is the Bergsonian sensitivity to the *élan vital* and to the flow of time; the theme of Progress is essentially a theme of Time. By both poets the work of art is offered not as something "tout fait," but as "se faisant" before our eyes.[7]

Who says rhythm says metrics. We will not find in Claudel any regular system of rhyme or meter. Language, with him, is not subjected to the coercion from without of preordained metrics, as is the case with orthodox French poetry; it is conditioned by an inner motivation and impulsion whose intensity and direction may vary at any moment. And the divisions which the poet usually indicates by metrical devices are here suggested by the recurrence of word-motifs—what we have called the flood-and-wave technique. Within the expanse of the strophe, which is like a sea sending forth its floods, there cannot be the sharp division of fixed stanzas—only the tenuous limits we have been able to discern by following the wave-movement to its crest: indeed, it is possible to find double or triple crests, as in 22-23 and 48-49-50. As for the "stanzas" so discerned, we may observe the diminishing size of the three units: the poem starts slowly, with a gradual acceleration of its course until the end is reached—which prolongs itself into the infinite. The corresponding efforts of understanding called for from the reader must be given a chance to gain sufficient strength for the final synthesis or apotheosis. And, to the progressive intensification of the reader's effort, corresponds a growing firmness on the part of the poet; the stiffening of his will is reflected in the variation of tenses suggestive of three stages of decision: (1) "Et je voudrais compasser un poème" (still wavering) ; (42) "Je chanterai le grand poème . . ." (prediction of a firm decision) ; (48) "Je le ferai avec un poème" (*faire* emphasizes the practical realization of this purpose).

Up to now we have followed the verbal-metrical scheme of the strophe only insofar as it throws light upon the ideological purpose of this proem. But in a proem there is generally present a second topos: in order to fulfill his purpose the poet calls upon the Muse for inspiration. In our strophe the Muse is mentioned in the title and in the opening line (as in Homer's Ἄνδρα μοι ἔννεπε, Μοῦσα, πολύτροπον) but, as the poem proceeds, her influence seems to fade; she is mentioned for the last time in lines 31-32, where the vocatives and imperatives addressed to her come to an end. It is as though the "flood" of the Muse-motif had completely receded at this point. But in our strophe Claudel's Muse is a force, not invoked for his help but, on the contrary, rejected by him; this attitude, strange enough on the part of a poet, takes definite shape as early as the fifth line: "Laisse-moi te refouler[8] dans cette strophe; avant que tu ne reviennes sur moi comme une vague . . ."[9] (here Claudel himself uses the "wave" metaphor —which, I may say, was not suggested to me by this line but occurred to me independently when I was attempting to define his technique). And the recession of the Muse-flood forms a movement contrary to the movement by which the program of the poet gradually takes shape: she is an antagonistic power in whom is incarnated all that he would shun, that he fears or loathes; the inebriation caused by the gods of pleasure, of licentiousness, of casualness (her animality is emphasized by *cri félin*,[10] line 5, and *le bouc*, line 14). Now, if we seek to discover a "Muse" word-motif comparable to that descriptive of the poetic program, we shall find signs of this only in the series of vocatives and imperatives (which suggest the presence of an influenceable being and which must cease when the poet's new-found determination releases him from dependence on the Muse) ; this being, who must be "refoulée," is distinguished by no motif as graphic as that which was used in allusion to the positive purpose of the poet. The presence of the Muse as it acts on the poet is indicated only indirectly by allusions to his attitude toward her, and this attitude expresses itself in words with a climate of their own. First, we find humorously slighting expressions and a particularly flippant tone, as though the poet, in a gesture of withdrawal, sought to taunt her and make light of his previous inclination toward her.[11] The particular flavor of this vocabulary, fickle, wavering, unprecise, is, perhaps, primarily due to the poet's state of mild intoxication inspired by the capricious pagan Muse—against whose influence he is on guard (". . . en sorte qu'un autre mot parfois / Vient à la place du vrai, à la façon que tu aimes").[12]

The poet is only "un peu ivre," not drunken (as he must have been earlier, since he fears being invaded again by the Muse: "que tu ne reviennes sur moi . . .")—not drunken, that is, with the heavenly enthusiasm and sweet frenzy celebrated by the pagan poets from Plato to Ronsard.[13] One of the first of the expressions used about the Muse has a popular, even a vulgar ring: "Laisse-moi avoir explication avec toi" ("thrash things out with you"), as if tipiness encouraged vulgarity, freeing the poet from the obligation of using the vocabulary of a cultured man. The teasing tone continues: "Va-t-en de moi *un peu*!" "laisse-moi faire ce que je veux *un peu*"; a pouting child that wants to be left alone would indulge in such stubborn, monotonous phrases.[14] Again, "quoique je fasse et *si que* je le fasse de mon mieux" has the deranged syntax that is to be heard in any French *bistro*. These humorous[15] expressions may seem at first glance strangely aberrant from the sublime tone characteristic of the ode. And indeed, the very fact that they are transplanted into an exalted environment serves to bring out in strong relief the lack of harmony and poise in the poet's attitude at this point: not yet having attained finality of decision, he can show his aversion only through (a humorous assumption of) childish petulance.

But humor recedes as a more serious guide makes an appearance—an anonymous force which bans the casual: "Bientôt je vois un oeil se lever *sur moi en silence* comme vers quelqu'un qui feint. Laisse-moi être nécessaire . . ." (as opposed to "avant que tu ne reviennes *sur moi . . . avec un cri félin*"). This silent being whose gaze he feels—and which may remind us of Hugo's silent eye of conscience—is evidently Christian grace, which will ultimately assume the role of the poet's true Muse and which now, mutely, within his conscience, rebukes him for his infidelity with the pagan Muse. And, with "nécessaire," the motif of "l'homme soustrait au hasard" appears for the first time; the poem, which will sing of man freeing himself from the casual, must not be casual. For what Claudel censures most in the pagan Muse is not sensuality itself so much as the arbitrariness of a spirit not oriented on Christian, on "necessary" principles. It would be a betrayal of his own nature to indulge in the irrelevancy of Bacchic frenzy or dionysiac corybantism (13-14); there is an insidious danger to the Christian soul in the laughter of Bacchus, "ce rire qui gagne des couches plus profondes"; laughter *per se* is, for Claudel, not "le propre de l'homme" (as Rabelais has declared); it is not "nécessaire," it is juvenile, worthy of a "jeune homme, avec son menton orné de. . . ."[16]

And now that the poet feels more free to follow his true and necessary nature, we will find again that technique associated with his positive purpose: word-repetition; "nécessaire" is the first wave which will ultimately lead to the "crests" of "Et je voudrais compasser un grand poème," "Je chanterai le grand poème de l'homme soustrait au hasard"—which can be achieved only after pagan enthusiasm has completely subsided. It is only gradually that this intoxication recedes: even after the poet has expressed his desire to write "un grand poème plus clair que la lune," the frivolous note reappears (though here, as always, he uses frivolity to exorcise the pagan world of frivolity): in verset 24 he describes Pegasus in words which limp, as if to mimic the erratic gait of this absurd beast (for, with Claudel, the heavenly courser of the Greeks, limps): "dans sa course cassée qui est à moitié aile et bond."[17] Here, the whimsicality of pagan poetry appears in the form of hybridism. And Claudel spurns the hybrid, which had been exalted in pagan poetry; like the medieval poets in their treatment of classical demigods, he (cynically) pretends to see in such blends only the imperfect and incongruous.

Now, after following the poet in his excursion into frivolity and animality, let us return to the line (9) where the motif "nécessaire" first appears. This impressive line is followed by a hemistich which may astonish many readers: after the poet has proclaimed inner necessity to be his moving force, we hear the request: "laisse-moi remplir fortement une place reconnue et approuvée, / Comme un constructeur de chemins de fer, on sait qu'il ne sert pas à rien, comme un fondateur de syndicats." The poet asks to play a role in society! This premium placed on *fama*, this acceptance of the "ut in pluribus" principle is evidence of the Thomist trend in Claudel; the inner necessity which guides him in his poetic activity asks for the complement of a necessary role among his fellow men. In Claudel's opinion, the poet should not be a peripheral phenomenon: he should occupy a place in society,[18] he should be necessary as a modern railroad executive is necessary, or a trade-union leader. And, since Claudel would like to join the ranks of the workingmen (to be himself a "writing-man"), he must adopt their language; his words have the bluff, hearty flavor of the speech of a Parisian workingman who talks straight from the shoulder ("on sait qu'il ne sert pas à rien")[19]—as "one sensible person to another." With this shift into the practical, commercial and political world of today, we are given the first indication in this strophe of the complex of ideas represented by the "siècle nouveau"[20] mentioned in the title of the collection: it is the material progress of our world which Claudel hails. The poet must not despise the world of his day, as Vigny did in *La Maison du Berger*, as Duhamel does in *Scènes de la vie future*."[21] But this gigantic program is not presented in one piece, a manifesto "tout fait"; it emerges only gradually out of conflicting tendencies; and the solemn resolve is first expressed childishly, almost petulantly ("laisse-moi *du moins*")—though it is immediately recast in accents of dignity: "remplir fortement une place reconnue et approuvée." The expression "art studieux" joins the ideological complex of "nécessaire" in its reminder of that laboriousness necessary to one who would be a workingman. The best examples which Claudel gives of the "art studieux" are drawn not from ancient Greece and Rome but from Egypt and Assyria: the Egyptian "scribe"[22] (which word is an etymological pun on *écrivain*, 27)[23], who was a tabulator, and the Assyrian engraver of cuneiform, bring to mind not the reverie of a poet withdrawn from the world but a technical skill which is socially useful (Claudel would share the professional pride of the Assyrian workman who rejoices in his skill), as well as precision of craftsmanship; from "pointe minutieuse," "attrapé avec la massette et le ciseau"[24] there is a smooth transition to "compasser (un poème plus clair que la lune)"[25] and "tracer (une grande voie au travers de la terre)"—which brings us to that main artery we have distinguished before. This vastest of enterprises which the poet envisages must be worked out with the greatest minuteness of detail, and this he proposes in lines which themselves have been chiseled with a painstaking precision that retards for the moment the oceanic sweep of the verse. The poet, then, must be an *écrivain*, a scribe—a simple "writing man." What Dante-like modesty (coupled with Dante's ambition) on the part of one of the greatest poets of all times![26]

With line 25, which is situated exactly in the middle of the poem, man makes his first appearance, in the phrase "l'oeuvre des hommes" (anticipatory of "l'homme," in 42)—as if to imply that man is the center of a universe created for him; this idea (which, for all of Claudel's disregard of serious pagan thought, is a Thomist derivate of the ancient πάντων μέτρον ἄνθρωπος will be outspokenly stated in line 34. In this same line, where the program motif "chanter" appears, we also find the last of Claudel's defensive "laisse-moi's" addressed to the Muse—whose "wave" must recede as his assurance gains in strength. His "chanter" is immediately followed by "et que chacun retrouve dans mes vers ces choses qui lui sont connues";[27] this is an echo of the motif "une place reconnue" wherein was suggested the poet's association with the practical things of modern everyday life—of which he will act as tabulator: "tenir des comptes" (27) may remind us of the duties of the Egyptian scribe. Thus, in Claudel's modest-ambitious definition of the role of the modern poet, there is no suggestion of a *poeta vates* on the scale of a Tyrtaeus or a Victor Hugo. Because the universe God has created is finite, the task of the poet can be only to recreate what has been created—or, better, to "take stock of" (*re-*

censer) things already existing. The ποιητής of Claudel is no divine artifex or Maker, but an artisan or recording-clerk, gathering together the work of God (drawing up a *summa* in medieval fashion); his public should not seek for novelty in his poetry but should recognize therein old familiar things.

But, though a tabulator rather than a creator, the modern poet must not abandon his lofty vantage-point, his eyrie, from which his gaze embraces infinite space, within which he can descry the single points. The poet is equally at home in the micro- and in the macrocosmos (26-28). In order to express this fusion of the macro- and the microcosmic, which is basic to Claudel's vision of the world, he uses a particular stylistic device discovered by Walt Whitman (after the way had been prepared by Gautier and Balzac): this is a presentative device which I have called, in a study published in Buenos Aires (1945), "chaotic enumeration," and which bespeaks the same inspiration, on another plane, as the modern department-store with its agglomeration of wares brought from the four corners of the globe. While the exuberant enumerations, the lists, the "catalogues" to be found with Rabelais or Quevedo still respected the distinctions between the different realms of Nature, the post-Whitmanian writer can enumerate things and thoughts detached from their frames, in order to evoke the plenitude of the world. Thus Claudel will list, among "ces choses qui lui sont connues" (note this pleonastic demonstrative, incorrect according to school grammars, which takes for granted our close association with "these" familiar objects): "sa maison," "la gare," "la mairie," "ce bonhomme avec son chapeau de paille," "l'espace," for he must keep "les comptes" (and here again there is an indiscriminate listing: "les siens," ". . . d'un magasin de chaussures," ". . . de l'humanité tout entière.") The whole and the part, the far and the near, the concrete and the abstract, the important and the inconsequential, can all appear side by side because they are fused in Claudel's vision. The more confusing and inchoate our civilization appears, the firmer seems to become the poet's grip on the essentials. But Claudel does not meet the confusion of our world by imposing thereupon a rigid orderliness of his own making: he is able to *accept* it without letting himself be distracted from the essentials: he can calmly depict the apparent disorder, for he sees it in a higher order. His faith remains unshaken. Evidences of this same faith that can so easily accept the juxtaposition of part and whole can be found in any Catholic church, where a painting presenting a single scene from the life of Christ, or of one of his saints, may hang side by side with one which represents the totality of God (the Trinity). And the juxtaposition of the sublime and the trivial ("ce bonhomme avec son chapeau de paille") is paralleled by the arrangement of those medieval towns in which, from out the midst of booths and shops and sheds, there emerges the Gothic spire—or, perhaps by the medieval mysteries in which comic and solemn scenes are made to alternate. By adducing such parallels I would seem to be assuming a religious inspiration for a passage which speaks only of the "choses connues" of everyday life and where the "Gothic spire" is missing. But I contend that it is indeed Claudel's religious nature which has enabled him to see together the trivial and the transcendental.[28] It is true that in our strophe the religious note is greatly subdued; but, later, it will sound forth gloriously in the poem.

But there is still another justification for the device of "chaotic enumerations" in our poem. According to the pattern fixed by Pindar, an ode must be rhapsodic, since this genre in contrast to others calls for the perpetuation, by the work of art, of the poet's original fervor: that "first fine careless rapture." In order to achieve this effect of enthusiasm, Ronsard, in his Pindaric odes, went to great pains to introduce drastic breaks (change of thought or of scenery) within his balanced stanzas; Claudel, having banned prophetic frenzy and Pythian obscurity from his poem, could not follow the Pindaric trend which Ronsard tried to imitate. It is the "disorderliness" of the chaotic enumerations, reflecting the diversity and fullness of the world, which offered the best approximation to the rhapsodic style of the ode. Thus Claudel does not, in the manner of the classicist André Chénier, seek, to make new poetry with ancient devices but, rather, to reach the effects of ancient poetry by means of new devices. His attempt is comparable with that of the modernist architect who designed the Catholic cathedral in Barcelona.

But now that he has defined the activity of the modern poet by inclusion of the trivial and the practical, Claudel cannot but think back to the idealism and sublimity of the ancient art which he has left behind him. In his last address to the pagan Muse (29-32), a new note informs his imperatives: behind him are the half-hearted, nervously joking maneuverings of self-defense ("laisse-moi," "laisse-moi"); now that he has decided to cut old ties, he is free squarely to appraise the totality of the being he abandons; for the first time he forces himself to contemplate her bitter beauty and sublimity; now he can call the Greek Muse his "bien-aimée," of whom he has loved the prophetic spirit ("ô soeur de la noire Pythie!")[29]—though admitting the bodily ugliness which must accompany prophetic frenzy ("et un filet de salive verte coule du coin de sa bouche");[30] the great Nike-like wings of freedom ("ô géante!"); and the winds of spaciousness that blow about her ("ô vent sur le désert!")—though he extends the background of the Greek goddess to include Egypt ("les quadriges de Pharaon").

But now the poet finds the strength and clarity of vision to oppose to the majesty, the enthusiasm, the propheticism, the freedom and spaciousness of Greek art, the fundamental objection of the Christian poet: Greek poetry cannot be ours because the Greek gods it praises have no "presence" (similarly, Lucretius had imagined the pagan gods as envious of man's reality), they have, that is, no action on man.[31] But, in the Christian conception of "natura rerum," all things are addressed to man's intelligence. And at this point the word-floods "man" and "earth" ("earth"="Nature," "things") again coalesce; "les oeuvres des hommes," "au travers de la terre" are revealed in their full dimensions: it is to man that the works of Nature have been addressed[32] (we remember the Biblical account of Adam completing creation by giving things created their names). Nature, that is, is as purposeful in her workings ("rien . . . qui soit fait sans dessein et propos") as is man in his—and as the poet, a simple workingman, must be, according to Claudel who opposes the dionysiac and the enthusiastic. Nature addresses herself to man through the mediation of the senses (Claudel shares the Thomist, the non-Kantian [originally Greek] trust in the senses, the belief that "nihil est in intellectu quod non fuerit in sensu"); the observations carried out by means of the senses contain the results of an intellectual admixture of a "continued" intelligence, penetrate to the elements of Nature.[33] It is characteristic of the Thomist Claudel that he sees religious belief as based not on emotional and mystical fervor, not on a feeling of union with the divine which is realized in moments of rapture, but on the workings of human intelligence in the practical everyday world—progress promoted by intelligence is seen by Claudel as working to the glory of God. In the line "pour l'analyse de l'intelligence continuée avec l'intelligence qui la / Refait de l'élément qu'elle récupère," Claudel means to emphasize the motif of the continuity of the exercise of intelligence by his anaphoric repetition of *re-* in *refait* and *récupère*; the *re-* suggests the re-creation by man of what God has first created.[34] The continuity which, according to Christian belief, is established between the sense-data (Nature), the senses, and the intelligence of man, is precisely the opposite of the pagan presencelessness of the Gods. Nature's presence is manifested in her continuous "address" to man's mind. The versets "Et je puis parler, continu avec toute chose, / Parole qui est à sa place intelligence et volonté" follow up the motif of "lumière continuée" (i.e. the poet continues the work of Nature), of "moi je dis . . ." (a motif which is soon to reappear in the "crest" verse 42: "Je chanterai le grand poème de l'homme soustrait au hasard": when Claudel says "je puis parler" we realize how completely he has become disenthralled from the pagan Muse), of "nécessaire" ("à sa place": this anticipates "l'homme soustrait au hasard"), and of "natura rerum" ("toute chose muette": this, taken together with "moi je dis," "je puis parler," suggests that the poet is the voice of silent Nature). Nowhere in our strophe is there any word of the Christian divinity; apparently we are offered only the operation of Nature (as in Lucretius' poem). But when Claudel opposes to the presencelessness of pagan gods the workings of a Nature present at every moment to man's intelligence, the Christian reader knows that this Nature is the creation of the omnipresent God. We realize that there has been taking place in the strophe a psychomachy in which silent, intelligence-directed Nature has calmly defeated the winged, majestic and prophetic pagan Muse.

The crest line 42 is surrounded on both sides by new chaotic enumerations of the achievements of modern progress, wherein the plan of Nature is revealed. We shall not be surprised to find that in these lists man-made instruments, rather than man himself, occupy the foreground: the pen of the scholar is on the same level as the prospector's instrument; the Ingénieur-en-chef is dwarfed by "le canal qui remplit": indeed, he is made superfluous by the automatism of his creation which can be released at the touch of a child. Man can retire from the stage which he has set, to allow the drama to unfold: the drama between the stage-properties themselves. And this "play" is, in fact, that of Nature: we do not find in Claudel's poetry, as so often in modern indictments of the machine age, engines opposed to "natura rerum": rather, engines, which are the creations of man's intelligence, represent the continuation of "natura rerum" which addresses itself to man's intelligence.

The first of the two enumerations is concerned with the rudimentary tools with which man first learned to extend his range of influence over Nature; in the second are mentioned the more complicated modern machines, along with the vast achievements which are due to these instruments and which serve, in their turn, to produce new achievements. And just as, in Claudel's vision, "rerum natura" and machines are reconciled so, too, are man and Nature: it is Nature who encourages man to regroup its elements into new combinations, whereby he is enabled to free himself from the given in Nature—while remaining true to her essential designs. Claudel can sing, not only ἔργα καὶ ἡμέραι as did Hesiod in primitive times, not only "Georgica," as did Vergil in a primitivistic mood: with his face turned toward the future he joyfully hails the progress of industry, and is able to see in the industrial achievements of our age the modern variant of the primitive industries hallowed by traditional poetry: all human industry, all "industriousness" bespeaks the continuous communion between man and Nature. And so Claudel, by regrouping the elements and the fabricants of Nature, is working in accord with this great design. He need have no fear of scientific positivism since man, as he sees him, has never lost contact with the supernal forces.

It is in the second "chaotic enumeration" (43-47) that Claudel's imagination is given fullest expansion: his eye roves near and far[35] ("ce que les gens ont fait autour de moi . . ."— "le canot démontable qui remonte l'Aruwhimi"; "les ports tout bordés intérieurement . . ."—"le transatlantique qui signale au loin . . ."), embracing panoramas and single concrete details ("les frénétiques villes haletantes et tricotantes" —"quand la fille de l'Ingénieur-en-chef du bout de son doigt . . ."), the perennial or archaic, and the modern which invades them ("le canon qui ouvre les vieux empires" or again "le canot démontable qui remonte l'Aruwhimi"), technical civilization and Nature ("avec les frénétiques villes . . . et ça et là une anse bleue de la rivière dans la campagne solennelle" : a blue patch of river glimpsed in the midst of the industrialized area),[36] the prosaic and the poetic ("le transatlantique qui signale—au loin dans le brouillard"). Claudel dominates the chaos of the modern world, not by reducing its confusing manifoldness and concreteness to a regularized, abstract, skeletal design (which has been attempted with greater success in painting than in poetry) but by subordinating this confusion to established poetic patterns—which, precisely because of their modern content, are difficult to recognize at first glance. But we may recognize in his chaotic or rhapsodic enumeration of modern industrial achievements, the old, the Biblical patterns of anaphoric repetition ("avec . . . , avec . . .") and of "parallelismus membrorum" (44-47); and, grafted thereupon, the more modern device of successive expansion of versets: in 43-47 the versets grow in size in proportion to the increase of the achievements of modern technics.

This whole enumeration is contained within the framework of the simple statement: "ce que les gens ont fait autour de

moi avec le canon . . . je le ferai avec un poème." How revelatory is the phrase: "je le ferai avec un poème": by means of
the preposition *avec* a parallel is offered between the poem
Claudel is to write and the cannon, the collapsible boat, the
blast-furnaces, the harbors, the ocean liner, the locomotive.
We have already accepted that these industrial achievements
are "necessary" fulfillments; now the full measure of their
sublime and grandiose nature is brought out. How great, then,
will have to be the poem which shall equal these achievements
of modern civilization! And indeed, in the closing versets of
this tremendous sentence, Claudel reveals in its final form a
poetic program fit for a Conquistador.

And Claudel the Conquistador aims at nothing less than a
poem of a Lucretian scope: he will treat "la connaissance de
la terre"—in which phrase we recognize the combined motifs
of intelligence (cognizance) and of things (Earth, Nature).
He spurns the Homeric model of "unnecessary" adventurings
in exotic lands; he will not celebrate a hero in his casual
rovings over the earth: indeed, he will praise not a single man,
but man himself and his cognizance of Nature.[37] The temporal
indication given in his rejection of the Odyssean theme ("ne
sera plus . . .") is followed up in 49 by the "enfin" (conspicuous by its unexpected position in the verse): "finally"
is said from the point of view of the poet's inner struggle with
the Muse which has come to an end, and also from the point
of view of world history: Claudel feels strongly that the
reconciliation of man with the laws of Nature has, in our day
at least, become possible—and his affective "enfin" bespeaks
the intensity of his desire to ally himself with this great
cause.[38] Claudel does not use the expression "[réconcilié avec]
les lois de la nature"; he speaks instead of "les forces éternelles," which, of course, stand for Nature. But at the same
time, these are more than Nature. For the eternal forces are
"above" the "causae secundae": they can be only the "causa
primaria," or God. And again, just as we have noticed in the
passage above dealing with the pagan gods "privés de
presence," the Christian divinity has been evoked indirectly:
simply by mentioning one member of a binomial he forces us
to think in terms of the other: "force éternelle" in itself could

be interpreted in a purely naturalistic manner, but once it is
opposed to "causes secondes,"[39] it serves inevitably to suggest
the supernatural. By using a term so suggestive of medieval
Scholasticism, Claudel has been able to evoke the atmosphere
of centuries of Christian philosophy.

And only now, "finally," does the full implication of the
title of our ode "La Muse qui est la Grâce" stand revealed: the
poem, which treats of man's secular progress, is a polemic
against heathendom and an apologia of Christianity—the
poem of glorification of Christian Grace has assumed the
form of a Greek proem only in order to reject the core of
pagan poetry—an apologia which points to the reconciliation
of science and religion.[40] The progress of the twentieth
century is welcomed in this new "carmen seculare" which
traces the *via triumphalis* of man who is about to enter upon
a new Augustan age of *pax christiana* (we remember that
our poem was written in 1907!). "Reconciliation" is the final
word-wave lifted up in the surge of the last crest line (50), in
which, as we have seen, all the motifs of the strophe have
been integrated. And the working of Christian Grace has
been shown as well in the liberation of cognizant mankind
from chance as in the poet's inner liberation from pagan
seduction: the "Muse qui est la Grâce" has worked within
the poem without ever having been mentioned by name
(though from the ninth line on her silent gaze has rested on
the poet). She can have worked only through the inner development of the poet who was brought from the petulant
"laisse-moi" 's addressed to the pagan goddess, through "je
voudrais," "je puis parler," to the confident "je chanterai,"
and finally to "[ce que les gens ont fait . . .] je le ferai," in
which his poetic activity is aligned with the good works of his
fellow men.

This strophe, which reveals the activity of Grace, is entirely given up to praise of man's activity; and this can be so
because, to Claudel, human achievements (of which poetic
achievements form only one branch) represent the intramundane workings of Grace. It is as if Claudel would have us
recognize the divine in what is close at hand, familiar to us
all; he will not encourage us to look away from the things

of the earth toward heaven. The very fact that Grace is here not explicitly mentioned can be taken as proof of Claudel's deep belief that man is the field in which Grace silently and efficaciously works—this Grace who is Claudel's true Muse.[41] (Thus, in contrast to the procedure of conventional poetry, according to which the Muse is invoked at the beginning, our poem opens with a rejection of the traditional pagan Muse—without, however, following this up by an invocation of the Muse which is Grace. For Grace does not come at our bidding; we must abide the miracle of its coming.)[42]

This poem, which is so strongly opposed to ancient enthusiasm is intellectual rather than mystical—it has, that is, the orthodox-Catholic approach to the divine. To Claudel, whose motto seems to be "intellige ut credas," science and technics are intramundane "ancillae theologiae." It is possible to speak here of a miracle: the miracle by which Claudel becomes more and more aware of the necessity and nature of the poem that asks to be written. But the "miraculous" revelation that unfolds before our eyes implies no deviation from the intellectual, consisting as it does in the very working of intelligence for the glorification of intelligence.

Among the attempts made in the last century to reconcile aspects of modern civilization with values of the past, we may remember Renan's *Prière sur l'Acropole*, in which he offers the tortured image of modern man wavering between a Christian faith sentimentally retained and Greek clarity which his reason affirms, and the *Invocation à Minerva* of Maurras, who harmonizes French classical *raison* with Greco-Roman *ratio* and order—while Giraudoux, in his *Prière sur la Tour Eiffel* (in *Juliette au pays des Hommes*, 1924), simply ignores any such conflict and speaks only in terms of the general preeminence of *French* reason and taste. Claudel, for his part, without any similar symbolical localization, spreads before us the panorama of a pan-Christian harmony of reason and belief, offering us, in this panorama, the most "total" vision of our modern civilization I know of. Indeed, this is Claudel's *summa*, it ranks with such poems as the *Commedia*, as *Faust* and *Lear*; it is a "Weltgedicht," a world-ode. Such a *summa* must contain all the main strivings of the epoch it reflects and, if we survey the whole range of our strophe, we will see that no essential is missing here: we find references to art, to religion, technics, science, nature, society (and the relationship of these with art); the professions are fully represented, including that of the poet; the wide sweep and intricate nature of our civilization is revealed, its history and that of mankind (Egypt, Assyria, Greece, Japan; Rome is mentioned later in the ode); the spirit of Christianity blends with that of the Enlightenment, of the Industrial Revolution and of imperialism. This strophe, which purports to offer the prospectus of a poem to be written, is in itself "le grand poème de l'homme enfin par delà les causes secondes réconcilié aux forces éternelles." A complete factual commentary would have to extend over many pages if it were to clarify all the allusions to historical and technical details which the strophe furnishes; this poetry rivals in factual density that of Dante, while the French poet loses sight as little as the Italian of things eternal. One might say that it is just because these poets have their eyes calmly fixed on eternity that they can portray so well the "man of the world" and the things of their own century: for them (as Auerbach has pointed out in regard to Dante) the fullness of God radiates through the manifoldness of this earth. Dante, and Claudel, too (in spite of his polemics against the Greeks), cast a Greek eye on this world; in fact, it seems to me that Catholicism has been the most faithful continuator of things Greek, particularly that vivid pictorial sensitivity of the ancients to things seen in our world. This continuation is really symbolized, as Santayana has suggested, in the significant name of that Roman church *Santa Maria sopra Minerva* (and perhaps Claudel cannot be exempted from blame for his failure to see fully his indebtedness, as a Catholic thinker, to the θεία κόρη Pallas Athene-Minerva).[43]

In this poem Claudel has offered Frenchmen an example of the "Christian Ode," a genre which, properly speaking, was only to be found in England with Milton, in Germany with Klopstock, in Italy with Manzoni. In France, Ronsard had succeeded in re-creating the antique ode characterized necessarily by "enthusiasm" (Claudel suggests his opposition to the Pléïade in the words "loin d'immoler le bouc"), while Victor Hugo had shown his complete misunderstanding of the nature of the ode by mixing this with the ballad. Claudel has been able to renew an ancient genre[44] and to retain its main ingredient, mythology, by substituting a Christian mythology concerned with the intramundane working of Grace. And, what is still more important, he has (as certain critics have stated), made poetry sing of Christian subjects more than one hundred years after Chateaubriand had made the same attempt in his poetic prose. The difference between the two procedures is that between pious speech and pious work: Claudel's ποίησις is a doing, the doing of a working-man (perhaps he had in mind this revelatory etymological pun when he made the comparison between the poet and the worker); and its pious incentive is blessed by Grace, whose presence we feel in the poem. Chateaubriand, with much documentation couched in aesthetic language, is forever advocating piety, but his pages of magic and sweetness cannot achieve the simple evidence of the presence of Grace. It is interesting to inquire into the reasons why the two apologists of Christianity had to come so late, and why it was necessary that their two undertakings were separated from each other by a century. We must remember that, since the time of Classical Humanism, French poetry had teemed with pagan themes; this was possible, in a Catholic country, precisely because it represented simply a literary practice which subsisted quite apart from religious belief—and this tolerance of pagan themes could continue so long as faith remained unshaken (even today, in a Jesuit school, the inclusion of classical studies in the curriculum—though they are rigidly separated from Christian studies—is held to be without danger to religion—just as, in Catholic circles, there has never been any fear of scientific Positivism: "render unto Caesar those things which are Caesar's, and unto God those things which are God's"). But, with the period of the Enlightenment and the development of positivistic science, Christian beliefs were shattered: it was against this background that Chateaubriand reacted, as, later, Claudel had to react against the period of laicism in which the state (and its schools) were separated from the Church (our ode was written two years after the laws of separation were enacted) : both poets voiced a reaction and helped bring about a "renouveau catholique." Claudel had to revive the program of Chateaubriand one hundred years later, because the Romantics had deflected poetry from the path laid out by Chateaubriand and had continued certain eighteenth-century (scientific or pantheistic) trends, which they endowed with a new poetic halo. Claudel sings of Christian values to a laicized world, but his attack on laicism disarms the opposing forces by declaring them ultimately God-willed: this lay-science, which had been so proudly hailed ever since the Enlightenment as an arm against religion, is accepted by Claudel as the preordained instrument of Christian divinity! Instead of impugning the scientific tendencies of our age he suggests another inspiration behind them; he does not, like Chateaubriand, preach the aesthetic values of Catholicism as offering a supererogatory beauty to earthly life: he discloses to us the continuous presence of the "cathedral" in the midst of the secular beauty of the workshops. What the lay institutions of the state have purported to protect, the labor of the common man, is now revealed as under the protection of divine powers. Thus, that scientific positivism in whose name the cudgels had been taken up against religion is revealed to be an intramundane form of religion: science and faith are reconciled.

Turning from the aspect of practical policy which must have been underlying Claudel's poem, to its purely literary significance, it may be observed that Claudel has restored in our time that "poetry of ideas" once practiced by Lucretius, Dante, and Rabelais; in this, he joins forces with Valéry, who considers the true subject matter of poetry to be not the "poetic" or the emotional but the "intellectual": that which offers most resistance to the alchemy of poetry. Claudel, however, while endorsing Valéry's program of extracting poetry from the shock and integration of ideas ("faire chanter les idées"), opposes the arrant agnosticism of Valéry by stressing the harmony of intelligence and faith.

A world-poem of today must evidently find a new form, evenly balanced between the conservative and the progressive, reflecting our own time while reminding us of the past. The old alexandrine[45] and the old stanza-forms were inadequate for this task; the first, Claudel replaced by the Biblical and Whitmanian verset, which offered the possibility of retaining the parallelism of Biblical style and the caesura characteristic of the alexandrine; the second was replaced by the "flood and wave" technique: a system of metrics in which the fixed forms of earlier literature give way to a Bergsonian flow; the language of such a poem must find a place somewhere between prose and poetry, since it is to show the integration of the prosaic and the poetic of modern life. The hymnic and the sublime characteristic of our ode had to emerge from the trivial; the totality of the vista implies the representation of a diversity of styles within the poem.

In our analysis we have sought to show the ascending movement in language; the network of the forces which determine the "waves and floods" was the task of this study[46]— which becomes superfluous once we have performed the mental activity imposed on us by the poet's words. Once the architecture of the work of art has been laid bare, the scaffolding, which the critic had to erect provisionally for this purpose, can be scrapped. Stylistics, as I conceive it, is an exclusively auxiliary science. Just as, according to Pascal, for him who knows truth no style, no "art de persuader" is needed, so stylistics (and the devices of suasion) must abdicate once the true nature of the work of art has been apperceived. A study of the kind we have attempted could have been made entirely unnecessary from the start by a simple recital of the poem, if the performer were able, by various pauses and intonations, to suggest the main motifs we have taken pains to distinguish, and to show, within the crystalline ball of the work of art, the play of the conflicting forces in the equilibrium which Claudel has been able to establish. For Claudel's poetry is, above all, an invitation to the listener to "reconcile," to harmonize its *idées-forces*—and to rest harmoniously in contemplation of harmony.

NOTES

1. It must be borne in mind that, in our ode, Claudel changes the tripartite scheme of the Pindaric-Ronsardian form in two ways: he replaces the sequence, repeatable at will, of strophe, antistrophe, and epode (the first two of which are equal in structure) by three sequences of strophe and antistrophe of unequal length and structure, followed, only at the end, by an epode and preceded by an introductory stanza; in addition, only in the dialogue between the Muse and the poet is there any alternation of strophe and antistrophe (in this way, the dialogue finds a form reflecting the to-and-fro movement of dialectics). This tight cohesive pattern may be contrasted with the leisurely air of Ronsard's "Ode à Michel de l'Hôpital"—at the end of which the author confesses that "the law of the song" bids him stop: he could have continued indefinitely with his system of loosely connected stanzas.

In the other odes the tripartite scheme is completely abandoned in all its original length, thereby improving the error of Ronsard who, misled by the contemporary editions of Pindar, thought to respect the Pindaric scheme by using shorter lines.

2. This was the starting-point I took in my explanation of Claudel's *Ballade*, the subject of an address at the convention of the Modern Language Association in 1937, which could not be published in its *Publications*—although the secretary had asked to have the manuscript submitted for publication—because the editorial committee deemed it "schoolroom work," not "scholarship." As though school-room work should not imply scholarship, and as though "scholars" are not tempted to err often in delimiting scholarship arbitrarily! The article ultimately appeared in the December 1942 issue of *The French Review*.

3. The epithet *grand* appears, in fact (together with the initial reference in Strophe I), in the introductory lines (before Strophe I): "Ah, ce soir est à moi! ah, cette *grande* nuit est à moi! . . . Voici le dépliement de la *grande* aile poétique!" (the last line suggests an allusion to the Greek Nike of the Louvre).

4. The epithet "grand" applied to our poem will, in later strophes, be expanded to "entier" (in Strophe II we find: "Et cependant quand tu m'appelles ce n'est pas avec moi seulement qu'il faut répondre, mais avec tous les êtres qui m'entourent, / Un poème tout entier comme un seul mot tel qu'une cité dans son enceinte pareille au rond de la bouche, / . . . Et moi c'est le monde tout entier qu'il me faut conduire à sa fin avec une hécatombe de paroles!"), and, in Ode v (as well as in the "Processional"), to "catholique" in the two meanings of the word: "Je vois devant moi l'Eglise catholique qui est de tout l'univers! . . . Tout est à moi, catholique, et je ne suis privé d'aucun de vous" "Voici l'immensité de tous mes frères vivants et morts, l'unanimité du peuple catholique, les douze tribus d'Israël réunies et les trois Eglises en une seule basilique."

The progression "great" > "complete" > "catholic" is a progression, to some extent, from dimension to integration and finally to the signification informing the integrated whole: Claudel considers himself a husbander of this vast, finite universe (Ode v: "Mon désir est d'être le rassembleur de la terre de Dieu! Comme Christophe Colomb quand il mit à la voile, / Sa pensée n'était pas de trouver une terre nouvelle, / Mais dans ce coeur plein de sagesse la passion de la limite et de la sphère calculée de parfaire l'éternel horizon." (This is also the main idea of Claudel's Spanish Catholic world-drama *Le soulier de satin.*) Claudel subjects this plenary universe to the limits of Catholicity. The "grande ode" is thus an annunciation of the Catholic Ode. There is a willful violence in this procedure of setting limits to the boundless universe and of making it Catholic in the narrower sense of the word: it is inspired by that same "passion de la limite" which the poet recognizes in Columbus (and which explains better, perhaps, than do the epithets "stubborn and obstinate" of the modern historian S. E. Morison, the reason for Columbus' misinterpretation of his own discovery).

5. Here we could use as well the metaphor of the path hewn through the forest: "la grande voie tromphale au travers de la Terre" comes to view only after the reader has fought his way through the underbrush of wildly luxuriant verse-vegetation.

6. Anyone who has watched the energetic consistency with which, at high-tide, the assault on the beaches is carried forward by the irregular succession of master-waves, while the weaker and less far-reaching currents provide *intermezzi* of relaxation, will realize how well this simile fits the rhythm of our poem, with its bold forward dashes, alternating with spells of calm, during which the poem rests for a moment, before undertaking a new attack.

7. In fact, we may state here that Claudel's collection of odes constitutes an *ars poetica* dramatically enacted. It is no didactic work like those of Boileau and Verlaine—or like Claudel's own treatise *Art poétique*—but an *art poétique* "se faisant," which develops before our eyes while the poet is wrestling with all the contradictory strivings which he feels in himself.

8. This "refouler" in Strophe I must not be confused with the "refouler" of the *argument*—though there may be a relationship of motif between the two cases: in Strophe I Claudel rejects the pagan muse, in Strophe II (which is resumed in the *argument*) he rejects the poetic muse as such because she distracts him from his earthly communion with human beings.

9. The "wave" motif has been prepared by numerous references, in the introductory lines, to the "sea," with which the poetic frenzy was compared: "Encore! encore la mer qui revient me rechercher comme une barque . . ." etc. And it is, as we have said, an oceanic impression that we receive from the opening lines of the poem.

10. This motif recurs in Strophe II, where the poet rejects the inspiration of the pagan Muse who receives no light from the Gospel: "les ténèbres et le chaos qui n'a point reçu l'évangile. / Ténèbres de la privation de Dieu! ténèbres actives qui *sautent sur vous comme la panthère*" (= the *incursiones daemonum* of the Scriptures).

11. If we were to state a literary model for the inclusion of the teasing tone into a serious poem, we could think of Victor Hugo's "Le satyre" (in *Légende des siècles*)—especially of its first part where the satyr, who later is to become Pan and thus mightier than the Gods, is facetiously introduced as though seen from the point of view of the Gods before they have realized his power.

But nothing could be further from Claudel than the state of mind of a

Hugo who seems to suggest (though without full conviction or convincingness) that a satyr-like animality is the source of art, science, political freedom. *Pace* Thibaudet, Victor Hugo was not as "intelligent" a poet as is Claudel: his vague humanitarianism and his pantheism did not integrate. To use Claudel's terminology, Victor Hugo did not create the "necessary" poem.

12. Distrust of "enthusiasm" does not imply a lack of those qualities normally associated with enthusiasm: exuberance, power of expression, revolutionary striving for new forms. In Ode 1 Claudel declines to follow in the footsteps of Homer, Vergil (and Dante), when he says: "Rien de tout cela! *toute route à suivre nous ennuie!* toute échelle à escalader! . . . / O mon âme, il *ne faut concerter aucun plan*, ô mon âme sauvage, il faut nous tenir libres et prêts . . . / O mon âme impatiente, pareille à l'aigle sans art! . . . / Que mon vers ne soit rien d'esclave! mais tel que l'aigle marin qui s'est jeté sur un grand poisson, / Et l'on ne voit rien qu'un éclatant tourbillon d'ailes et l'éclaboussement de l'écume!" He hastens, however, to add: "Mais vous ne m'abandonnerez point, ô Muses modératrices"; that is to say, Claudel's poetic revolution amounts not to anarchy but to a new order. It is a revolution, nonetheless: Boileau's precept concerning the ode: "Son style impétueux souvent marche au hasard, / Chez elle un beau désordre est un effet de l'art" (which is concerned only with an *"effect* of disorder" given by a poem which should be, in reality, most well-ordered), is timid in comparison.

13. With this stipulation Claudel shows himself opposed to the "furor poeticus"—and this in an ode, the very genre for which poetic frenzy had been held indispensable ever since the rediscovery of Pindar by the humanists. We can see in these lines a direct rebuke intended for Ronsard (who has his Jupiter tell the Muse: "Votre métier, race gentille, / *Les autres métiers passera*, D'autant qu'esclave il ne sera / De l'art [= technical skill] aux Muses inutile, / Par art le navigateur / Dans la mer manie et vire . . . / Par art se font les ouvriers. / *Vous n'aurez de tel erreur;* / Sans plus, une sainte fureur / Polira votre science") and ultimately a criticism of Plato, who had put enthusiasm above *sophia* and *techne.* Claudel, by his theory (so at variance with his own practice and with the law of the genre of the ode he cultivates) that the poet should strive to be comprehensible to the average man, dissociates himself from the aristocratic poets of Humanism who despised the common people for their failure to grasp poetic enthusiasm (cf. also Strophe xv of Ronsard's "Ode à Michel de l'Hôpital").

14. In Strophe 11, where the poet rejects the Muse still more violently, the same childish *un peu* is repeated:

Ah! quoique mon coeur se brise, non! Je ne veux point! va-t-en de moi un peu! ne me tente pas ainsi cruellement!

and in the epode, where the poet finally turns away from the Muse, the *va-t-en* appears without the childish *un peu*:

Va-t-en! Je me retourne désespérément vers la terre! Va-t-en! tu n'ôteras point ce froid goût de la terre . . .

15. In other words, humor, with Claudel as with the medieval poets, appears subordinated to the sacred, whereas the paganistic Ronsard was able to introduce burlesque among the Olympians: in the "Ode à Michel

de l'Hôpital" he shows us an assembly of the Gods listening to the song of the Muses, with Jupiter laughing at Mars "qui tenait l'oeil fermé, / Ronflant sur sa lance guerrière, / Tant la chanson l'avait charmé."

16. We can sense here the paraphrase of a colloquial word (such as *béjaune*, *blanc-bec*, for example) as well as a transposition into Homeric style ("orné de . . ."!). We remember Claudel's words: "Pas aucune de vos phrases que je ne sache reprendre!"

The motif of the "jeune homme" recurs in Strophe II: "Alors ne permettez pas [ô Seigneur] à celle-ci [à la Muse] qu'elle vienne me tenter comme un jeune homme . . ." (here, without the epithet equivalent to "béjaune") ; cf. the parallel sublimation "va-t-en un peu" > "va-t-en" mentioned in note 14.

17. This motif of the "hybrid" nature of the paganistic poet is emphasized again in Antistrophe II, when the Muse, encouraging the poet to follow his path with the pride of a god, says:

> Afin que je te regarde et rie, et que j'imite, moi, la déesse, ton avancement mutilé!
> Je ne t'ai point permis de marcher comme les autres hommes d'un pied plan,
> Car tu es trop lourd pour voler
> Et le pied que tu poses à terre est blessé!

18. Here, Claudel is in accord with Péguy, the son of the *rempailleuse de chaises*, who always expressed pride in the craftmanship of the *homme de lettres* and who saw in Christ, the carpenter's son who did "de la bonne ouvrage," the patron of the intellectual.

19. It must also be remarked that the inclusion, in large periods, of such brief main clauses as though they were incidental clauses (a sentence-unification made possible by the breath), belongs to oral speech: this is one of the cases in which a great writer is able to conquer new areas of oral speech for artistic writing—which has a tendency to drift away from the spoken form. This incorporation of the spoken into the written is the great secret of innovation in writing. Compare in Antistrophe III: ". . . Jusque tu aies appris la mesure que je veux, à quoi ne sert point de compter un et deux, *tu l'apprendras*, serait-ce avec le hoquet de l'agonie!" where the interpolation is one of those benignly consoling sentences with which the Muse mocks the poet.

20. Claudel is writing a twentieth-century *carmen saeculare* as he will state later:

> Salut aurore de ce siècle qui commence!
> Que d'autres te maudissent, mais moi je te consacre sans frayeur
> ce chant pareil à celui qu'Horace confia à des choeurs de jeunes garçons et de jeunes filles quand Auguste fonda Rome pour la seconde fois.

Claudel's *carmen saeculare* will, of course, be a Christian and a Catholic one, in which progress and religion are reconciled: "un temple nouveau" will rise in the place of the French sanctuaries destroyed by "la pioche qui ne sait ce qu'elle fait"; "Je vois devant moi l'Eglise catholique qui est de tout l'univers" (to entertain such a hope in 1907, only two years after the laws separating Church and State had been enacted and when venerable sanctuaries were being desecrated, was most courageous). And he states in the "Processional":

> Je crois que Dieu est ici bien qu'il me soit caché.
> Comme il est au ciel avec tous ses anges et dans le coeur de la Vierge sans péché,
> Il est mêmement ici, dans la gare de chemin de fer et l'usine, dans la crèche, dans l'aire et dans le chais.

21. If, for a moment, I may step out of my role of linguistic-literary commentator of poetry, I may venture to say that this seems to me the most sensible view for a critic of our epoch to take. I have never understood the attitude of those critics of the mechanization of our world and of supposedly mechanized America, who see an unbridgeable gap between faith and technics. Duhamel, e.g. in his *Scènes de la vie future*, speaks with derision of the church he saw in Chicago which was located on the top floor of a skyscraper. What matters is that people preserve their faith and that they are not swallowed up by the machines: if the community *can* pray in that Chicago church, it is of little importance that they must use an elevator to enter the church instead of walking in through the front door. The moral significance of technics depends entirely on the moral purpose to which it is put: war or peace, irreligion or faith.

22. It may be noted that the two anaphoric *ainsi*'s in verses 18 and 20, introducing carefully developed "Homeric similes," correspond to the usage of ancient poets who compare (by means of sentences introduced e.g. by *sic . . . sic . . .*) the situation they are describing with parallels from the mythic or the historic past. But Claudel takes care also to vary the expression of the parallels by devices more modern: the "census" taken by the Egyptian scribe assumes the form of a Claudelian "chaotic enumeration" (*vide* later in our text); the picture of the Assyrian engraver is given in a *raccourci* by a participial construction ("l'antique sculpteur . . . attrapé") followed by an anacoluthon ("Et de temps en temps il souffle . . .") with the Biblical ring which will be described in note 30).

One would expect Claudel to mention the Greek and Roman epigraphists, who certainly did not lack a "pointe minutieuse," instead of the Egyptians and Assyrians; but we must face the fact that, in this context, the poet was forced to exclude a positive appraisal of the Greco-Roman civilization.

23. This is a medieval device, amply represented in St. Bernard and in Dante (cf. Schiaffini's book *Tradizione e prosa*), which Claudel has revived most felicitously. His equation *connaître - co-naître* is well known.

We may think that in this passage Claudel had another etymological pun in his mind: Lat. *ratio* means "accountancy" and "reason," hence Fr. *raisonable* "accountant" and "reasonable." Thus "tenir des comptes" can also evoke the ideas of "being rational, reasonable, using reason."

One may be reminded here of the words of the French historian Gabriel Hanotaux who asked to be no more than "le greffier de l'histoire." In Ode 1 Claudel defines the Muse of history as "Clio, le greffier de l'âme, pareille à celle qui tient les comptes." We may see in this idea the explanation for the outward biography of the poet: he can reconcile a bureaucratic job with his poetic métier. I, personally, am of the conviction that the idea was preexistent to his outward biography: celle-ci s'est mise à imiter celle-là. . . .

24. The motif of "massette et ciseau," a suggestion of technical precision, recurs in the following strophe containing the rejection by the Muse of Claudel's poetic program:

> Que m'importent toutes vos machines et toutes vos oeuvres
> d'esclaves et vos livres et vos écritures? . . .
> Ce n'est point avec *le tour et le ciseau* que l'on fait un homme
> vivant . . .

And, in Antistrophe III:

> Ce n'est pas *l'auge et la truelle* qui rassemble et qui construit,
> C'est le feu pur et simple qui fait de plusieurs choses une seule.

In Ode V ("La maison fermée"), the idea of the "necessity" of the poet, as well as the theme of the "accountant," recurs:

> Je sais que c'est moi qui vous [*sc.* aux grandes forces célestes]
> suis nécessaire . . .
> Et toutes vous êtes en ma possession, *comme un banquier* qui de
> son bureau de Paris fait argent avec l'écriture des gommes de la
> Sénégambie . . .

(Note the colloquialism *faire argent* and the bureaucratic flavor of *écriture!*) In *Positions et propositions*, I, 19, Claudel explains the French aversion to excess and superfluity, as a "besoin de nécessité," deeply rooted in the French national character: "Le Français a horreur du hasard, de l'accidentel et de l'imprévu. . . . Il a le besoin de justifier devant lui-même chacun de ces actes, et, avisé d'ailleurs des regards acérés que chacun de ses voisins dirige sur lui, il s'arrange comme s'il avait à répondre à une accusation continuelle de détournement et de gaspillage. Le Français s'est toujours senti actionnaire d'une société dont chaque membre *doit des comptes* à tous les autres. Il ne veut rien laisser perdre. Un bien inutile et gâché, un agrément qu'on se donne, lui paraissent de mauvaises actions." What he is describing here is the Jansenist streak in the French national character.

25. Why should Claudel's poem be "clear like the moon," not "like the sun"? Evidently, not only because the Muse traditionally appears at night (a fact which troubled so greatly Alfred de Musset, who wished us to visualize in his *Nuits* the rebirth of Nature and his own nature-like spiritual rebirth—at night!), but mainly because the moonlight is clearly defined, cool and calm, not diffused, and not dazzling like that of the sun; and because the *via triumphalis* Claudel wants to draw must be coolly, calmly designed, must be clear-cut and sharply visible in the midst of the maze of the earth.

The simile of the "scribe" may have been prompted by Scriptural passages such as Ps. XLIV: "Lingua mea calamus scribae, velociter scribentis" which is interpreted by St. Jerome in Ep. LXV (Migne, *Patr. lat.*, XXII, 627): "Debeo ergo et linguam meam quasi stilum et calamum preparare, ut per illam in corde et auribus audientium scribat Spiritus Sanctus." Claudel, however, with his aversion to enthusiasm will not be the "stenographer writing (*velociter!*) under the dictation of the Holy Spirit": he will adopt only the skill and meticulousness of the scribe.

Claudel's poetry admits of no ambiguity behind which the poet may hide: he addresses himself to the whole of the nation and of humanity, and takes pride in being understood. His is not the "Mes-vers-ont-le-sens-qu'on-leur-prête" attitude of the esoteric Valéry, who could smile as he sat in the balcony of that Sorbonne amphitheater listening to Gustave Cohen explaining one of his poems. Claudel's poetry can be clearly, unambiguously explained—as we are trying to do here.

26. Similarly, Claudel's contemporary, Valéry, also insists on the ideal of "craftsmanship" for the modern artist, as opposed to the ideals of the enthusiastic romantic poetry of yore. And, today, one hears that the great and original Stravinski asks to be considered as a "craftsman," to the indignation of the lesser and more conventional Malipiero who retains the name of "musician."

27. In the introductory lines (before Strophe 1) Claudel himself says:

Les mots que j'emploie, ce sont les mots de tous les jours, et ce ne sont point les mêmes
Vous ne trouverez point de rimes dans mes vers ni aucun sortilège. Ce sont vos phrases mêmes. Pas aucune de vos phrases que je ne sache reprendre! [note the vulgarism *pas aucune!*]
Ces fleurs sont vos fleurs et vous dites que vous ne les reconnaissez pas?

In Antistrophe 1 the public is shown in its incapacity to understand, i.e. to recognize the things presented by the poet who is, at the moment of writing, under the impact of enthusiastic frenzy: he sees "Les choses comme elles sont et comme elles ne sont pas et les gens commencent à ne pas comprendre ce qu'il dit." In Ode v the public, recalcitrant to Claudel's esoteric poetry, is presented as saying: "Est-ce langage d'un homme ou de quelque bête? / Car nous ne reconnaissons plus avec toi, ces choses que nous t'avons apportées."

If we should attempt to define, in terms of the Roman tradition, the position claimed by Claudel for the poet, it would be neither that of the poets in archaic Rome (of whom it was said "in quibus nulla solida utilitas omnisque puerilis delectatio"), nor that of the *vates*, who is above society, claimed by Horace ("odi profanum vulgus et arceo"). Claudei looks upon his poetic activity as a *negotium* exercised in the interests of the people (cf., for these oppositions, Dag Norberg, *L'Olympionique, le poète et leur renom éternel*, Uppsala 1945). Thus the words of Claudel's poems will be those of Everyman.

One could also define Claudel's intention in Christian terms, if we remember the Church Fathers who ascribed to the Scriptures a style that "condescendit . . . ad eorum inscitias qui non intelligunt, et *simplici atque planiore atque usitato sermone* utitur, ut possit intelligi" (Ambrose); this is a language which, because of its clarity, wields all the more authority the more widely it is read: "et omnibus ad legendum esset in promptu . . . *verbis apertissimis et humillimo genere loquendi* se cunctis praebens . . . *ut exciperet omnes populari sinu* . . . multo . . . plures quam si non tanto epice auctoritatis emineret nec turbas gremio sanctae humilitatis hauriret" (Augustine: cf. Auerbach, "Sacrae scripturae sermo humilis" in *Istanbuler Schriften* no. 5, 1944)—terms which have been echoed by hundreds of medieval poets (e.g. Berceo: "Quiero fer una prosa en roman paladino, / en cual suele el pueblo hablar con su vecino"; "quiero fer la pasion de Sant Laurent / en romanz, que la pueda saber toda la gent").

28. Evidence that the chaotic enumeration is in Claudel a development of the conception of the omnipresence of God in creation can easily be seen from this stanza of the "Processional":

> Je crois que Dieu est *ici* bien qu'il me soit caché,
> Comme il est au ciel avec tous ses anges et dans le coeur de la Vierge sans péché,
> Il est mêmement ici, dans la gare de chemin de fer, et l'usine, dans la crèche, dans l'aire et le chais.

It is significant that here the manger is referred to, not together with Heaven or the heart of the Virgin, but with the railway station and the wine-cellar. And the *ici* is most striking, which conjures up a momentary proximity, here, now, of all these disparate things which are inhabited by God.

Again, we find, in the "Processional," an enumeration of the saints:

> Voici tous les Saints du calendrier, répartis sur les quatres Saisons,
> Les saints de glace et de braise, et ceux qui annoncent la sortie des bêtes et la fenaison,
> Saint Médard et Saint Barnabé, Saints Crépin et Crépinien de Soissons,
> Saint Martin et Saint Vincent des vignerons, Sainte Macre de Fère-en-Tardenois où est la fête de ce bourg,
> Et Sainte Luce en décembre où le jour est plus court.

Though the choice of these saints is evidently determined by a definite pattern (the four seasons are represented, and the saints named are all patrons of labor), still the immediate impression is one of disorder and arbitrary selection—which serves impressively to evoke the richness of the Catholic calendar, able to furnish every day of the year with its saint, so that the menial can be continuously pervaded by the transcendental. (The patriotic note is inescapable in this list of exclusively French saints; we may also discern a parochial sentiment in "Sainte Macre de Fère-en-Tardenois où est la fête de ce bourg": Claudel, writing these words in China, visualizes, in immediate proximity, the annual feast-day in "ce bourg.")

For Claudel, no barrier between the two realms of the transcendental and the trivial is allowed to stand; the most daring example of barriers annihilated may be seen in the lines below from Ode v, in which he is depicting the solitary and silent immersion of his soul in Christ: "Moi tout seul, tout en bas, éclairant la face du grand Christ de bronze *avec un cierge de 25 centimes.*"

29. In this allusion Claudel has coupled the prophetic with the poetic enthusiasm. Plato, in addition to these, speaks of two other enthusiasms, those of the *mystes* and of the lover (and the same four are to be found, listed rather inorganically by Ronsard in his "Ode à Michel de l'Hôpital"). The enthusiasm of the *mystes* is also found in our strophe where it is represented by the dionysiac element—which Claudel wishes to repress. And the enthusiasm of love is embodied in the Muse who tempts the poet as a woman (Antistrophe 1: "Et moi, je suis une femme entre les femmes").

"La Muse" in our strophe (i.e. the pagan Muse) is evidently Erato, the muse of love songs, who had earlier (Ode 1) abducted the poet to her ship.

30. The anacoluthon in "ô soeur de la noire Pythie qui broie . . . *et un filet de salive verte coule* . . ." is figurative of disharmony: it is as though, in the phenomenon of prophetic enthusiasm, the bodily declares itself anarchically independent. Again, in the anacoluthon of line 26: "Comme de haut on a plaisir à reconnaître sa maison, . . . mais l'espace autour de soi est immense!" the syntactical yoke is shaken off by the exclamatory phrase: it is as though there is no easy transition from the pettiness of small-town existence to the immensity of space. Thus intellectual objections are figuratively mirrored by an anarchic syntax.

The most remarkable case of anacoluthon is offered by "Comme l'antique poète parlait de la part des dieux privés de présence, / Et moi je dis qu'il n'est rien dans la nature . . ." (33-34), where the flow of the sentence alluding to Lucretius is broken up by the impact of the phraseology of Jesus ("but I say unto you"). The anacoluthon, as found in Claudel, usually represents the deliberate introduction of the oral style into the written—though, at the same time, Claudel exploits the patterns hallowed by Biblical and Homeric traditions.

31. Cf. Lucretius, III, 18 *seq.*: "apparet divum numen sedesque quietae, / quas neque concutiunt venti nec nubila nimbis / aspergunt . . ."; II, 1039 *seq.* "nam pro sancta deum tranquilla pectora pace, / quae placidum degunt aevom vitamque serenam"—it is well-known that Lucretius, like his teacher Epicurus, sought not "to put the Greek gods into retirement as ex-service rulers, but to establish them as the images and prototypes of the Epicurean sage" (P. Friedländer, *Transact. of the Am. Phil. Ass.,* LXX, 373). This very life of the gods in the *intermundia,* without influence on the universe, but also without its griefs, must evidently have appeared to Claudel, who is conversant with the Judeo-Christian omnipresent God in whose "face" (= presence) everything on earth and in Heaven happens, as a "lack of presence." (Paradoxically enough Claudel uses, in denying real, spiritual presence to the pagan gods, the very word which for the ancients denoted their helpfulness: cf. such Latin phrases as *numina praesentia, praesentes divi,* etc.)

The reference to Lucretius as to a pagan poet superseded by Christianity, is quite outspoken in the following lines of Ode v:

> Maintenant je puis dire, mieux que le vieux Lucrèce: Vous n'êtes plus, ô terreurs de la nuit!
> Ou plutôt comme votre saint Prophète: "Et la nuit est mon exaltation dans mes délices!
> Réjouis-toi, mon âme, dans ces vers ambrosiens!"
> Je ne vous crains point, ô grandes créatures célestes! Je sais que c'est moi qui vous suis nécessaire . . .

This idea of a Nature who needs Man complements that of Nature addressed to Man.

32. The wording "il n'est rien dans la nature qui soit fait sans dessein et propos à l'homme adressé" is resumed in Antistrophe II when the Muse who has become Grace says: "Entre tous les êtres qui vivent, je suis la parole de grâce qui est adressée à toi seul" (and in the *argument*: "c'est à lui [au poète] personnellement que la Muse qui est la Grâce ne

cesse de s'adresser"). It is significant that what was the action of Nature has, in the progress of the poem, become that of Grace.

33. When Claudel presents the visual and acoustic senses as "intelligent" senses, he must have had in mind the Thomist hierarchy of senses in which the highest are those which involve material alteration of the sensing organ by the things sensed, the accuracy of the eye being the closest to the operation of the intellect (cf. E. Gilson, *Le Thomisme*, p. 201).

It may be assumed that here Claudel offers a paraphrase of the Thomist *vis cogitativa*, an "internal sense" (on one level with imagination, memory, etc.), and therefore superior to the external senses, but still a sense and, accordingly, inferior to the operations of the intellect and separated therefrom by an unbridgeable gulf because it is directed toward the individual and the material, whereas the intellect is directed toward the universal and the immaterial. In the following lines, we see how a modern psychologist versed in Thomism defines one of the activities of the *vis cogitativa* (Rudolf Allers, "Intellectual Cognition" in *Essays in Thomism*, New York, 1942) : "Whenever the value-aspect of a thing is emphasized it is the *vis cogitativa* which is operative. To act upon something, the psychological power must have got hold of this value-content . . . [St. Thomas] frequently refers to the *vis cogitativa* as a *ratio particularis* and assigns it the task of co-operating with the rational faculties in the formation of judgments pertaining to action. Action by its very nature is destined to realize some value and, accordingly, presupposes an awareness of the value as well as a capacity of referring the will to the particular good in question." Thus man, acting with his will upon material and individual sensorial reality (that is, isolating and regrouping the elements thereof, as Claudel speaks of doing in our strophe), is still operating on the level of the senses, with his *ratio particularis* or *vis cogitativa*: he has not yet lifted himself up to the spheres of intellectual cognition of the immaterial and the universal. And Claudel, in our collection, reaches only in Ode v the stage of cognizing the universal and the immaterial. In our strophe the most important words are "at their place"—where we have to do with the pattern of medieval gradualism which stabilizes things at the "right place." The "word of the poet," on one level with the element isolated by the scientist, is the field for the *vis cogitativa* which, as Allers has said, "co-operates" with reason, but is not identical therewith.

34. It is time for us to recapitulate what the prefix re- means to our poet, who is so "prefix-conscious" (cf. his well-known puns on *connaître - conaître*, on *com-poser*, etc.). The words with re- which Claudel uses are apt to be words quite current in French but, by repetition or groupment and by semantic expansion, he is able to create a *re-*cluster which reflects a group of ideas dear to him. Any single formation may be unobtrusive but, when all are taken together, they have an impressive power.

First, the poet declares himself to be simply a "recenseur" (similar to the Egyptian scribe, 18), a garnerer of things existing and already created in a finite world. In Ode II he will say: "J'ai recensé l'armée des cieux et j'en ai dressé l'état . . . J'ai tendu l'immense rets de ma connaissance" (note the reference to a net, which, with its clear lines, delimits the catch). When he speaks of the martyrs of whom he will sing (in "Processional"), it is of those "dont les noms sont recensés au ciel et sur nos diptyques."

Secondly, since the poet is not a creator but a re-creator, the public that listens to him must "recognize" the things already created: "et que

chacun dans mes vers retrouve ces choses qui lui sont connues" (25)—
a variant of the passage, in the Introduction of our ode: "Pas aucune de
vos phrases que je ne sache *re*prendre! Ces fleurs sont vos fleurs et vous
dites que vous ne les *re*connaissez pas!"

Thirdly, the "recognition" as a procedure that repeats the process of
original creation is in the nature of our human intelligence, which only
continues the "intelligence of the senses" (36-37): "[l'intelligence] continuée avec l'intelligence qui la / *Re*fait de l'élément qu'elle *ré*cupère."
God's creation was the creation of the intelligent senses.

Fourthly, poetic activity is nothing but the continuation and repetition
of the God-given human intelligence: to integrate, in the catholic manner,
things garnered and catalogued ("recensées") brings unity into the poet's
own mind and into the universe as cognized by it: contrary to Corneille's
Auguste ("Je suis maître de moi comme de l'univers; / Je le suis, je
veux l'être . . ."), the poet Claudel gives freedom, the freedom of cognition, to himself and to the universe. In Antistrophe III of Ode v he announces his intention "De connaître Dieu dans sa fixité et d'acquérir la
vérité par l'attention et chaque chose qui est toutes les autres en la *re*-
créant avec son nom intelligible dans la pensée"; and he glorifies "cette
énergie divine de l'esprit qui ouvres les yeux, *Re*commençant sa journée
et qui trouve chaque chose à sa place dans l'immense atelier de la connaissance." He wants to be "le *rassembleur* de la terre de Dieu" (this is the
theme of Claudel's baroque drama, *Le soulier de satin,* in which he portrays the conquest, at the hands of the Spanish Conquistadores, of the
whole world by the Catholic God); "et moi aussi, toutes les figures de la
nature m'ont été données, . . . pour que je les *rassemble* dans mon esprit."
Thus the poet is only a copyist (another variant of the accountant or
the surveyor), comparable to the monk (of whom Claudel tells us in
Ode v) whose task it was to copy the Gospel and who, returning to his
devastated monastery, takes up once more his work where he had stopped:
"*Re*commence l'initiale d'or sur le diplôme de pourpre."

And finally, since all activity of human (and poetic) intelligence consists in continuing, repeating, retracing God's creation, the poet is a
"reconciliator" of what seems discordant ("le grand poème de l'homme
. . . *ré*concilié"). "*Re-*" is, so to speak, the principle by which, in the
medieval system of thought of an Alanus ab Insulis, the God-created
universe is kept functioning by Nature.

As for the metrical break: "qui la / Refait de l'élément qu'elle récupère,"
this is introduced to make us draw breath before the important word
refait, which stands out before us in relief; in "qui la / refait" Claudel
would have us pronounce *re-fait* with a distinct separation of the two syl-
lables, the stress being laid on the first—as is the practice of a French-
man in oral speech when special emphasis is called for. Thus, by
means of this metrical break, Claudel is able to indicate the intonation of
oral speech (in a way that is generally impossible with the usual system of
printing): oral speech and a technique of breathing. Here, indeed, metrics
does reflect the measure of human breathing, but the modulation here indicated is due, not to the limitations of human nature but to its "intelligence et volonté."

Compare the separation of the versets in the lines of the introduction
to Ode IV: "Ce n'est pas pour eux [les hommes] que je suis fait, mais pour

le / Transport de cette mesure sacrée." The words of the last verset are isolated from the rest and are held up above earthly contamination like a pyx. Again, the poet must pause for breath—which is a pause of reverence before the transcendental revelation. Compare also the lines in Ode v: "Faites que je sois entre les hommes comme une personne sans visage et ma / Parole sur eux sans aucun son comme un semeur de silence . . ."— the phrase "parole sur eux" seems to hover aloft over the believers. In Ode I, when Claudel imagines himself on the bark with the muse Erato, he exclaims: "Toujours / Plus avant, jusqu'au coeur de la mer luisante" —the quest "plus ultra!" adapted here to his own state of mind, must detach itself from the rest: it is "quoted" reverently.

35. We may note here a variant of the chaotic enumeration which is particularly Claudelian and, at the same time, characteristic of our time, in which distances are annihilated: the device of the "geographically chaotic enumeration": "le canon qui ouvre les vieux Empires" is evidently the artillery of Admiral Perry in Japan, the "Aruwhimi" represents Africa, the blast-furnaces are Pittsburgh, while, in the transatlantic steamboat we have an allusion to the ocean separating continents. Compare, in Ode v:

> Et toutes [choses] vous êtes en ma possession, comme un banquier qui de son bureau de *Paris* fait argent avec l'écriture des gommes de la *Sénégambie*,
> Et de la pelletée de minerai sur le carreau de la mine *antarctique*, et de la perle des *Pomoton*, et du grand tas de laine *Mongol*

(here Claudel adopts the capitalization of the ethnic adjective as in English, in order to make the geographic entities stand out more independently). And, in Ode II:

> . . . je tire, j'appelle sur toutes mes racines, le Gange, le Mississippi,
> L'épaisse touffe de l'Orénoque, le long fil du Rhin, le Nil avec sa double vessie. . . .

Again, from his *Art poétique* (1907): "Cependant à toute heure de la Terre il est toutes les heures à la fois. Pendant que l'ouvrière en plumes voit qu'il est Midi au cadran de la Pointe-Saint-Eustache, le soleil de son premier rayon ras troue la feuille Virginienne, l'escadre des cachalots se joue sous la lune australe. Il pleut à Londres, il neige sur la Poméranie, pendant que le Paraguay n'est que roses, pendant que Melbourne grille." (This passage is probably influenced by *Purgatorio*, XXVII, I *seq.*, where Dante states that when it is sunset in Purgatory it is sunrise at Jerusalem, midnight in Spain, noon in India; but Dante admits of no chaotic disorder: he merely points out the synchronic relationships of the four fixed cardinal points.)

36. How touching is this parenthesis which suggests a "parenthetical interpolation" of Nature and which seems somehow related to the main effect of the poem intended by Claudel; we were told that this poem should be "plus clair que la lune qui brille avec sérénité sur la campagne dans la semaine de la moisson"—the moonlight and the patch of blue river combine to the same color sensation of clarity and linearity, serenity and solemnity. Claudel sees the cities framed by Nature: in his vision the two

are not opposed to each other, but are fused—a fusion which is so characteristic of our modern landscape (I think I shall never forget the impression made on me by the noisy streets of Istanbul teeming with gesticulating and screaming Southerners and the solemn quiet of the Bosporus and the mountains of Asia—boundless beyond man's gaze). A still further step would be to see the landscape character of our modern cities themselves: for example the "canyon" of Wall Street.

Should "et ça et là une anse bleue" be constructed grammatically together with "avec les frénétiques villes"? That is, should we understand: "ce que les gens ont fait avec les villes . . . et avec . . . une anse bleue"? Evidently not. We have here to do with a quite independent expression "et ça et là une anse . . . !" and this syntactical break is indicative of the cleavage man has forced between civilization and Nature. The brusqueness of the break, however, is mitigated by the inclusion of the exclamation within the sentence structure.

37. It must be noted that Claudel's *carmen saeculare* is a glorification of his century, not of any one august personality of the times, as was the case with the poem of Horace, and with those of the court poets of the baroque age (Ronsard and Boileau) who had accepted this limitation. It is true that Claudel, in more recent times, seems to have descended to the obsequious level in his "Ode to Marshal Pétain" (which I have not seen).

38. Grammatically speaking, "enfin" is an ἀπὸ κοινοῦ: you may construct "le grand poème de l'homme enfin" (*finally* the great poem comes into being) or "le grand poème de l'homme / enfin . . . réconcilié" (of mankind finally reconciled . . .). Sometimes Claudel places an ἀπὸ κοινοῦ in a clause to which it would not seem to belong naturally, thereby suggesting two contrasting forces which draw, as it were, the adverbial phrase toward themselves with equal force—compare the *dans mes vers* in the motto of this chapter.

39. In order to realize the full impact of this line, we must remember that Thomist philosophy, while centering all activity of creation in God, recognizes, at the same time, that things created act out of their own impulse: this is the so-called efficacy of the *causae secundae*; it is a gift of God's love just as creation is the act of His power. Etienne Gilson (*Le Thomisme*, p. 174), represents the convergence of God's activity (that is, the activity of the *causa principalis*) and the activity of things created, by the simile of a hatchet swung by a carpenter: although the hatchet has been made and is wielded by the carpenter, it is undeniably true that the hatchet, the *causa secunda*, does the chopping. Claudel, faithful to Thomism, seems to share the belief that "detrahere actiones proprias rebus est divinae bonitati derogare." And, accordingly, he puts the *causae secundae* in the foreground; he feels, nevertheless, the estrangement which has taken place in the modern world between the *causae secundae* (our material civilization) and the Prime Cause. Claudel offers no complaint against the "evil" modern world; he simply works by means of his harmonizing poetry toward the necessary "reconciliation": "oportet omnes causas inferiores agentes *reduci* in causas superiores sicut instrumentales in primarias."

40. At the celebration of the 400th anniversary of the University of Marburg in 1929, I heard a Catholic delegate quote a sentence he had heard from the mouth of the Pope: "Gaudet ecclesia studio veritatis." Or, as Claudel would say: "Gaudet Deus studio veritatis."

41. It is worthy of note that Claudel does not use the Ovidian technique of metamorphosis: he states suddenly the achieved transformation of "la Muse qui est la Grâce." In the *argument* Claudel speaks of (a gradual) "devenir," but in the poem there is only stage A followed by stage B—and declared identical therewith. A Christian miracle does not admit of gradual transformation: Segismundo, in "La vida es sueño" *is*, suddenly, from a particular scene on, enlightened.

Has not the idea of "la Muse qui est la Grâce" been suggested to Claudel by Ronsard's "Ode à Michel de l'Hôpital," which opens with the line: "Errant par les champs de la grâce" (where the particular "grace, or gift of poetry" is meant), and which contains such passages as: "C'est lui [Michel de l'Hôpital] dont les grâces infuses) / Ont ramené par l'univers / Le choeur des Piérides Muses" (where the wording seems to suggest the fusion of "grace - gift" and Divine Grace)? But with Ronsard there is rather an unconscious shift from the pagan to the Christian meaning, whereas Claudel maintains the opposition between the two extremes.

42. One could doubt whether I have not overstated the facts as far as our strophe is concerned: is Christian Grace really the Muse of the poet, *by the end of the first strophe*? It is true that, in the answer given by the Muse in Antistrophe I, we find only ideas which are quite at variance with Christianity and which can only be intended as a temptation to the poet—a temptation to which he almost succumbs (Strophe II); again, in Antistrophe II, the Muse presents creation as an amoral fire and appeals to the flamelike in the poet's nature. In Strophe III, where the poet reaffirms the inner necessity he feels of representing the whole world in his limited poetic activity, there is no word to indicate that he appeals to the Muse as to Grace. Only in Antistrophe III do we find the words, spoken by the Muse: "Tu m'appelles la Muse et mon autre nom est la Grâce," and later she explains her personal message to him: "je suis la parole de grâce qui est adressée à toi seul." And yet it is this envoy of Heaven that the poet, in the epode, rejects in his desire to cling to the earth and to his sainted earthly love: "Va-t-en! Je me retourne désespérément vers la terre." And we are asked to suppose that in the interval between the composition of Odes IV and V the poet has found happiness with his love, the "épouse nocturne." It is only in Ode V that the poet is fully ready to reconcile his private and circumscribed family-life ("la maison fermée") with the task of "collecting" the whole world for God. Thus it would appear that the moment when he was able to formulate his program in Strophe I of Ode IV was only an anticipation of that state of Grace-given inner freedom reached in Ode V. "La Muse qui devient peu à peu la Grace" (as she is called in the "argument") has only in Ode V truly become "la Muse qui est la Grâce." Ode IV ends on a desperate note: the poet had already understood, in our strophe, his superhuman task, but could not reconcile it with his earthly love; only in Ode V does he gain the strength necessary both for his superhuman and his earthly task. Still, our strophe remains a first and interimistic stage on the long and wavering road toward the final conquest of Grace. The miracle of the revelation of his task to the poet takes place, in fact, in our strophe, but it finds him yet not quite prepared to accept it. Grace is a gift coming to those who are not yet great enough fully to deserve it.

And now we are in a position to recognize the development of form, and the inner connection, in the sequence of the odes. Whereas, in Ode I, the Muses (and particularly the muse Erato) are invoked without any response on their part, we have, in Ode IV, a dialogue between the poet and the Muse. Such a dialogue is meant, with all modern poets (we may remember Musset) to symbolize the conflict between the creative forces of the poet and the rest of his being. This comes to an end in our ode: in Ode V the dialogue takes place only with the public. From this we may infer that the poet no longer has need of communication with his creative forces, since the latter have been integrated into his being. We can also understand now the alternation, in our collection, between paganistic and Christian odes: Ode I, "Les Muses"; II, "L'Esprit et l'eau"; III, "Magnificat"; IV, "La Muse qui est la Grâce"; V, "La maison fermée"; VI, "Processional"—of which III and VI, the liturgical pieces, show two fairly clear stages in the gradual process by which the pagan element in the poet's soul is absorbed into Christianity. Ode III ends in the meditative serenity and confident peace of a vesper service, at a time of day when sharp contours are blurred "avant que la nuit ne commence et la pluie, avant que la longue pluie dans la nuit sur la terre ensemencée ne commence." The setting of our Ode IV is the night—a night in which the poet, after his triumphant wrestling with the pagan muse is, at the end, brought to a temporary defection from poetry altogether, and seeks happiness with his wife. In V, he is able to reconcile his avocation of poet with earthly happiness in "La maison fermée," where he finds the ultimate peace which sets the tone of the Processional: "Procedamus in pace in nomine Domini." Thus our collection of six odes embodies the whole drama of the separation and reintegration of the spiritual forces of the poet—a psychomachy.

There is still another development underlying the sequence of odes: the unfolding of the autobiographical element. It is as if the development by which the Muse becomes Grace is paralleled by the settlement of the practical existence of the poet in his house and his family—as if the abstract suffering due to his position between earth and heaven gave way in proportion as he took firmer roots in the concrete and necessarily narrower life: the more protected by God he is, the more "la maison fermée" comes into its own, and the more concrete becomes "la Muse qui est la Grâce." Whereas the "je" of the Introduction and of Strophe I of Ode IV is a quite general "poetic I," it tends, in the following stanzas, to become more and more the particular "Claudelian I" who identifies himself not only with the universe but with his family. In Strophe II of Ode IV Claudel will still complain to God: "Mais vous m'avez placé dans la terre, afin que j'endure la gêne et l'étroitesse et l'obscurité"; in Strophe III he will formulate his own situation in this narrow world in general terms: "Celui qui a acheté une femme à l'âge juste, ayant mis l'argent de côté peu à peu, / Il est avec elle comme un cercle fermé et comme une cité indissoluble. / Et leurs enfants entre eux deux comme de tendres grains mûrissants"—the motif of the "maison fermée" appears here for the first time, but the Biblical "acheter une femme" still veils the existence of his particular wife. In Ode V, however, she appears as "la gardienne du poète," to explain to the public (in the words of the *argument*) : "Je sais que la clôture lui est nécessaire; il est temps que toute sa vie soit ordonnée vers l'intérieur; et par moi il a cet intérieur." Claudel includes the autobiographical element not at all moments but "chemin faisant," as his being is allowed to affirm itself in life: the autobiographical matter is not a fixed quantity, and nothing would be more contrary to the spirit of this poetry than for pragmatistic literary critics to operate with that matter as if it were something primordially given. Much earlier, Claudel had disclosed that he was writing from exile; only after he has, helped by Grace, made his peace with the world and heaven does he write the lines (reminiscent of Ovid's *Tristia ex Ponto*): "Mon Dieu qui m'avez conduit à cette extrémité du monde . . . , / Ne permettez point que parmi ce peuple dont je n'entends point la langue, / Je perde mémoire de mes frères qui sont *tous les hommes, pareils à ma femme et à mon enfant.*" When the biographical makes its appearance, it is fused with the ecumenic or Catholic concern of the poet; it has no exhibitionist purpose, as with some of the Romantic poets.

Our remarks about the gradual recession of the pagan theme and the final enthronement of the intramundane Christian element, as embedded in the practical biography of the poet, lead to another observation: the extension of the "poetic I." Claudel has beautifully exploited the wide range that is inherent in the personal pronoun. This type of pronoun is a kind of proper name that stands for a human person in his unquestionable evidence: "I" speaks of a human being as *existing*, as imposing his evidence on the interlocutor; we may use it before being "introduced" to someone: by means of "I" we introduce ourselves sufficiently without giving our name, presenting ourselves as "this human being before you, whatever his name." When the interlocutor becomes better acquainted with the person calling himself "I," he is in a position to fill out the empty framework of the being indicated only as "I," without sensing any interruption of continuity: "I" becomes not only an unquestionable existence as such, but a filled-out ("étoffée") existence. In Odes I-IV Claudel furnished us only the "poetic I," accepted in its vagueness by the reader; in Ode V, the "poetic I" has truly become that "Paul Claudel, the French ambassador who is living in China with his family." The autobiographical filling-out of the pronoun is meant for the reader (the interlocutor of the poet) and surely gives him the feeling of having come closer to the poet; at the same time, however, the poet has gained confidence in his "I"—that is, in the relevance of his autobiography—ever since the moment when Grace has affirmed him in life. The struggles whereby the "poetic I" is enabled to take root in life are the content of this sequence of odes. We have here a paradigmatic example of the poet's capacity of widening and deepening, in an individual manner, the meaning of a simple grammatical tool which is given to any individual speaker, quite matter-of-factly, by his mother-tongue. Or, in other words, the poet shows us the inner, the human struggle hidden behind the screen of the word "I"—that word on which rests all poetic and all human activity.

A last question remains to be solved: Why does Claudel write *five* odes ("followed by a processional")? And why are there 50 versets in the strophe we have here selected? The symbolism of numbers is in line with medieval practice (Dante), but why is Claudel's symbolism based on the number 5 (or 6)? One may think immediately of Manzoni's five *Inni sacri* (though these five odes simply happen to be the only ones preserved of the greater number Manzoni originally intended to write). But such literary parallels are less instructive than are Claudel's own words: in Ode v, on the cardinal virtues, we find the following lines on "Justice":

> Elle considère la terminaison de toutes choses et le jour quand il se consomme . . . ,
> Ce jour qui est le sixième, celui qui précède le sabbat et qui suit les cinq premiers.
> Elle acquitte mes comptes; elle règle pour moi ce qui est dû....
> D'autre part je sais que toute chose est bénie en elle-même et que je suis béni en elle.
> Car l'homme, héritier des cinq jours, qui l'ont précédé, reçoit sur sa tête leurs bénédictions accumulées.

In this passage which shows the workings of Providence-in-Time (or, Justice), a Providence which was at work in the creation of man at an appointed time (the sixth day) and which still works in bringing things to their just ends and in settling human accounts, Claudel figures the week (as a division of time) as divided into the Sabbath, the day before the Sabbath, and the remaining five, relatively undistinguished workdays. Perhaps this division can serve as a clue to the arrangement and the theme of the collection as a whole: the block of the five odes corresponds to the block of five days (the five working days); the sixth ode ("Processional") corresponds to the day preceding the Sabbath, and treats of the ritual of purification in view of the heavenly Sabbath—a theme which Claudel (unlike Dante) makes no attempt to treat: his poem takes us only to the threshold of Heaven (Ode v ends with the lines: "Le custode seulement et non point la coupe, car nous ne goûterons point de ce fruit de la vigne avant que nous le buvions nouveau dans le Royaume de Dieu"). The idea of the whole collection, then, is to prepare us for the heavenly Sabbath and to lead us, by way of everyday chores, through the particular purification of the Sabbath, to the threshold of eternal joy.

43. As an exception I venture here to voice criticism and not to apply only the *critique des beautés*. I feel justified in so doing because I have tried to understand Claudel's world of thought from within, and only after my apperception of his art was (in a manner of speaking) completed have I found a flaw which is inherent to the very conception of his poem. This "historical" flaw is conditioned by the basic idea of having Grace replace the Muse, or of having pious rationality replace secular enthusiasm: since there had to be the Muse (who was also made necessary by the invocation in the proem) she had to become the *repoussoir*: the personification of the Greek culture which had to be rejected. Claudel could then not admit in his poem a Pallas Athene as a prefiguration of the numerous Catholic patron saints of skills and technics.

My objection cannot be met by the argument that a poet is free to alter historical facts in accord with the laws of poetry: since Claudel's poem implies a historical picture of our civilization, this picture must be in harmony with at least that historical picture which our civilization calls its own, and which forms a part of it. When Dante alters history he is in accord with what his civilization taught him about history: Vergil could be his *duca e maestro*. When Villon makes of the Greek Alcibiades a lovely woman Archipiada, this was in accordance with what his civilization thought of Alcibiades. But when Claudel willingly shuts his eyes to *his own knowledge* that Greek philosophy and religion anticipate Christian philosophy and religion, he puts himself in opposition to himself, and the rift makes itself felt within the poem (the Egyptians and the Assyrians must replace the Greeks and Romans!).

44. According to Karl Viëtor, who (in *Geschichte der deutschen Ode* [1923]) seeks to define the ode on the basis of all the examples of this genre from antiquity to our day, the ode is characterized by its position between the *lied* and the hymn: its style ends toward the sublime and the elaborately poetic, its mood is that of heightened feeling coupled with reflection —Herder's definition "die poetische Ausbildung eines lebhaften Gedankens" can, according to Viëtor, be maintained if we grant to the terms used their full range of significance (*poetisch* - "elaborately poetic"; *lebhaft* - "animated by heightened feeling"; *Gedanken* - "mood of reflection"). From these basic characteristics Professor Viëtor derives other features: the mythical element must be in evidence and there must be that "beau désordre" which Boileau posited; the poem must have been inspired by a solemn occasion; rhyme must be absent (according to the Horatian model). Professor Viëtor states that the pure type of the ode which would contain all those elements together in perfect harmony is rarely to be found in the actually existing historical representatives of the genre; I would venture to claim for Claudel's odes the harmonious presence of *all* these essential features (in spite of the fact that the French poet was not able to read Viëtor's treatise!). And, when we read Viëtor's lament over the inability of contemporary German poets to breathe into their odes a new spirit uniting "Freiheit und Gesetz" (the freedom of artistic creativity and the law of form), we Romance philologists can point with pride to Claudel.

45. As if out of a feeling of pique against the alexandrine—which he has criticized in his treatise on French versification ("Positions et propositions," 1)—Claudel carefully avoids giving his shorter lines (generally descriptive of energetic decision, of concentration of forces, etc.) the correct form of an alexandrine:

lines: 3 . . 7 + 7 (with two hiatuses)
          4 . . 12   (without a caesura; one hiatus)
        15 . . 5 + 7
        17 . . 3 + 9 (one hiatus)
        27 . . 7 + 8
              etc.

46. The reader may have noticed that, from the moment I had pointed out, with the help of the word-motif, the main structure of the poem, my study shifted more and more away from Claudel's words.

I have sought to obey the Claudelian motto of this study by first disobeying it: by starting with the attempt to cut a path through the poetic labyrinth in order to reach the "center." In clearing my path, it was necessary to brush away, for the moment, much of the underbrush—which later on had to be properly accounted for: hence the thicket of notes which could not be avoided if we were to respect the labyrinthine aspect of the poem willed by the poet. Thus it was necessary, for the purpose of exposition, to split into two (text and notes) what appears in the poem as a unit.